CONTESTING MORALITIES

CONTESTING MORALITIES

SCIENCE, IDENTITY, CONFLICT

Edited by

Nanneke Redclift

WITHDRAWN

UCL
PRESS

First published in Great Britain 2005 by UCL Press,
an imprint of Cavendish Publishing Limited, The Glass House,
Wharton Street, London WC1X 9PX, United Kingdom
Telephone: + 44 (0)20 7278 8000   Facsimile: + 44 (0)20 7278 8080
Email: info@uclpress.com
Website: www.uclpress.com

Published in the United States by Cavendish Publishing
c/o International Specialized Book Services,
5824 NE Hassalo Street, Portland,
Oregon 97213-3644, USA

Published in Australia by Cavendish Publishing (Australia) Pty Ltd
45 Beach Street, Coogee, NSW 2034, Australia
Telephone: + 61 (2)9664 0909   Facsimile: + 61 (2)9664 5420

© UCL Press   2005

British Library Cataloguing in Publication Data
Redclift, Nanneke
Contesting moralities: science, identity, conflict
1 Ethnology
I Title
305.8

Library of Congress Cataloguing in Publication Data
Data available

ISBN 1-84472-014-4
ISBN 978-1-844-72014-9

1 3 5 7 9 10 8 6 4 2

Printed and bound in Great Britain by Cromwell Press, Trowbridge, Wiltshire.

LIST OF CONTRIBUTORS

Sara Corben de Romero is a specialist registrar in public health. She is currently placed at the Kings Fund in London where she is a visiting research fellow working on the management of long-term health conditions. She has previously worked in the NHS and local government, and in addition to HIV/AIDS has research interests in prison health and the health of asylum seekers in the UK.

Oonagh Corrigan is a Lecturer in Sociology at the University of Cambridge, at the Centre for Family Research, the Faculty of Social and Political Sciences and the Cambridge Genetics Knowledge Park. Her work focuses on biomedical technologies, the ways these are shaped by social, political, economic and ethical forces, and the relationship such technologies have with various key players and stakeholders. She has published numerous articles and her most recent publication is a co-edited book entitled *Genetic Databases: Socioethical Issues in the Collection and Use of DNA* with Routledge.

Sahra Gibbon is a Wellcome Trust Postdoctoral Research Fellow in the Anthropology Department at University College London. Having completed her PhD examining the social and cultural context of the knowledge and technologies associated with 'BRCA' genetics, she is continuing her research work in the field of cancer genetics by examining the dynamics between science and publics in relation to a range of bio/tissue-banking initiatives and developments in bio-informatics.

Michelle Lee Guy is a Lecturer at the Centre for Social, Development and Environmental Studies, Faculty of Social Sciences, National University of Malaysia. She completed her PhD on Filipina domestic servants in Malaysia at University College London. Her research interests and publications are on transmigration, gender and social stratification, and transgendering, in southeast Asia and Malaysia.

Carlos Novas is a Wellcome Trust Postdoctoral Fellow at the BIOS Centre for the Study of Bioscience, Biomedicine, Biotechnology and Society, London School of Economics. He is currently working on a project titled 'The political economy of hope: private enterprise, patients' groups and the production of values in the contemporary life sciences'. This project investigates the ways a range of values are produced in the contemporary life sciences, and the intersection between business and bioethics.

Michael Mahrt received his MA in Anthropology from the University of Aarhus in Denmark in 1998. Since then he has taught at universities in Denmark and Eritrea. He has done three years of fieldwork in the highlands of Eritrea (1994–95 and 1999–2001). He is currently finishing his PhD at University College London and working with UNHCR in the lowlands of Eritrea.

Nanneke Redclift is Senior Lecturer in Social Anthropology at University College London. She has carried out field research in Spain and Latin America and her interests are in gender, the anthropology of the body, new forms of cultural production and the social context of genetics. Previous publications include *Engels Revisited: New Feminist Essays* (co-edited with Sayers and Evans, Tavistock), *Beyond Employment: Household, Gender and Subsistence* (co-edited with Mingione, Blackwell), *Working Women: International Perspectives on Labour and Gender Ideology* (co-edited with Sinclair, Routledge), and *Genetics: Critical Concepts in Social and Cultural Theory* (co-edited with Gibbon, forthcoming from Routledge).

Sara Skodbo received her PhD from University College London for research on the development of Norwegian food biotechnology from the perspectives of scientists, regulators and consumer groups. She now works in the Research Office in the Home Office Drug and Alcohol Research Unit.

Kathryn Tomlinson completed her PhD in social anthropology on the displaced Meskhetian Turks of southern Russia at University College London in 2002. Thereafter she worked for over two years as a Senior Research Officer at the National Foundation for Educational Research, undertaking qualitative research into issues of social inclusion in education. Her work included research and evaluations in relation to the education of children in public care, children with special educational needs, and the relationship between education and conflict. Interest in the wider application of anthropology led to her establishing Apply: the ASA Network of Applied Anthropologists in 2004. Dr Tomlinson is presently working for Peace Brigades International in Indonesia, providing protection for local human rights defenders.

Paul Twinn is currently completing a doctorate at University College London based on fieldwork in St Vincent and the Grenadines for which he received an Emslie Horniman award from the Royal Anthropological Institute. He is currently working as an Associate Lecturer in the Faculty of Social Sciences at the Open University.

Tony Watling is a Netherlands Organisation for Scientific Research (NWO) Research Fellow in the Faculty of Theology at Leiden University in the Netherlands, researching religous views on ecology and environmentalism. Previously he worked as a Wellcome Trust Research Fellow looking at Christian views of genetic engineering in the Department of Anthropology at University College London, where he was also an undergraduate and studied for his PhD on religous discourse among Protestants and Catholics in the Netherlands.

ACKNOWLEDGMENTS

Many people have contributed, directly and indirectly, to this collection. First and foremost I would like thank to Carla Risseeuw. On a grey London afternoon over a cup of coffee our conversation led gradually towards this theme. Later, it became the subject of a conference, hosted by Carla, at the Research School CNWS, University of Leiden, the Netherlands, in June 1998. The financial support provided by the EU Socrates Programme, the University of Leiden and University College London was fundamental in facilitating this event, which became material in shaping the research of some of the authors in this book. The meeting carried on a stimulating collaboration between our two departments started by Els Postel, who has been an inspiration to researchers on gender throughout her long career. I would particularly like to extend my gratitude to all the speakers at this conference. They provided a rich and varied range of ideas and approaches, which we all took away with us for further reflection. Among them special thanks are due to Els Postel, Carla Risseeuw, Kurti Singh, Maitreyi Krishnaraj, Rajni Palriwala, Takyiwaa Manuh, Dzodzi Tsikata, Selma Sevenhuijsen, Joyce Outshoorn, Annemiek Richters, Lily Ling, Jose van Santen, Ellen-Roos Kambel, Philip Havik and Jolien Harmsen. Their contributions had a formative effect on much of the material we publish here. Karin Willemse also played the role of indefatigable co-ordinator and administrator for the event and helped to ensure the good working environment that emerged. The four contributors to Part 1 of the book, two of whom also participated in the Leiden debates, were founder members of the Genetics, Anthropology and Technology Group at University College and I would also like to thank everyone who has been part of this discussion forum for the lively and acute analyses they have brought to our reading. For their insight, humour, warmth and perceptiveness, as well as for a certain forbearance and for many formative kitchen table conversations, to Michael, Ben, Rebecca and Victoria much love. Finally, Cavendish/UCL Press have been both supportive and flexible and the editors, Jon Lloyd and Ewan Cooper, have made a valuable input. Ewan deserves our particular thanks for his professionalism, precision and meticulous attention to detail in the latter stages of production.

CONTENTS

PART 3: MORAL RHETORIC:
MEANINGS OF CONFLICT AND VIOLENCE

INTRODUCTION:
FIGHTING FOR THE HIGH GROUND:
ANTHROPOLOGICAL PERSPECTIVES
ON MORAL CONFLICT

Nanneke Redclift

Why have questions of public and private morality become such important areas of contemporary discussion? What are the implications of the increasing concern with ethics that has emerged across a number of different fields? Questions of personal and collective conduct have always been central to social life. However, divergent moral standpoints on a range of issues, such as sexual and reproductive choice, the politics of food, the rights and responsibilities of parenting, care of the elderly, human-environment relationships, animal welfare or the definition of life and death, have become highly confrontational. While it might be argued that moral evaluation has decreased its hold on aspects of behaviour for particular social groups, for example in relation to sexual activity, behind broad statistical trends countervailing processes are also significant. Moreover, moral questions and value-based politics have increasingly moved into other arenas. The more than 20 'Truth and Reconciliation' Commissions that have been convened in the last 30 years are one testimony to the enhanced significance of ethical debate as a powerful dimension of social and political practice.

In this book we explore these questions in a series of detailed case studies and examine some of the sources of moral debate in the diverse contexts of Europe, Asia and Latin America. Foucault's view of ethics as 'the kind of relationship you ought to have with yourself, *rapport à soi*, which determines how the individual is supposed to constitute himself as a moral subject of his own actions' (1986: 352), sees the impulse to assign value to action as a general aspect of subjectivity and consciousness. It is thus amenable to philosophical reflection, but only within historically changing ideas of the specific content of the moral values of any epoch. This raises questions, not touched upon by Foucault, about the ways in which people actually constitute themselves as the moral subjects of action in the many specific arenas where self and collectivity meet. It also suggests issues about the nature of an ethics of the self in culturally diverse and interacting moral worlds. The research brought together here was particularly concerned with three broad sets of issues that have come to dominate an increasingly global public culture. First, the ethical dilemmas surrounding scientific advance and the kinds of subjectivity and relationship that new kinds of knowledge bring into being; secondly, the worth attributed to different ethnic and religious communities, including the power of moral language to constitute boundaries between groups; thirdly, the 'moralisation' of the political sphere, the use of morality as a weapon, and conflicts over the legitimacy of governments, violence or militarism. The social movements and identities thus brought into being enable us to see the posing of moral questions as forms of social action in their own right.

Our research suggests that these debates reflect significant shifts in the function of knowledge, expertise and authority in contemporary society. They are also responses to major changes in the role of the State, and the disassociation of people and territory, which have bought different ethical systems into increasing contact and produced new patterns of ethnic identification and conflict. Latent uncertainties about the proper scope of the political domain and the limits to violent intervention have also come to the fore. In a post-9/11 world, the traditional rules of engagement have become suddenly obsolete and assumptions about the ethical mandate for intervention have been questioned. Even non-violent aspects of international relations and their 'moral' basis are issues for a mass audience to consider. The cynical or benevolent dimensions of 'humanitarian' aid, strategic political coalitions or international markets, which have long been the targets of critical academic analysis, are now the subjects of a broader popular discussion.

Such responses to extreme events can also be seen as the manifestation of a more pervasive process that has unfolded gradually with the demise of ideological super-powers. The so-called 'end of history' has left a fragmented political map where old alignments must be re-examined. Francis Fukuyama's essay of the same title argued that the end of the Cold War represented the final conclusion of the ideological conflict that had been the motive force for historical action until the present. He saw this as the apparent victory of 'free' market liberalism, ushering in a new global consensus (Fukuyama 1992). This controversial thesis provoked considerable debate at the time and it might be argued that critics who identified a misleadingly triumphalist note in his perspective have been vindicated by the events of September 2001, which suggest the moral fragility of such an argument as well as the significance of challenges to it.

Other kinds of social and cultural transition run parallel to this. In parts of the world where alignments between peoples, territories and States have become increasingly unclear (as in the former Soviet Union or the 'conflict diamond' States of Africa, for example) the connotations of citizenship and the moral efficacy of government have become problematic. Although the technological capacity of governments has in some cases expanded, their ethical hegemony has been weakened. The empty heart of global capitalism seems to leave a vacuum into which a diversity of interests can insert themselves. In European nations, the existing frameworks of 'welfare' are being challenged by demographic shifts and fiscal crises, leading to new insecurities. In both cases, though for different reasons, there are growing conflicts about the division of rights, obligations and responsibilities in relation to the ethics of basic human relations, the social regulation of personal needs, and the duties of care giving and receiving. Notions such as the 'end of history', however contentious, are paralleled by suggestions that we are also witnessing the 'end of nature'. Anxieties about the relationship between societies and their environments, as well as about the connections between bodies, people and kin represent a further source of ethical assessment, social division and re-definition. It has also been argued that the immediacy of information, particularly the heightened visual connections between spectators and victims, create new kinds of moral imagination (Ignatieff 1997: 90) and make collective reaction and evaluation especially potent. The speed and ubiquity of media representation intensify acts of witnessing and can turn distant events into public and practical moral concerns, which are nevertheless highly ambiguous and problematic (Humphrey 2002, Redclift Chapter 9, this book).

Moral questions have always been central to the work of ethicists and philosophers (Gewirth 1978, Singer 1979/1993, Bauman 1995, Maclean 1993, Raz 1994, Beauchamp and Childress 1983/2001). But the use of hypothetical examples to explore moral reasoning or the logical basis of different positions is not primarily designed to examine the formulation, development or modification of moral standpoints as a social process. Nor is it best suited to an exploration of their relationship to other aspects of social life, such as authority, legitimacy, knowledge or identity. Abstracted from specific cultural context such enquiries also tend to take for granted a 'Western' frame of reference. Public and social policy analyses, too, have been elaborated in the context of advanced industrial economies and when they have been addressed within the context of 'development' studies they have naturally been most concerned with the barriers to the implementation of specific objectives (Sevenhuijsen 1998, Mwabo, Ugaz and White 2001). Where comparative cultural questions have been considered, attention has mainly been directed to evaluating the debate between 'absolutists' and 'relativists', treating these as philosophical and disciplinary debates and in relation to anthropological evidence (Edel and Edel 1959/2000, Moody-Adams 1997, Cook 1999). Cook argues, in fact, that the division of labour between anthropologists and philosophers 'has produced nothing but misunderstandings' (1999: 4). In his review of the academic shift from the interest in ethics within philosophy, stimulated by Rawls' work on justice in the 1970s (Rawls 1972), to a broader concern with the ethics of difference in the work of Derrida, Levinas and Bauman in the 1990s, Scott Lasch (1996a, 1996b) has suggested that the analysis of the moral sphere should be developed, beyond the abstractions and dichotomies of philosophical positions, towards an 'ethics in the street' which 'takes the problem of community and ... sociality very seriously indeed' (Lasch 1996a: 76).

Our aim in this collection of essays, therefore, is to explore the notion of 'practical ethics' (Singer 1979/1993) from an empirical, ethnographic and comparative perspective. The rapid changes taking place in the post-modern public sphere suggest that values need to be understood as both discourse and practice. Marilyn Strathern has used the term 'literalization' to describe the ways in which an idea, object or entity that was formerly tacit or hidden, can be brought in consciousness and made explicit, thus revealing its 'conventional points of reference' (1992: 5). While this is particularly applicable to the effects of techno-scientific change, a more generalised contemporary literalization of moral positions also generates new forms of social engagement and experience. It also uncovers underlying values and commitments and it forces us to confront divergences, discrepancies and cleavages within particular societies and between them. It was our view that there were few bodies of literature that had fully responded to this challenge.

MORAL CULTURES?

Sociologists and anthropologists have always been interested in the values, concepts and norms of the communities they study (Overing 1985, Parkin 1985, Pocock 1986, Parry and Bloch 1989, Appell and Madan 1988, Pardo 1996, Gullestad 1996, Howell 1997, Cohen 2000). They have explored the internal divisions exemplified through different prescriptions, rights and duties: for example, between castes, between men and women, or between aristocrats and commoners. They have explored the underlying values of incommensurable acts such as head-hunting, for example, or the morality of money and the market.

Early anthropological discussion of morality often had a static quality, in which values tended to be seen as one element of a given form of cultural script. Redfield's ideas about the 'limited good' (Redfield 1955), or Banfield's work on 'amoral' familism in Italy (Banfield 1958) are classics in this regard. They saw moral action as an aspect of the debate about 'self-interest' versus society, or as an indication of the kinds of value system that supported or inhibited notions of 'progress'. Moral codes were often read as indicators of other things: for example, as characteristic of the archetypal closed corporate community, or the social world of the poor, and sometimes as a symptom of backwardness which could thus provide a cultural rationale for levels of development. The (unconscious) assumptions of the anthropologist sometimes provided the implicit template against which the moral systems of the informants were measured. For an indication of the distance travelled between the middle and later periods of the 20th century we might compare Nancy Scheper-Hughes' account of 'mother love' in a Brazillian favela (Scheper-Hughes 1992), which challenges assumptions about both the words 'mother' and 'love', showing how a practice which may look both immoral and unnatural from one standpoint can reveal its logic, thus providing an insight into, even if not an endorsement of, 'local moralities'. For a fictional working through of similar concerns we could consider Toni Morrison's marvellous and troubling novel *Beloved*, which puts the reader inside the soul of a woman who would kill her children rather than having them sold into slavery and who somehow makes us understand how this could be the case.

Ethnography has always had a special mission to uncover the gap between 'ought' and 'is'; this is one of the hallmarks of an approach to social analysis that is rooted in detail and an awareness of everyday local complexities. Revealing the cultural logic of specific moral orders and showing that they are located in wider webs of meaning has been one of the key themes of the discipline. Ethnographies frequently give detailed accounts of the ways in which ideas about what is right, good or true shape personal ontologies and particular courses of action. However, as Howell noted (1997), this is a pervasive but largely implicit interest, seldom the focus as such. Similarly, moral reasoning is often treated as a reflection of the constitution of cultural meaning of the group in question. Moral codes are thus read as cultural characteristics or interpreted as 'world-view', reflecting particular commitments to kinship or understandings of selfhood. These relativising approaches have been fruitfully deployed to explain forms of behaviour that might seem morally problematic (or even 'immoral') to the outsider, challenging ethnocentrism. However, it becomes difficult to distinguish the domain of morality from the notion of culture as a whole, and such contextualisations also run the risk of over-reifying social groups, approaching them as if they were homogenous and relatively bounded (Howell 1997: 3).

It has also become common to criticise anthropologists themselves for being embedded within an implicit 'Western metaphysics' and to argue that this provides a distorting lens through which to look at other cultures. The post-colonial production of knowledge is morally charged. Both Marilyn Strathern and Gananeth Obeyesekere have pushed this position to its logical conclusion, although on different grounds (Strathern 1988, Obeyesekere 1996). Each has suggested that this problem is not simply a philosophical hitch which could be cured by some academic consciousness raising, but an effect of presuppositions that are even more deeply rooted than we supposed, creating a viewpoint which becomes so naturalised as to be intractable.

Strathern, for example, implies that it is the very rare 'Western' student of Melanesian cultures who can really step outside the embodied and taken-for-granted connections between a notion of the individuated self and the material sense of a bounded body, which would enable them to 'accurately' perceive the flow and transactions between substances and persons that seem to be characteristic of Melanesian experience. Similarly, Obeyesekere's provocative contention is that it takes an academic quasi-'native' such as himself, as a Sri Lankan (albeit American-based) intellectual, to point out that a 'Westerner' may fail to be aware of the hold that the myth making of his own culture has exerted on his analysis of the myths of 'others' (in this case Sahlins' 1981 discussion of 18th century Hawaiians). In these analyses, the neutrality of the anthropological viewpoint is vigorously challenged yet again and epistemology acquires a moral force.

Such interventions provide an important reminder of the continuing need to situate the observer and to acknowledge the power inherent in any form of analysis (Battaglia 1999). However, the map of meaning systems is not so clear or simple. As commentators on this discussion have already pointed out, in the very act of trying to give greater agency to local meanings, the apparent gulf between qualitatively different kinds of knowledge, 'West' and 'non-West', is firmly re-established (Borofsky 1997). There is the obvious danger of stereotyping each, and of fetishising an ultimate dualism with 'others'. Moreover, the very debate runs the risk of reinforcing outworn images and models. Through the globalisation of aspirations and images, Westerners have exported their conceptual predispositions and history, so that these have become rooted, reincorporated and transformed in relation to many other local settings. 'Western' or 'Northern' conceptions of person and identity have been traded, sold, imposed and resisted, through politics, legislation, consumption, the media, among other channels, throughout the world. Meanwhile, individualism, thought to be so much the hallmark of everything that is Western, is changing its shape, decomposing and being re-elaborated in a number of different ways.

'Rationalism', usually regarded as the centrepiece of Western individualist ontology, is now sometimes seen as under threat, and popular disenchantment with science appears to find outlets in celebrations of the 'irrational' through intuition, the paranormal, chance, new age magic or 'special powers'. At the same time the cultural configuration of human individuality associated with rationality, far from being abandoned, is being extended and elaborated, through the language of 'choice', 'consent' and 'efficiency', and through a global order increasingly based on supposedly rationalising institutions, such as free trade, environmental protection and planning, or legal responsibility for war crimes. In Dumont's words:

> To the extent that the individualistic ideas and values of the dominant culture are spreading worldwide, they undergo modification locally and engender new forms ... the new modified forms can pass back into the dominant culture and operate there as modern elements in their own right ... the acculturation of each particular culture to modernity can leave a lasting precipitate in the heritage of global modernity. (1986: 17)

The anthropological critique of enlightenment thinking suggests that 'Western' knowledge is not always the right kind of tool for understanding cultural difference. However, such a perspective tends to lose sight of such knowledge as lived consciousness. While researchers have become increasingly interested in the social nature of personhood in other cultures, they have left a somewhat homogeneous idea of the 'Western' person as analyst largely intact. Injunctions to take stock of Western viewpoints might therefore need first to ask exactly what kinds of viewpoints these are. The West itself is full of contradictions and needs closer examination, or it remains over-generalised and ambiguous. Polarities between West and elsewhere restrict an ability to explore the mutual cultural flows, which are much older than some contemporary discussions of globalisation imply. Thus, the model of West and Other is already a complex half-truth the moment it is formulated and the notion of each is itself a complex mosaic of shared and disparate elements. Rather than a geographic distinction, it has itself become part of a moral and political discourse. We may debate the impact that the exportation of 'our' science, technologies, goods and values to others, but the conceptual status of these cultural products is itself changing. The neutrality of analysis and the ethical position of research itself must also be an integral part of this inquiry.

A starting point for this collection of essays is that there is a gulf between philosophical rigour, normative distinctions and everyday experience. The research discussed examines the 'substantive moral concerns of everyday moral inquirers' (Moody-Adams 1997: 6) and suggests a more diverse picture of contest and negotiation. The contributors make visible the heterogeneity and the contradictions of value and 'right' conduct within and between the worlds they study, encouraging a processual view of moral practice and social life. Following the important collection of essays edited by Howell (1997), they also endorse the growing recognition that values are constantly manipulated and constitute self and action. The 'contested moralities' of the title, therefore, allude to the layered, overlapping and contradictory nature of contemporary experience, and invoke the diversity of struggles to define truth and conduct at a number of different levels and spaces in the social fabric. The perspective taken here also pays particular attention to the individual claims and personal narratives through which groups, kin and peers, play out the dramas of selfhood and relationship, the arena of personal life and subjectivity where people struggle to defend positions, beliefs and identities. The moral imagination and the social imaginary, with their eddies and whirlpools of shock, blame, praise, fear, panic and adulation are not merely reflections of deeper realities. They actively constitute new frames of reference, posing social choices increasingly in terms of personal moral behaviour. Our aim is therefore to illuminate the actual ways public moral anxieties are generated, how they are expressed through political imagery, media representation and policy formulation, and how people and communities make complex choices and decisions in this context.

From the research considered here three concepts were helpful in thinking about the material. The first is exchange, a classic term in anthropological analysis but one that, applied to a new context, helps us to conceptualise the many ways in which morality and agency are linked. It is particularly useful in illuminating the processes through which new kinds of knowledge, for example in relation to science or medicine, are incorporated into particular social worlds through ethical debate. Discussions between clinicians, scientists, regulators, counsellors and patients can be seen as a series of transactions in which particular activities are made possible or prohibited and in which new individual or collective identities are brought into being or resisted. Then, the continuing importance of claims to memory, history and the moral basis of a shared past is examined through the concept of boundaries, reflecting the use of shared values as an indication of present identity and identification. As Kathryn Tomlinson shows in this book, the concept of boundary-making is indissolubly connected with the moral basis of cultural affiliation. Four of the chapters discuss ways in which different kinds of relationship are marked though moral claims, including those between men and women, between ethnic groups, between religious congregations and between servants and their employers. Finally, we examine the notion of rhetoric and the ways in which moral language is used as a discursive strategy in instituting power over others, in justifying the use of violence, or in defining oneself against events. Applied to the domains of science, identity and conflict that are the focus of our analysis, the concepts of exchange, boundaries and rhetoric provide an organisational structure for the book, which can also be read across each section. The case studies are drawn from different cultural settings, which include Britain and Europe. A number of the chapters indicate that knowledge as a form of practice is itself in flux. The examples show that, even within specific cultures or religions, forms of personal embodiment are more various than a uni-dimensional model would suggest. Through moral argument and debate individuals struggle to fit the language of the past to the changed conditions of the future.

NEW KNOWLEDGE, NEW SUBJECTS: SOCIALISING TECHNO-SCIENCE

The opening chapters of the book lay the ground for this discussion. The theme of the first part, 'Moral Exchange', is that morality is a dynamic field of discourse and transaction which itself gives rise to new forms of subjectivity; a domain where social and ethical questions intersect explicitly with cultural understandings of the human person. The pervasiveness of image and information, and new relationships between science, technology and society, and between nature and culture, create perceptions of uncertainty, even if the factual basis of this novelty if questionable. Techno-scientific development in particular has become 'the terrain where humanity, morality, ethics and the law collide' Riddell 1996: 22–24). It is therefore a sphere that is particularly significant for examining formative aspects of moral debate. The emerging capacities and materialities, which scientific knowledge makes possible, transcend the political framework of states and nations, as well as creating new kinds of boundary and exclusion. They expand their purpose as solutions to problems, but in themselves pose new ethical dilemmas.[1] The very ability of science and technology to successfully manipulate the material world creates dilemmas of capacity versus control, generating conflicts over the legitimate ownership of decision making in relation to human experience (Franklin 1997). The power to save life or to prolong it provokes questions about exactly which lives these should be, and changes the locus of responsibility for choice.

Anthropologists such as Marshall (1992: 51) have suggested that there is 'a deep seated ambivalence toward scientific developments and their implications for control over life and death'. There is a persistent 'lack of consensus regarding normative standards', which is rooted in a contradiction between possibility on the one hand, and individual emotional response and the need for personal control on the other. Marshall criticises the philosophical style of current bioethical debates on two counts. First, that they take the Western Cartesian framework of individualism, autonomy and self-determination for granted as a general model of the person, and therefore cannot deal with these issues as they become increasingly important in other cultures. Secondly, that they 'contribute to a distancing of moral discourse from the complicated human settings and interactions within which moral dilemmas are culturally constructed negotiated and lived. In this discourse, issues of personhood, body parts, organ replacements, genetic cloning and the like are confronted as abstractions rather than experiential realities'. As she points out, 'morality is created and enacted through experience' and there is a relevant role for anthropology to play in its emphasis on situatedness, contradiction, lived experience, ambiguity, power and legitimation.

Understandings of the place of the human being in creation, the ethic of the sanctity of life and the sense that it must be preserved at all costs are metaphysical, and often tacit perceptions that may be hard to articulate. When confronted by the power of possibility that advances in technology have given to specialists and knowledge holders, new struggles for expression ensue. Because we *can* do anything, deciding what exactly to do may become a more conflictual and anxiety-laden process (Singer 1979/1993). At the same time the public space in which moral discourse is shaped is vaster and more global, no longer merely the province of kin and neighbours, but more widely 'imagined' in Benedict

---

1   For a comment on the use of bioethical 'principles' from the perspective of the sociology of knowledge, see Evans 2000. On challenges to ethics posed by developments in reproductive medicine, see Chadwick 1987/1990, 2001, Strathern 1992, and on the growth of the market, see Busch 2000.

Anderson's sense, as we participate virtually in moralising the actions of distant others, in ways that also infuse local codes.

These issues are taken up in first four chapters of the collection, which focus on practical aspects of morally-based social relationships with others in the context of new forms of knowledge. The contributors deal with different facets of the ethical dilemmas and struggles that result from the changing nature of science and technology. The examples analysed include food biotechnologies, cancer genetics, predictive tests and pharmacology. The debates between scientists, legislators and publics, which surround these technologies, reveal the complex bioethical landscape of contemporary Western European societies. The research presented discusses the implications of such exchanges for the kinds of individuals we will become and the choices that will be socially sanctioned.

Sara Skodbo's ethnography of the cultural impact of new biotechnologies in the food industry in Norway explores the different ethical arguments put forward by governments, industry, regulators and consumer groups in relation to the manipulation of 'nature' and the human modification of organic material. In Norway genetic technology, modern biotechnology and its human representatives, the biotechnologists, are considered morally suspect. As a consequence they are excluded from 'good society' in the form of relations with and influence on policy-makers. The chapter presents data on the terms of inclusion and exclusion in relations between regulators and biotechnologists. It suggests that exclusion is due to the technology's/technologists' inability to adhere to a core project of sociality, which is based on central Norwegian moral values of equality as sameness. The impossible task of reconciling two competing value systems condemns biotechnologists to exclusion from the sphere of social relations that make up daily life in the technological field of biotechnology.

Sahra Gibbon also takes the ethical consequences of new knowledge as a central theme, looking particularly at the way morality is defined and made explicit by those involved in the provision of health care in breast cancer genetics. This is explored in relation to a key aspect of developments in the new genetics, the patenting of genes. The chapter takes a single event as a focus for this discussion: a conference convened in May 2000 by a group of health care practitioners and managers to look at the impact on the NHS of an American pharmaceutical, Myriad, which had offered licences to a UK biotech company for private testing of the two breast cancer genes BRCA1 and 2. Representatives for the company, and the UK molecular genetics society, together with patients, practitioners and a lawyer, vied with each other to define what the ethics of care was or could be. The issues of patient rights, an equitable NHS and technological and research advances competed to claim this space. Exploring the microcosm of this event reveals the way that morality and ethics are used to bolster or critique different contesting positions, as those involved in developments in breast cancer genetics try to negotiate the tensions between altruism and consumerism.

Oonagh Corrigan turns to another aspect of contemporary biomedicine, the development of clinical drug trials, as a case through which to further examine the moral context of notions or risk. Clinicians have a duty to 'inform' patients and to gain their consent and their willingness to 'bear' the implications of participation. However, constraints on both sides make this a very imperfect process. The author's examination of the protocols, process and investments of doctors, patients and volunteers reveals a complex environment in which the morality surrounding acceptable risk is only partially understood.

Using the example of the development and subsequent implementation of a predictive genetic test for Huntington's disease in a medical genetics clinic, Carlos Novas approaches ethics as a form of pastoral practice which creates new forms of personhood. He argues that moral arguments are also profoundly technical. The discourses of medical geneticists, genetic counsellors, psychologists, neurologists, ethicists and patient organisations construct the person who is genetically at risk as an 'uncertain subject' who is in need of a technology to help them plan for the future and enable them to realise their lives in the light of their biological destiny. Building on the work of Michel Foucault, his chapter shows that the realities of decision making in the medical genetics clinic involve a kind of pastoral power in which the principles of informed consent, patient autonomy, voluntary action and choice are translated into a range of micro-technologies for the management of the conduct of the genetic counselling team. This form of pastoral power organises the responsibilities of the counselling team in ways that are both individualising and totalising, but that nevertheless attempt to govern the at-risk individual through the very exercise of their freedom.

Although some people have argued that Western cultures seek increasingly to distance themselves from basic life events, removing birth from the home, handing the washing of the dead over to paid specialists, leaving graveyards to languish under the weeds, diminishing the links between ancestors and descendents (Norgaard 1994), it is also a society in which some of these very life events and 'life itself' (Franklin 2000) have become increasingly central to public consciousness. As these chapters make clear, the ability to manipulate physical/biological existence as part of a redefined social existence has its expression in the domain of new popular moralities and the moral imagination.

MORALITY AS MARKER: IDENTITY, GENDER AND DIFFERENCE

It may be a truism to regard women as the keepers of cultural value, and there has been a longstanding debate within feminist analyses about the nature of female altruism, as for example in relation to the association of women and peace building (Ruddick 1989, Roseneil 1995, Warren and Cady 1994, Macdonald, Holden and Ardener 1987), or the gendered division of community involvement (Moser 1989, Oakley and Williams 1994). Concern with moralities and a concern with gender come face to face in the concept of 'care', a term which is almost a definition of what it means to be social, suggesting both an emotional response of sympathy towards another, and a practical activity in which individuals are drawn together through physical support and security. Feminists pointed out long ago that in analysing the formal economy account should also be taken of the 'caring economy', importantly labelled an 'economy' so that its contribution and worth could be fully recognised. Yet the idea of care can also be seen as both integrative and divisive, since the association of women with caring plays into the conflictual debates which have taken place about women's 'essential nature'.

Carol Gilligan's famous and controversial book *In a Different Voice* (1982/1993) described the young women she interviewed as speaking about their life's experiences in 'a different voice' than that of men. This was a voice that emphasised an ethic of care, based on the link between relationship and responsibility, and which identified the origins of aggression in the failure to make connections with others. Listening to the voices of her informants, both children and college students, she identified contrasting images of hierarchy and network in the ways in which children and young people thought about moral conflict and choice. In the language forms and images chosen by her subjects, she claimed to find evidence that the male self is defined though separation, the female self through connection. Jake and Amy, two children (who almost become the hero and heroine of her book), thus reflect opposing images of 'a self, measured against an abstract ideal of perfection and a self assessed through particular activities of care ... providing evidence of a conflict between responsibility to others and responsibility to self' (1982/1993: 35). Thus Amy's responses were diffident and contextualised, she was always prefacing her answers with 'well it depends ...'; 'to her, responsibility signifies response, an extension rather than a limitation of action ... doing what others are counting on her to do regardless of what she herself wants' (1982/1993: 38). For Jake, on the other hand, choosing a right course of action meant not doing what he wanted because he ought to try to think of others, acting categorically, weighing up moral choices almost mathematically, searching for a general standard of fairness according to the rules.

This image of female other-directedness may sound stereotypical and Gilligan has certainly been roundly criticised for over-generalising and essentialising her subjects. Certainly from the anthropological point of view, not only the moral dilemmas presented to elicit the information, but also the narratives themselves stand out as thoroughly of their (American) time and place. Nevertheless, despite its possible ethnocentrism, her standpoint does resonate with the view, which is of course also widely supported by statistics and research, that women's orientation to families and communities is often one of struggle, sacrifice and the sublimation of the individual in the collective in order to make ends meet. Much recent research has underlined that under conditions of restructuring and neo-liberal economic policy it is indeed often women's care that has held things together. The gendered nature of care is also a central tenet of environmental and eco-feminist perspectives, where Gilligan's interpretation of the relational morality expressed by the other-directed social selves of girls and women finds surprising echoes (for a dissenting voice, see Jackson 1993).

In a sense, then, an attention to caring work has always been woven into analyses of divisions of labour, production, resources and income. But until recently it was often simply a way of describing what women *did*. The actual process and meaning of caring as a social process subject to reformulation and change, connected with other aspects of cultural life, was taken largely for granted. Nor were the moral implications of such work or their connections with self worth or social value examined in great detail. The 'survival strategies' framework adopted by development sociology has also had contradictory implications. It has emphasised agency and rational action to challenge stereotypes of female passivity. However, it may also have encouraged an economistic viewpoint, which does not pay enough attention to the issues of subjectivity or moral identity which are crucial to sustainability of survival over a longer time span (Cornia 1987).

For example, in an interesting study of agricultural projects in India, Ruth Alsop demonstrated how possible economic gains from the new activities could all too easily be cancelled out by loss of social capital, as shifting relationships between women and men, as well as between groups of women divided by caste, became fractured by moral deprecation and stigma (Alsop 1993). Similarly, in her study of Guadalajara, Mercedes Gonzalez de la Rocha (1994) found that despite their entry into the waged labour force and apparently increased autonomy, women's management of subsistence and their responsibility for children's wellbeing remained the central defining aspect of their social worth and value. In 'post-scarcity' or conflict situations, women's resources or ability to carry out caring roles may well evaporate, undermining their social worth.

In the policy domain, privatisation and the commoditisation of everyday life have created a new social policy jargon of 'the mixed economy of care' and created debates about the relationship between health, wellbeing, caring and cost, and an increased emphasis on managerialism. In both North and South, a search for new forms of public social provision and changing ideas of citizenship confront a re-definition of caring roles that result from political conflict, migration, economic and reproductive change (Neale 1995, Green 1988, Colen 1986, Gupta 1996, Lewis and Keirnan 1996, O'Donovan 1993). Perhaps therefore we need to ask instead – under what conditions can, or do, men and women care? Risseeuw and Palriwala (1996: 38) raise the problem well in relation to economic restructuring when they write, 'Paradoxically, it is these very economic policies, which implicitly assume the continuance of extended and functional kinship and family units that have intensified the fragility and disinterest of members to provide for others'. When the spatial ties of community and the bodily bases of kinship and relatedness are shifting, as described by many of the authors in this volume, what patterns of interest and disinterest, connectedness and responsibility emerge?

To address the issues of risk, security and vulnerability we need to know more about the social practices of care, who will carry them out, within what definitions of moral responsibility and relatedness (Redclift 1996, Redclift 2001, Tomlinson, Corben de Romero, Lee Guy, Gibbon, this book). We develop this further in Part 2, 'Moral Boundaries'. Two themes emerge from this: a continuing interest in the constitution of the person through moral debate, and a new urgency in looking in more detail at how people actually think, act and construct the ethics of care and responsibility, whether in co-operative, individualistic or violent ways, as the political and economic context is re-defined.

Kathryn Tomlinson's chapter focuses on the respect given to bread by displaced Meskhetian Turks, who share their Russian neighbour's attachment to bread as a symbol of both sustenance and equality. She begins by examining their relationship with the State, both Soviet and now Russian, as mediated through the State's literal provision of bread. The faults of the present authorities are made acceptable by its policy on bread distribution, which echoes the Soviet ideology of equality, to which the Meskhetian Turks remain attached. She argues that the centrality of bread in daily life is partly due, but not limited to, its importance as the key daily foodstuff, that it is also an important expression of the role of women's labour and care within the household and therefore of their social identity. Furthermore, the sharing of food, actually and linguistically represented by bread, is central to the construction of kinship and to the process of enacting and developing relatedness.

Debates about who can or should take responsibility for the welfare of others lie at the heart of the moral sphere and have also been central, and contested, issues in analyses of gender. They are also an intrinsic aspect of the discourse and implementation of social policy both national and international. Nowhere are the issues more acute than in the case of the management of illness, and perhaps none has received more international visibility or raised more complex moral questions than has the case of HIV/AIDS. Sara Corben de Romero's research considers sexual practice and moral understanding in Pueblo, Mexico. Studying the transmission of information about illness and the complexities surrounding the negotiation of sexual behaviour, she suggests that moral codes affect men and women in extremely different ways. Her chapter underlines the point that international health policy and prevention programmes need to take much greater account of local moral meanings and practices than they yet do. She considers how individuals incorporate a new awareness of body and self in the context of HIV/AIDS and suggests that such perspectives could usefully inform health policy and provision. The locally contested aspects of rights are most clearly seen in reproductive and bio-political debates, where ethics, morality and science meet ideas of identity, ownership, self-fulfilment and desire. A changing demography and a changing political culture are also indivisible from these issues as far as their application in personal experience is concerned.

In both North and South, it is often argued that breakdown of the State and its retreat from social provision can be compensated for by increased reliance on 'informal' caring and the resilience of households and families. But the evidence we have does not necessarily support this view. In many parts of the world communities are becoming more fragile, and kin networks less able to support their members (Redclift 2001). In many others the ability to purchase care sharply divides class or ethnic groups, creating what Ginsburg and Rapp have called 'stratified reproduction'. Michelle Lee Guy examines precisely this gendering and ethnic differentiation of moral codes in a transnational context. She describes the lives of Filipina migrants who work as domestic servants in Malaysia, and the power of the moral values of selflessness, loyalty and sacrifice that they express in discussions and narratives. Commenting on the tensions that they experience with the moral world of their host communities she points to the paradox of personal and communal values in the growth of a transnational community.

Finally, drawing on ethnographic research from the Netherlands, Tony Watling, discusses the conditions under which religious pluralism and diversity of religious affiliation and identity can be accommodated and assimilated. His chapter sets present debates about religious division in the context of the specific historical development of the Dutch State, and examines the conditions that were conducive to the philosophical negotiation of ecumenism and tolerance.

DEBATING RIGHTS AND VIOLENCE

Moral claims are also intrinsic to the political process, to integrate or to exclude, to endorse or to reject. Ethically inflected struggles over the validity of the use of force, the legitimate basis of power or the justifiable behaviour of opponents are central to the pursuit of political action. Proclaiming moral purpose or moral authority is a strategy used to purify the use of force and to 'sacralise' political intentions (Falk Moore 1993: 1). It can be used to defend them from debate and even to suspend the normal conventions of government or law. Far from being timeless cultural truths, these questions are often crystallised in acute moments of crisis, through which the definition and the congruence of familiar concepts is reinforced or called into question. Alternatively, they may involve longer-term cleavages between opposing groups, who draw on moral rhetoric as a justificatory discourse. The definition of external threats posed by others helps to endorse the moral legitimacy of force. Morality in action comes to be constituted through history, myth, symbol and memory and appeals to universal 'fact' become indistinguishable form moral conflicts.

Recent attention to post-conflict processes has demonstrated this in a number of striking ways. The divergent interpretations surrounding the values of 'forgiveness', 'justice' or 'reconciliation' reveal that the same terms carry widely different connotations. They indicate some of the difficulties surrounding the definition of the boundaries of moral communities or cultures. For example Wilson (2001), discussing the South African Truth and Reconciliation Commission, argues that township courts were constituted around a (moral) notion of the necessity of punishment that was diametrically apposed to the model of restorative justice guiding the Commission. In the context of Sri Lanka, Argenti-Pillen (2003) shows how a subtle and disguised moral conversation full of euphemism and avoidance is used to enable the co-existence of perpetrators and victims, but without reconciliation.

Such opposing definitions are also evident in discussions of 'rights', a moral concept rooted in a specific cultural history that has been generalised to form the founding value of the first embryonic international community (see Rawls 1984). In one sense, the question of the Western origin of human rights may be redundant, as human rights come to be seen as the first 'universalist' ideology (Anheier, Glasius and Kaldor 2001). This is not to imply homogeneity, but rather to stress the interpenetration and changing definitions of moral values in a newly global arena despite the plurality of local interpretations. The power of generality conferred by the international system produces a mosaic of endorsement or of resistance, for both *local* as well as global reasons. Central here are conflicts over the redefined or redefining State, which generates public policy-making and forms of disciplinary power, however tenuous and contingent this may be. In its assemblage of regulation and resources, circumscribed by private or multi-national forces, legitimacy for various processes of distribution and entitlement must be sought through the manipulation of moral justifications and political claims. The traditional term 'government' describes a series of roles and functions. The current usage of 'governance', on the other hand, implicitly responds to newer debates about exactly what the proper, most equitable relationship between persons and powers should be. Thus the recent concern with 'good governance' seeks to promote public institutions, which are informed by virtues of rights and representativeness, an explicitly moral concept of authority.

It is therefore becoming particularly important to understand more about how specific interpretations of rights articulate with the discourses of national institutions and particular interests, and how they interact with international and juridical systems in the global arena (Wilson 1997, Wilson 2001, Wilson, Cowan and Dembour 2001). More importantly for the purposes of this book, such a perspective helps to make us critically self-conscious of Western value systems, as a web of contested meanings and representations of its own.

In Part 3, 'Moral Rhetoric', we discuss the use of moral language and imagery by the State and by specific social and ethnic groups. The contributors explore the suggestion that we are increasingly witnessing the reinforcement of dichotomies between opposing local value systems and between 'Western' and 'other' forms of meaning, while at the same time we can also identify the inter-penetration and hybridity of values. The real world companions of rights and justice are discrimination, violence and terror and the three chapters in this section complement the abstraction of philosophical debate by considering the ways in which rights are negated through stigma or violence and the language through which such practices are naturalised or disputed. They explore the ways in which representations of good or bad conduct, proper or transgressive behaviour, valued or despised belief, create citizenship, political participation, membership and legitimacy.

Paul Twinn's account of racialisation in the Caribbean examines the process in which an oppressed group, part of the Carib population of St Vincent, was denigrated through the re-working of a historical event. The chapter argues that the moral stigmatisation that followed also helped, paradoxically, to created the conditions for contestation, consciousness and resistance. His chapter indicates the power of moral codes to shape the historical record, their ability to inflict symbolic violence to endorse the memorialisation of those accorded moral rectitude, while further pathologising and excluding those who are regarded as marginal. The story of 'Jack Iron' is a powerful reminder that history lingers, and that later generations carry the burdens of evaluations inherited from the past.

Contemporary moral debates can also be trans-local in scope, spreading out from central points and creating a web of culturally diverse responses and positions. To examine these 'migratory' meanings, Nanneke Redclift takes the attacks of 11 September 2001 as a critical event that was witnessed and discussed simultaneously from a multitude of different contexts. The chapter contrasts views *from* and views of America, drawing on ethnographic research from Yucatan, Mexico to suggest that the events, as they were experienced in one particular location, created a moment of 'disclosure' in which tacit understandings and moral evaluations were made explicit. As new cultural encounters begin to unfold, or in the attempt to wrestle with unfamiliar events, 'meanings are re-valued as they are practically enacted' (Sahlins 1981). The chapter draws on a series of responses and moral conversations to suggest some of the ways that events 'outside' a particular frame of reference can be used to position and define speakers within. It is possible to identify a mosaic of such practical enactments which lead to diverse chains of consequence, provoking contests of meaning, and in some cases to revaluation (Weeks 1995, Ginsburg and Rapp 1995).

Finally, research in Eritrea by Michael Mahrt compares two important contexts of violent conflict, the Liberation War (1961–91) and the Border War (1998–2000). Mahrt analyses the various institutions for dealing with different kinds of violence in the area. He examines the perception of space, which he argues is related to who gains legitimacy to perform violent acts, against whom violence is thought to be legitimate, and how they claim such legitimacy. He sees violence as an extension of the body, both of the perpetrator and the victim, and thus raises questions about 'the moral implications of distance' which have wider applicability, namely that of the victim's perception of his or her distance from the perpetrator, arguing that this relates to the perception of the extension of the body and agency of other people.

CONCLUSION

In the 21st century we can continue to talk about human values and the ways people seek to realise them, but there has been a shift from a concern with moral codes to an exploration of moral arguments. There is greater recognition that moralities are constantly manipulated, and above all that 'morality constitutes the self and makes for action in the world' (Howell 1997). The heterogeneity and contradictions of morality are also more visible, leading to a processual view of moral practice and social life, and an interest in the way people construct their 'own moral image among significant others' (Pardo 1996).

There are therefore two areas to which the contemporary anthropology of morality can make a particular contribution. One is that of the many and various injunctions, prohibitions, sanctions, endorsements and affirmations that constantly generate and produce identity, particularly gender identity, and work to create the interpersonal construction of the self. The other is a deeper understanding of social process, enabling us to see the various ways in which new kinds of knowledge become culturally incorporated through debate about things that are seen as 'good', or desirable, threatening or dangerous, and about hopes and aspirations in everyday life.

This collection opens up some connections that might be drawn between political, technological and personal change. If definitions of physical essence are undergoing a metamorphosis, the kind of connectedness we have to past and future and the kinds of relationship we establish with future generations may also be shifting. The State can be seen as retreating, but also as becoming more involved in aspects of personal life. The changing location and meaning of sexual pleasure and freedom has also contributed to ongoing redefinitions of gender. It has led to struggles to define and contest responsibility. The domestic domain occupies a different location in the wider social structure. The cultural meaning of children and childhood is being reworked. Reproduction and the ability, or choice, to care for others is dependent on context and stratified rather than merely repetitive.

In bringing together these essays we are both carrying on a tradition and opening a new debate. By locating the study of moralities in the language of contest and discourse, and setting it within the global dynamic of North and South, our aim is to transcend old polarities and to indicate some challenging ways of thinking about contemporary society and culture.

BIBLIOGRAPHY

Alsop, R (1993) 'Whose interests? Problems in planning for women's practical needs' 21(3) *World Development* 367–77

Anheier, H, Glasius, M and Kaldor, M (2001) *Global Civil Society Yearbook*, Oxford: OUP

Appell, G and Madan, T (eds) (1988) *Choice and Morality in Anthropological Perspective: Essays in Honor of Derek Freeman*, Albany: State University of New York Press

Argenti-Pillen, A (2003) *Masking Terror: How Women Contain Violence in Sri Lanka*, Philadelphia: University of Pennsylvania Press

Banfield, E (1958) *The Moral Basis of a Backward Society*, New York: Free Press, London: Collier-Macmillan

Battaglia, D (1999) 'Toward an ethics of the open subject: writing culture in good conscience', in Moore, H (ed), *Anthropological Theory Today*, Cambridge: CUP

Bauman, Z (1995) *Life in Fragments: Essays in Post-Modern Morality*, Oxford: Blackwell

Beauchamp, T and Childress, T (1983/2001) *Principles of Biomedical Ethics*, 5th edn, Oxford: OUP

Borofsky, R (1997) 'Cook, Lono, Obeyesekere and Sahlins' 38(2) *Current Anthropology* 255–82

Busch, L (2000) *The Eclipse of Morality: Science, State and Market*, New York: Aldine de Gruyter

Chadwick, R (1987/1990) *Ethics, Reproduction and Genetic Control*, London: Routledge

Chadwick, R (2001) *The Concise Encyclopaedia of the Ethics of New Technologies*, San Diego, California and London: Academic Press

Clarke, J (1996) 'Public nightmares and communitarian dreams: the crisis of the social in social welfare', in Edgell, S, Hetherington, K and Warde, A (eds), *Consumption Matters*, Cambridge, MA: Blackwell/Sociological Review

Cohen, A (2000) *Signifying Identities: Anthropological Perspectives on Boundaries and Contested Values*, London: Routledge

Colen, S (1986) 'With respect and feelings: voices of West Indian childcare and domestic workers in New York City', in Cole, JB (ed), *All American Women: Lines that Divide, Ties that Bind*, New York: Free Press

Cook, JW (1999) *Morality and Cultural Difference*, New York and Oxford: OUP

Cornia, G (1987) 'Adjustment at the household level: potentials and limitations of survival strategies', in Cornia, G, Jolly, R and Stewart, F (eds), *Adjustment with a Human Face: Protecting the Vulnerable and Promoting Growth*, Oxford: OUP

Dumont, L (1986) *Essays on Individualism: Modern Ideology in Anthropological Perspective*, Chicago: Chicago UP

Edel, M and Edel, A (1959/2000) *Anthropology and Ethics: The Quest for Moral Understanding*, New Brunswick, USA and London: Transaction Publishers

Evans, J (2000) 'A sociological account of the growth of principlism' 30(5) *Hastings Center Report* 31–38

Falk Moore, S (ed) (1993) *Moralising States and the Ethnography of the Present*, Arlington, VA: American Anthropological Association

Foucault, M (1986) 'On the genealogy of ethics: an overview of work in progress', in Rabinow, P (ed), *The Foucault Reader*, Harmondsworth: Penguin

Franklin, S (1997) *Embodied Progress: A Cultural Account of Assisted Conception*, London: Routledge

Franklin, S (2000) 'Life itself: global nature and the genetic imaginary', in Franklin, S, Lury, C and Stacey, J (eds), *Global Nature, Global Culture*, London: Sage, pp 188–227

Fukuyama, F (1992) *The End of History and the Last Man*, London: Hamish Hamilton

Gewirth, A (1978) *Reason and Morality*, Chicago: Chicago UP

Gilligan, C (1982/1993) *In a Different Voice: Psychological Theory and Women's Development*, Cambridge, MA: Harvard UP

Ginsburg, F (1989) *Contested Lives: The Abortion Debate in an American Community*, Berkeley: University of California Press

Ginsburg, F and Rapp, R (eds) (1995) *Conceiving the New World Order: The Global Politics of Reproduction*, Berkeley: University of California Press

Gonzalez de la Rocha, M (1994) *The Resources of Poverty: Women and Survival in a Mexican City*, Oxford: Blackwell

Green, H (1988) *Informal Carers: A Study Carried Out on Behalf of the Department of Health and Social Security as Part of the 1985 General Household Survey*, London: HMSO

Gullestad, M (1996) *Everyday Life Philosophers: Modernity, Morality and Autobiography in Norway*, Oslo, Boston: Scandinavian UP

Gupta, JA (1996) *New Freedoms, New Dependencies: New Reproductive Technologies, Women's Health and Autonomy*, unpublished PhD thesis, University of Leiden

Howell, S (ed) (1997) *The Ethnography of Moralities*, London: Routledge

Humphrey, M (2002) *The Politics of Atrocity and Reconciliation: From Terror to Trauma*, London: Routledge

Huntington, SP (1996) *The Clash of Civilizations and the Remaking of World Order*, New York: Simon & Schuster

Ignatieff, M (1997) *The Warrior's Honour: Ethnic War and the Modern Conscience*, New York: Henry Holt

Jackson, C (1993) 'Environmentalism and gender interests in the Third World' 24 *Development and Change* 649–77

Lasch, S (1996a) 'Introduction to the ethics and difference debate' 13(2) *Theory, Culture and Society* (Special Issue) 75–77

Lasch, S (1996b) 'Postmodern ethics: the missing ground' 13(2) *Theory, Culture and Society* (Special Issue) 91–104

Lewis, J and Keirnan K (1996) 'The boundaries between marriage, non-marriage and parenthood: changes in behaviour and policy in post-war Britain' 21(3) *Journal of Family History* 372–87

Macdonald, S, Holden, P and Ardener, S (eds) (1987) *Images of Women in Peace and War: Cross Cultural and Historical Perspectives*, London: Macmillan, for Oxford University Women's Studies Committee

Maclean, A (1993) *The Elimination of Morality: Reflections on Utilitarianism and Bioethics*, London: Routledge

Marshall, P (1992) 'Anthropology and Bioethics' 6(1) *Medical Anthropology Quarterly* 49–73

Moody-Adams, M (1997) *Fieldwork in Familiar Places: Morality, Culture and Philosophy*, Cambridge, MA: Harvard UP

Morrison, T (1987/1997) *Beloved*, London: Vintage

Moser, C (1989) *Community Participation in Urban Policy in the Third World*, Oxford: Pergamon

Mwabo, G, Ugaz, C and White, G (eds) (2001) *Social Provision in Low-Income Countries: New Patterns and Emerging Trends*, Oxford: OUP

Neale, B (1995) *The New Parenthood?*, Research Working Paper No 13, Leeds: University of Leeds School of Sociology and Social Policy

Norgaard, R (1994) *Development Betrayed*, London: Routledge

Oakley, A and Williams, AS (eds) (1994) *The Politics of the Welfare State*, London: UCL Press

Obeyesekere, G (1996) *The Apotheosis of Captain Cook*, Chicago: Chicago UP

O'Donovan, K (1993) *Family Law Matters*, London: Pluto

Overing, J (1985) *Reason and Morality*, London: Tavistock

Pardo, I (1996) *Managing Existence in Naples: Morality, Action and Structure*, Cambridge: CUP

Parkin, D (1985) *The Anthropology of Evil*, Oxford: Blackwell

Parry, J and Bloch, M (eds) (1989) *Money and the Morality of Exchange*, Cambridge: CUP

Pocock, D (1986) 'The ethnography of morals' 1(1) *International Journal of Moral and Social Studies* 3–20

Rawls, J (1972) *A Theory of Justice*, Oxford: OUP

Rawls, J (1984) 'A theory of justice', in Sandel, M (ed) *Liberalism and its Critics*, Oxford: Blackwell

Raz, J (1994) *Ethics in the Public Domain: Essays in the Morality of Law and Politics*, Oxford: Clarendon, New York: OUP

Redclift, N (1996) 'Human and divine: the female body and the second reformation', unpublished paper given at the Anthropologies of Modernity: Identity, the Body and Material Culture Conference, Athens

Redclift, N (2001) 'Contexts of caretaking: privatism, diversity and households in social provision', in Mwabo, G, Ugaz, C and White, G (eds), *Social Provision in Low Income Countries: New Patterns and Emerging Trends*, Oxford: OUP

Redfield, R (1955) *The Little Community: Viewpoints for the Study of a Human Whole*, Chicago: Chicago UP

Riddell, M (1996) 'The pragmatic humanitarian wants doctors to do one thing: take the burden of guilt from killing the mentally ill – Mary Warnock' *New Statesman*, 25 October, pp 22–24

Risseeuw, C and Palriwala, R (eds) (1996) *Shifting Circles of Support: Contextualising Kinship and Gender in South Asia and Sub-Saharan Africa*, London: Sage

Roseneil, S (1995) *Disarming Patriarchy: Feminism and Political Action at Greenham*, Buckingham: Open UP

Ruddick, S (1989) *Maternal Thinking: Towards a Politics of Peace*, Boston: Beacon Press

Sahlins, M (1981) *Historical Metaphors and Mythical Realities*, Ann Arbor: University of Michigan Press

Scheper-Hughes, N (1992) *Death Without Weeping: The Violence of Everyday Life in Brazil*, Berkeley: University of California Press

Sevenhuijsen, S (1998) *Citizenship and the Ethics of Care: Feminist Considerations on Justice, Morality and Politics*, London, New York: Routledge

Singer, P (1979/1993) *Practical Ethics*, Cambridge, MA and New York: Cambridge UP

Strathern, M (1981) *Kinship at the Core: An Anthropology of Elmdon, a Village in North-West Essex in the Nineteen-Sixties*, Cambridge: CUP

Strathern, M (1988) *The Gender of the Gift*, Cambridge: CUP

Strathern, M (1992) *Reproducing the Future: Anthropology, Kinship and the New Reproductive Technologies*, Cambridge: Cambridge UP

Tronto, J (1993) *Moral Boundaries: A Political Argument for an Ethic of Care*, London: Routledge

Warren, K and Cady, D (1994) 'Feminism and peace' 9(2) *Hypatia* (Special Issue)

Weeks, J (1995) *Invented Moralities: Sexual Values in an Age of Uncertainty*, Cambridge: Polity

Wilson, R (1997) *Human Rights, Culture and Context: Anthropological Perspectives*, London: Pluto

Wilson, R (2001) *The Politics of Truth and Reconciliation in South Africa: Legitimizing the Post-Apartheid State*, Cambridge: CUP

Wilson, R, Cowan, JK and Dembour, MB (eds) (2001) *Culture and Rights: Anthropological Perspectives*, Cambridge: CUP

PART 1

MORAL EXCHANGE: SOCIALISING NEW KINDS OF KNOWLEDGE

CHAPTER 1

'AMORAL' BIOTECHNOLOGY AND A NORWEGIAN MORAL DOMAIN

Sara Skodbo

INTRODUCTION[1]

In Norway, genetic technology[2] and its human proponents, biotechnologists, are considered morally suspect and are excluded from 'good society' through regulatory processes that embrace consumer protest, environmental activism and manufacturers' reluctance. This chapter presents selected ethnographic data on the terms of inclusion and exclusion in the relations between government regulators and biotechnologists. It is argued that exclusion is actually due to the technology's/technologists' challenge to central Norwegian moral values of 'equality as sameness'. Genetic technology enters the field as a would-be amoral agent, and those who interact with it are subsequently set the impossible task of reconciling amoral genetic technology with existing value systems, leading to personal and professional distress. These conflicts offer insight into the identity forming processes of persons and things, and the contours of a Norwegian social and moral domain where amoral science is irreconcilable with social inclusion.

The Anglo-American and European response to the emergence of genetic technology in the food industry and other areas has been marked by explicit moral debate and concern (see, eg, Nelkin and Lindee 1995, Ho 1998, Reiss and Straughan 1996). 'Evil scientists' and 'dangerous genes' are perceived to threaten a peaceful and beneficent nature. Government and research ethics committees debate the ethical aspects of scientific endeavour, as 'ethics' emerges as a powerful social and political discourse in its own right (Badiou 2001). This is nowhere more true than in Norway, where the main trait of response to genetics has been one of 'moral concern' (Nielsen *et al* 2001, Nielsen, Monson and Tennoe 2000, Skodbo 2003c). Such discourses are indicative of the moral nature of our relationship with

1   This article draws on PhD research (Skodbo 2003c) funded by the British Federation of Women Graduates, ESRC, UCL Graduate School and the Norwegian Research Council (NFR). Fieldwork was carried out in Norway during 1999–2001. This research, based on 14 months of field research using interviews, participant observation and document analysis, mapped the emergence of genetic technology in the Norwegian food industry, and draws on the anthropology of art to develop new approaches to the study of technology. Thanks are due to Nanneke Redclift, Simone Abram, and colleagues at UCL and Oslo University for their helpful comments on earlier drafts.

2   In the following I use 'genetic technology' and 'biotechnology' interchangeably to refer to modern, genetic engineering based biotechnology. I do not consider traditional biotechnology practices such as fermentation technologies.

nature and technology, but nevertheless only tell half the story. The underlying bases of these moral debates vary across cultures, and discourses must be explored in relation to deeper cultural processes and actions.

The chapter first introduces a theoretical position on genetics as a subject in society, one that acts and is acted upon. The second section provides a brief sketch of central Norwegian moral values as a basis for understanding people's interaction with genetics. This provides a context within which to examine regulators' struggles to include genetics in a regulatory field that is strongly guided by these values. I go on to examine the biotechnologists' view and their experience of moral exclusion. A contrasting example of a modern Norwegian ritual illustrates the moral uniformity at the heart of inclusion in the Norwegian social domain. Against this background I finally posit a model of Norwegian sociality as morality, defining a domain into which non-natives, including genetic technology, must tread with caution.

GENETIC TECHNOLOGY AS SOCIAL AGENT

The current chapter works from the premise that genetic technology is best understood as a Gellian 'index' (Gell 1998), which engages with others and is engaged with on an affective basis. I have explored this at length elsewhere (Skodbo 2003c). In essence this approach suggests that, like human agents, genetic technologies traverse national and global boundaries, engaging with and being engaged by others.

The agency of objects is increasingly studied in anthropology (see Strathern 1999, Gell 1998, Knappett 2002, Graves-Brown 2000, Ingold 2000); new foci are on the processes by which such agency is understood, perceived and given meaning. There has been a convergence around the need to understand the agency of objects as a route through which to overcome the opposition between external material worlds and the disembodied will of the human agent that acts upon it, where 'mind, body and world are seen as *codependent*' (Knappett 2002: 98–99). In the fieldwork from which the following analysis draws I explored the relations that genetic technology engendered with government administrators, consumer association representatives, environmental activists, scientists, food companies and others in Norway during 1999–2000. This was a multi-sited, *affect*-based project, which unpacked the linkages between actors in the technological field, as depicted in Figure 1, and allowed a deeper understanding of the processes underlying the moral debate surrounding genetics.

Figure 1 Technological field

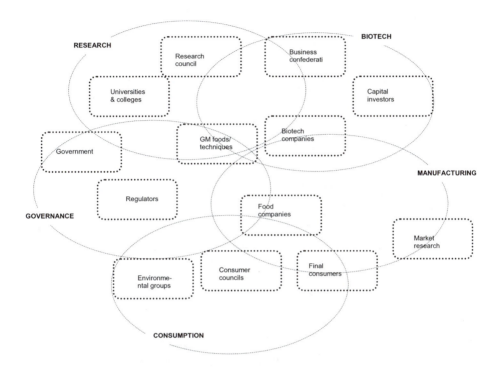

This affect- and agency-based approach depends on the notion that genetic technology and knowledge (apparently disembodied and abstract entities) act like 'things', and 'things' act like people (Strathern 1999, Gell 1998). Not in a Latourian sense, where rational self-interested actors strive to establish networks to advance their cause (eg, Latour and Woolgar 1985, Callon 1986, Latour 1988, 1996), but rather out of a complex of factors. As I have argued elsewhere, love, enchantment, fear and trepidation, sadness and above all a sense of desire to engage with moral values guide actions in relation to the genetic technology and to other agents in the field.

Figure 2, drawing on Gell's (1998) work on art objects and their relationships to the social agents surrounding them, illustrates aspects of how genetic technologies are enmeshed in social relations as social agents. It prefigures some of the relationships that emerge later in the chapter.[3]

---

3 See Skodbo 2003c for further discussion of the manner in which these figures can be used to make explicit the assumptions that we bring to our analyses. This research, based on 14 months of field research using interviews, participant observation and document analysis, mapped the emergence of genetic technology in the Norwegian food industry, and draws on the anthropology of art to develop new approaches to the study of technology.

Figure 2 Selection of relations embedded within genetic technology

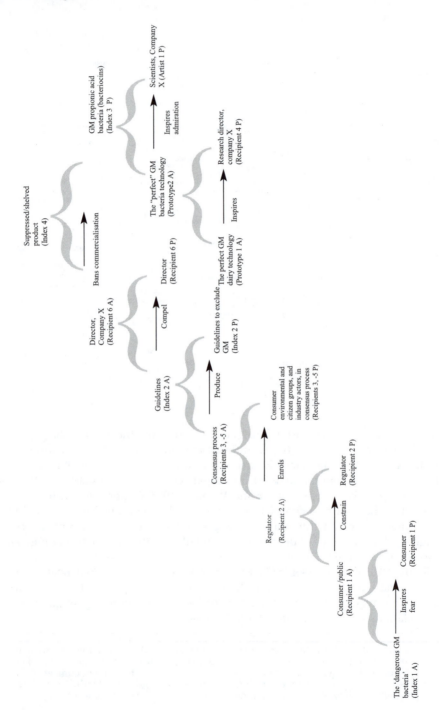

The figure is read from bottom to top, with each set of interactions leading on to and embedded within the next. It shows how the technological 'indexes' (Index 3 and Index 4) combine the actions of both its designers ('artists') and recipients (cf Latour's (2000) Berlin key). The final genetic index (4) embodies or contains within it the sets of relations conditioning their design, use and prohibition.

The figure reveals to us sets of relations that are contained within each other, in a manner similar to Strathern's 'partible' or distributable person (1988), thus opening for analysis relationships that are usually bracketed off under rubrics such as 'economic pressure', 'political interference' or 'technical feasibility'. Instead we see that a genetic technology (here a genetically modified propionic bacteria) has within it many relations, and is drawn into relations with others. Consumers fear it and seek to expel it. Research directors are fascinated by it, scientists dedicated to it. The Company Director is both fascinated and suspicious. There is a definite paucity of neo-classical rational economic actors; instead we are able to unpack and consider the fears, anxieties, enchantment and desires underlying actions and relationships (Skodbo 2003c).

In the current context, such an approach allows us to examine how moral debate on genetics is connected with deeper cultural anxieties surrounding the moral boundaries that constitute the Norwegian social field. Anxieties about and fascination with the technology are expressed in certain types of relationships; some relations are allowed, others banned. People and technologies are excluded or included, in response to fears or fascination. The reasons behind these acts of inclusion and exclusion are revealing about the nature of Norwegian sociality. I turn now to a brief consideration of values underlying Norwegian sociality, as a basis for discussing how genetics throws light on the morality of sociality.

THE MORAL BASIS OF NORWEGIAN SOCIALITY: EQUALITY AS SAMENESS

A number of commentators have noted that, in contrast to many other western European cultures, an explicitly and fundamentally moral basis of sociality is particular to Norway (Barnes 1954, Gullestad see especially 2001, Skodbo 2003a, 2003c). It has been shown that the primary or dominant value – the moral axis against which people's actions are measured (Strathern 1997) – is the value of 'equality as sameness' (see especially Gullestad 1989, 2001, Barnes 1954, Graubard 1986, Odner 1996, Lien, Lidén and Vike 2001). This needs some clarification, since as I argue, it is central background to understanding the anxieties about genetic engineering.

The Norwegian term for 'equality', *likhet*, is also the term for 'sameness' (Gullestad 1989). This means that the concept of *likhet* has within it an ambiguity or tension, in that in order to think of oneself as *of equal worth* one must also be *of the same kind*. Social intercourse will generally seek to establish that participants are *the same* (Gullestad 1984, 1989, 1992, 2001). Gullestad stresses that while 'Norwegian culture is fundamentally individualistic in the sense that each human being is ideologically in the foreground … the Norwegian form of individualism coexists with a strong emphasis on equality defined as sameness' (1996: 2). These values are made explicit in Norwegian sayings such as *'Like barn leker best'* ('similar children play best together'). The infamous *Janteloven* (Jante Law), which expresses both anti-hierarchy and anti-difference sentiments, states for instance 'Do not think you are anything special' and 'Do not fool yourself into thinking you are better than we are'.[4] These core values 'lead to forms of interaction where similarities are emphasised and differences are tactfully ignored' (Gullestad 2001: 35, my translation; see Dahl-Jørgensen 1997 and Vabo 2000 for ethnographic examples from working life that relate to these tensions).

Thus it is a common perception in Norway that people belong to the same general 'middle class'; that everyone owns their own home and generally have a *hytte* (cabin in the mountains or by the sea). There is a corresponding tendency to fail to recognise deeper social inequalities. The moral necessity of appearing the same is encountered in the way that misbehaving children are chastised; '*oppfør deg som folk!*' ('conduct yourself like [other] people!'), they are told. Tensions between sameness and difference mean that differences must be under-communicated in order to maintain social cohesion; differences are submerged as much as possible, and conflict is avoided (Gullestad 1984, 1989, 1992, 2001).

The Norwegian social, political and economic realms are dominated by these values, and by the tension between moral and immoral behaviour along this central measure (Skodbo 2003c). Hierarchies are considered immoral; to feel superior to others is immoral; earning a lot of money, and especially the display of that wealth, is immoral. Similarly, consensus-based processes are highly praised; not being boastful or bragging, playing down difference and conforming to uniform behaviours are highly valued and morally good (Skodbo 2003c). This is expressed in huge rates of participation in shared collective events such as volunteering rates (30% of the population is well integrated in volunteering: see Andresen 1999), cycle to work schemes, 'Get the people fit for the Olympics' (see eg, Ommundsen and Aarø 1994) and other health schemes, and so on.

THE ENTRANCE OF GENETICS

In recent decades, genetic technology entered the Norwegian realm as it did in the rest of western Europe and the US. It has caused anxiety in Norway as in other countries, and is strictly regulated by two Acts, the 1997 Gene Technology Act and the 1993 Biotechnology Act. In the (human) food industry, where I did my fieldwork, no genetically engineered products, processes or ingredients were permitted without formal approval by the Ministries or the Food Authority (SNT). No such permissions have been granted. Nevertheless, genetic technology is present in Norway. It is found in research laboratories, where scientists pursue it. It is found as ingredients in food products such as tortilla chips or soya milk (cf

---

4   The Jante Law comes from Dano-Norwegian writer Aksel Sandemose's misanthropic novel (1933) about a town called Jante, in which he examines the dark side of small town mentality. This mentality is encapsulated in moral laws called Jante Law. These laws appeared in everyday conversation in the field as representative of Norwegian thinking, both disparagingly and jokingly. For example, an informant tells me: 'Everyone says that [the Jante Law] is terrible, but then we're just like that. It's hard to admit.' Gopal (2000) considers the Jante Law to act as a signifier of doxic knowledge, an observation that my experiences in the field would tend to affirm.

SNT and Veterinærinstituttet 2001). Medical and diagnostics companies make use of it; additives, enzymes used in baking, brewing and the dairy industry are often produced through genetic engineering (imported to Norway from Denmark). Regulators and government are faced with a tricky task in controlling it, as it is often invisible, unreported and difficult to detect.

In Norway, genetics is feared as potentially dangerous and as an unknown entity. It does not (yet) have a social use or role, as its agency is difficult to discern. People are particularly concerned to establish the nature of genetics' moral agency; whether it will be a force for good or evil. On the one hand, people ask whether it will simply increase the efficiency of manufacturing processes and produce greater profits for companies and individual entrepreneurs. Environmentalists thus argue that it is simply a 'technology for profit' (fieldnotes). A contrasting vision is put forward by a small number of actors who claim that genetics will be a good and useful tool for society, and indeed the world as a whole. These (generally scientific) informants argue that genetics will save lives, and that attitudes will change 'when the choice is between going blind or eating genetically modified rice' (fieldnotes).

People are thus committed to establishing whether genetics is 'good' or 'bad'. However, as I have established elsewhere (Skodbo 2003a, 2003b, 2003c), genetic technology brings with it something that is difficult to handle in the Norwegian sphere, namely abstract scientific knowledge that claims to be *amoral*. Scientific knowledge, knowledge for knowledge's sake, is deeply suspect in the Norwegian context. Hakken (1999), for example, explores IT development in Norway and shows how IT must be subjected to social control and made *useful* before it can be permitted to exist. Similarly, other successful and central Norwegian scientific technologies such as petroleum and chemicals industries are deeply *useful* sciences with clear practical application. Genetics, I argue (Skodbo 2003c), is not (yet) so clearly useful, except, of course, in the medical realm where it has indeed met with a degree of acceptance in Norway (Nielsen *et al* 2001).

Genetic technology makes no claims to being either good or bad, but insists on remaining at the level of abstract, potential (and in many claims universal, in the sense of being concerned with DNA, the very stuff of life) scientific knowledge. This amoral, anonymous expertise that is associated with modern global science (Shapin 1994) is deeply troubling to the Norwegian moral and social field (Sirnes 1996).

REGULATION: THE PRACTICE OF MORAL GOVERNANCE

Genetics has as yet no socially comprehensible role. It nevertheless asks for inclusion in the social technological field (see Figure 1 above), as its allies invite it in, or it sneaks in unannounced through imported processed foods. It is government regulators who are in the frontline of negotiations over this entry into the Norwegian domain. The way in which regulators negotiate the concern and frustration of consumers and biotechnologists, faced with amoral genetics, is revealing about both the agentic nature of genetics and the particular, local cultural aspects of Norwegian concerns.

Norwegian regulatory processes have traditionally taken place in accordance with the dominant values of sameness and equality discussed above. Anonymous expertise, in the sense most often understood in for example the UK context, (ie, as amoral, apolitical knowledge) does not provide a legitimate basis for policy-making or regulation. Lien, Lidén and Vike (2001: 23) remind us that 'abstract principles' cannot justify policy or action in Norway. Where global traditions of regulation appear more hierarchical and differentiating in nature, they are based on appeals to 'amoral' principles such as 'economic law' (Carrier 1998) and are cloaked in the amoral language of scientific discourse (Foucault 1991, Rabinow 1996a, Hacking 1991, Rose 1991, Abram and Vike 2003, Vike 1997, Shore and Wright 1997), Norwegian regulatory traditions are instead based on explicitly 'moral' principles.

Instead, personal integrity is the measure by which politicians and regulators tend to be judged, as they seek to place themselves as morally good.[5] They assure moral amity through commitment to sameness and equality; political legitimacy is gained through commitment to consensus processes, dominant morality and the moral majority. Regulation in the food industry was strongly characterised by these values. Control and inspection in the area of foods is based on a process of consultation, education, and guidance. Regulators distance themselves from punitive measures or scientific evidence of wrongdoing. Rita, a specialist in this area, drew a critical contrast with traditions in the Netherlands:

> The Dutch state has a liberal tradition for the individual. But they're control obsessed ... No consultant services, no discussion ... Just fines. Chemists or managers are in charge of inspection. Inspectors are strictly certified. Norway is the only country that doesn't have specific qualifications for inspectors. [In Norway] it is based on the inspection itself [ie, the visit, the social event] not on work in the laboratory ... Their [the Dutch] inspection system is built on mistrust. Institutionalised mistrust. (Fieldnotes)

In contrast to the mistrust of anonymous scientific systems, the Norwegian system is based on the idea of institutionalised trust. Rather than scientific testing being the point of contact between regulators and regulated, the 'visit' is most important. We find basic moral values of consensus, education, co-guidance at the heart of the Norwegian tradition (Elvbakken 1996). In contrast see Vike (1997) for an interesting example of governance floundering after failing to base itself on strict adherence to common moralities.

Such commitment to sameness and equality became evident in the commitment of genetics regulation to 'ethics'. Thus the Norwegian Gene Technology Act insists that the Norwegian government must:

> ... ensure that production and use of genetically modified organisms takes place in an *ethically and socially* responsible way, in accordance with the principle of sustainable development and without negative consequences for health and the environment (Gene Technology Act 1993, Chapter 1 § 1, emphasis added)

In Norway 'ethics' is closely associated with the common good and responsibility to the whole of Norwegian society. Individual decisions to use genetics must be

---

5   Reminding us of Shapin's (1994) characterisation of the pre-modern scientist, where personal integrity rather than anonymous expertise was primary.

considered by the broadest selection of society's members. This imperative to be responsible to the broadest common denominator is put into practice through the enactment of the precautionary principle (*førevar prinsippet*), which forms the basis for decision-making both locally and centrally (Skodbo 2003c). It ensures that a broad range of actors – preferably all those who are affected by an issue – are involved in decision-making.

Thus, individual applications to use genetics are considered by actors as diverse as the Housewives' Society and the Ministry of Health before decisions are made. In this way regulatory practices value as equally as possible disparate members of society and respect their essential sameness and right to be heard (Vike, Lidén and Lien 2001, Skodbo 2003c), and scientific knowledge is subject to democratic control.

SAMENESS AND EQUALITY FOR ALL: THE FOOD REGULATORS' DILEMMA

The Norwegian food regulators *Statens Næringsmiddeltilsyn* (SNT) are responsible for regulating food manufacture. Early on, their regulation of genetics reflected attempts to adhere to these traditions and subject scientific knowledge and genetic engineering to control at the hands of 'the people'.

Early guidelines on genetically modified ingredients, developed by SNT, were thus the result of consensus processes (see Recipient 2, Figure 2). SNT held workshops and seminars with industry, the consumer association and environmentalist groups. Rather than imposing guidelines at a distance, regulators brought all the parties together and developed a consensus.

This process of discussion, negotiation and deciding in unity were praised by regulators:

> The labelling demands were accepted in July 1997. We had lots of dialogue with the Environmental Organisation and the Consumer Council. We had consultation meetings in the auditorium here. People were very passionate; everyone was open and talked a lot. It was good, every one was happy. (Regulator, fieldnotes)

Such co-operation is positive and fair, and is characteristic of moral governance.

The outcome of these consultations was a consensus that genetics engineering was undesired. Food manufacturers would rather avoid genetics, the consumer association wanted to ensure that the authorities took full responsibility, environmentalists feared the unintended consequences of genetic modification. Regulators subsequently issued strict guidance on GM ingredients (a lower limit for labelling was set at 2% of any single ingredient):

> We're the strictest in the world. The 2% limit was a compromise that everyone could live with. (Regulator, fieldnotes)

However, regulators were in principle committed to treating fairly not only consumers, environmentalists and food manufacturers, but also all those involved both willingly or unwillingly with genetic technology. During fieldwork an underlying anxiety emerged amongst regulators that genetics and biotechnologists weren't being treated fairly by the political system. It was the view that politicians and regulators were in danger of reactively allaying consumer fears and consequently failing to pursue truly moral governance.

One regulator put it like this:

> The [biotech] industry isn't having an easy time. First ... I thought it was great that consumers had so much power. My attitude was that ... well, the authorities get cross if people don't eat what they're told to and so on. But then ... the consumers take the stage by storm and it all takes off ... and then industry has a really hard time ...

Another regulator added that it was simply as though 'consumer fears are made into regulations' (extracts from fieldnotes). Clearly, while initially genetics was seen as an external threat that was being unfairly forced onto an unwilling and powerless population, now regulators felt that in fact genetics and scientists were being treated in an unequal and unfair way. Genetics and biotechnologists, it was felt, deserved fair treatment, deserved inclusion. Any other approach was a betrayal of core values.

The heart of this unfairness was the way in which genetics was not allowed a fair hearing, as a regulator explained as he showed me a copy of SNT's information pamphlet *Genmat på våre fat* ('GM food on our plates'). Turning to a table which listed the pros and cons of genetic engineering technology, he explained in slight frustration that scientifically proven benefits, such as increased crop resistance to viruses, were given equal weight with unscientific or unproven fears such as genes spreading from one species to another. In his view this just wasn't right; how could consumer fears be valued equally with scientific facts or professorial views?

Herein lies the heart of the problem for Norwegian regulatory processes: if they were to treat genetics fairly, regulators would have to include scientific knowledge as a basis of decision-making *that has greater value than other inputs*. Valuing science, that is, anonymous expertise and amoral knowledge, is the only legitimate way to treat genetics if it is to be treated in a way that is reasonable and fair. Genetics is a highly specialised subject and should therefore be treated differently from others, in order to be treated fairly. Such difference (*ulikhet*) is not easily reconciled with fairness (*likhet*), in a context where fairness (*likhet*) by necessity implies sameness (*likhet*). This is deeply contradictory and not at the present time possible to maintain.

So far, genetic technology has largely been excluded, both from the shops and the regulatory process.[6] The following section looks at how such exclusion, difference and perceptions of unfairness are experienced by Norwegian biotechnologists.

---

6   Regulatory attempts by SNT to allow companies with GM ingredients in their products to continue to trade until a decision was made on their applications to use GM ingredients (to their mind a fair treatment of these companies) were politically unacceptable. Subsequently a government minister overturned SNT's decision on a consumer affairs show on live television, giving further cause for regulatory anxiety that consumer fears were driving a 'reactive' and 'unfair' process of governance in the case of genetic engineering.

DIFFERENCE, TEARS AND AMBITIONS

The biotechnology industry held a 'Strategy Conference' in the autumn of 1999. This conference aimed to bring genetic technology into Norwegian society, to 'build a bridge' between science and society. The conference formed a good fieldwork opportunity to understand the sector's experience. Exclusion and the desire for inclusion were recurrent themes that emerged in conversations at dinner and coffee breaks as well as in the conference papers themselves. Two complementary approaches to ensuring inclusion emerged.

On the one hand, several speakers insisted that the government and Norwegian society needed to change, and to respect global forms of governance and values, in order to include genetics and science. Thus the conference opened by focusing on the need to value scientific knowledge, as the chair bemoaned the fact that Norway was at the bottom of OECD ranking on R & D (research and development) as a percentage of GNP (gross national product). One of the opening speakers declared:

> Norway *must* become a technological country … we need to invest in R&D. From the laboratory to the business world, the conference aims to be a practical step towards achieving technological development.

Participants articulated a need for the government, for regulators and Norwegian society as a whole to incorporate more science and greater respect for knowledge. This could be described as a strategy to alter or transform Norwegian society so that it could include genetics and the biotech sector as equal parties, through developing a respect for (amoral) science.

On the other hand, a slightly contrasting approach which emerged was the way in which genetics is maybe 'misunderstood', and that perhaps genetics itself could be redefined in order to make it more acceptable to Norwegian society and regulators. Several speakers sought to change the understanding of their activities away from 'science' (a difficult, amoral, non-Norwegian activity) and into 'commerce' (in many ways 'immoral' but fundamentally 'Norwegian'). By this I mean that there was a clear desire at the conference to translate 'difficult' and 'a-social' biotechnology into something that could be understood within the existing moral/immoral sphere. For example, there was great laughter and relief when one of the participants put up a slide that showed a fistful of dollars, and declared that this, after all, was what genetic technology was about. The fact that they could talk about greed and making money was greatly appreciated. This image and his sentiments appealed to the notion of capitalism, entrepreneurship and wealth creation. If only the rest of the country would understand that all they were doing was just 'making money', like any other entrepreneur. Then they would be socially acceptable.

Entrepreneurs are not ethically 'good', but they are not beyond the pale. They are measured against the moral axis of sameness, albeit in a hierarchical and thus less attractive or morally good position. Capital accumulation and commercial success may not be entirely admirable according to the dominant moral ethos, but it is at least not 'un-Norwegian'.

DISTRESS FELT

The tensions experienced by biotechnologists at a personal level were articulated and displayed through their angry sense of hopelessness at the way in which they were treated by 'their fellow Norwegians' (or by 'these four million nutters' as one informant characterised them). However, their position as excluded and ostracised was brought home to me by the sight of one speaker wiping tears from his eyes in response to an 'artistic interlude'.

The artistic interlude came after the introductory speech to the conference, which had stressed the 'need for biotechnologists to build bridges between the laboratory and industry', to 'bring science into the society'. There were a number of such cultural framing events, for instance the performance of medieval music and songs at the gala dinner. Such performances are common in Norwegian conferences, both in industry and academia.

The lights were dimmed and two young men stepped up on the stage; one played the piano and the other the flute. Behind them on a screen a succession of photographic images were projected: classic images of Norwegian landscapes in winter and spring. We saw the sea, rocks, fjords, fields, snowy branches, snow on a broken fence, children playing, running water. The images suggested purity; water in the many forms that it is found in Norway, as ice, snow, liquid, as vapour (thin, frozen winter clouds).

The music and the images combined to produce a silent, church-like feel in the auditorium. When the next speaker got up on stage once the lights were back on, he appeared to be wiping tears from his eyes:

> [He] started by saying that he himself played the violin and that he had been moved to tears by the music. He carried on to the main talk and started by discussing the local elections in Norway … how political discussions focus on how to divide and share welfare, and focus very little on the issue of value creation which is needed in order to have welfare in the first place. (Fieldnotes)

This moment of music and imagery evoked many things: purity and cleansing, Norwegian identity, land[7] and an almost religious togetherness. I suggest this moment, like other moments of 'art' at later points in the conference, signalled a need to identify the conference as a highly Norwegian event, despite the fact that English was the conference language, and that biotechnology was considered a global technology. It was also despite the fact that the conference participants were all keen to identify themselves as global players and to distance themselves from the Norwegian general public both in public and in conversation with me. (It was frequently pointed out to me that the Norwegian public are were fools, ignorant of science, unworldly and hysterical.) The 'artistic interlude' exposed an underlying tension within the apparently global identity, and signalled the participants as first and foremost Norwegian.

---

7   Norwegian concepts of *landet* (the country, nation, land) are closely associated with the concept of 'culture' (*kultur*) as something connected to the person through blood (kin) as well as loyalty. See, eg, Gullestad's (2001) discussion of how the term 'we who built the land' in anti-immigration debates signals close affinity between the notion of the concepts 'land' and 'culture'.

My interpretation of this moment is that the speaker's tears signalled sadness and nostalgia. He himself as a violin-player, as a Norwegian by blood and loyalty, was now obliged by the moral codes of sociality in Norway to be excluded from the centre. He could not consider himself the 'same' as other Norwegians, as he based his career, his personal aspirations, on adherence to a system of knowledge and science that is unacceptable. The images of Norwegian cultural markers provoked an awareness of these tensions, and sadness at the situation. This interpretation is substantiated by the speech he then went on to give, in which he stressed the fact that Norwegian society (in the shape of government and citizens) was too preoccupied with distributing welfare and too little with the creation of welfare. Biotechnologists, on the other hand, were pursuing the necessary means by which to create wealth for their nation, but they would not be rewarded for that through respect or inclusion.

KNOWLEDGE, THE BODY AND PERFORMING THE NATION

To understand how and why scientific knowledge such as that embedded in and represented by genetic technology is excluded from the Norwegian social and moral domain, it may be helpful to look briefly at a phenomenon which I explore in greater depth elsewhere (Skodbo 2003c). What appears at first glance to be an entirely unconnected phenomenon can throw surprising light on the conflict experienced by biotechnologists between their science-based careers and their Norwegian identity, and also on why regulators struggle with their desire to include science in regulatory processes as a privileged voice.

During fieldwork I attended 17th of May celebrations (marking Norwegian independence from Sweden in 1907) two years in a row. On this day, all the schoolchildren in Norway join processions through their local town or city, waving flags and wearing their best clothes. Parents, relatives and almost everyone else gather to watch the procession, to walk around and look at other events (the royal family waving at the crowds, the firing of cannons, and the soldiers in their uniforms).

At the same time another group is present, in a disruptive and sometimes unpleasant way. This group, the *russ*, is made up of 18–19 year olds who are about to finish their school leaving exams (similar to A-levels). They weave in and out of the children's parade (Sande 2000), run around town in uniformed groups, drive their uniformly red and blue buses and vans rigged up with sound systems, displaying through bodily adornment and performance their wayward behaviour during the last 17 days. The *russ* formed a strong and unruly presence in their uniforms. They handed out 'business cards' with their name and mottoes printed (often obscene in tone). My daughter (at four and a half years old) quickly got the idea – these were specifically intended for younger children to collect from as many *russ* as possible.[8]

---

8   It reminded me of my own glee at a card that I was given as a (then Norwegian) child, the motto of which translates as 'If Adam hadn't stuck, where Eve had cracked, we wouldn't be sitting here today, drinking' (it rhymed! *Hvis ikke Adam hadde stukket, der Eva hadde sprukket, ville vi ikke sittet her og drukket*). My being permitted to collect, handle, and ultimately to own cards with such obscenities was quite thrilling.

Russ dress in uniform red or blue boiler suits, red for humanists, blue for economists and scientists, with special *russ* hats. They begin partying on or before 30 April, the 'night before 1 May' (*natt til 1 mai*), and continue until the national day on 17 May. Partying involves drinking large quantities of alcohol, as well as other risk behaviour: staying up for as many nights as possible, displaying nudity in public places, having sex, and playing tricks on non-*russ*. In return for these acts *russ* are rewarded by being able to display symbols of their achievements on their boiler suits and hats. Burnt matches signify staying awake all night, tufts of pubic hair in sticky-tape signify sex, beer-bottle tops signify drinking twenty-four bottles of beer in as many hours and so on. The *russ* are a nation-wide phenomenon.

Sande (2000) interprets the *russ* celebrations as a rite of passage which makes sacred the individual identity project. It is an expression of the challenges that young people face as a result of increasing individualisation and globalisation, and resolves tensions between the collective and the individual (2000: 351). In such an interpretation the extreme, alcohol-based acts are seen as dissolving previous identities in order to create possible futures; the risks involved in such behaviour challenge existing structures of authority between parents and children.

I suggest that a different interpretation can be interesting in the current context, in relation to the question of *examinations and knowledge*, which Sande does not touch upon. The *russ*, through their behaviour on the national day and through their drunken partying, are performing a particularly problematic relationship to knowledge. In fact, I argue that they act to expel abstract and amoral knowledge, knowledge for knowledge's sake, *vitenskap* (science), from their bodies in order to subsume it to the more important value of sociality through equality (sameness) in Norway.

Norwegian commentators observe that, through their debauchery and misbehaviour, the *russ* show that there are, after all 'more important things than education' (Vibeke Borgersen, *Aftenposten* 15 May 2000, my translation). When I asked neighbours, friends and colleagues about this educational aspect, no one seemed to even know whether they had already finished their exams and were celebrating, or whether their exams were after 17 May. People were quite puzzled by the question. The issue of education, exam-time, and knowledge were simply a non-issue. They described *russ* as typical, or amusing; often people related how they had been *russ* when they were younger.[9] I later learned that the *russ* are in fact now performing their 18-day ritual of drunken debauchery *before* their final exams (Sande, pers comm). The contrast with for instance British traditions could not be stronger.[10] Debate about whether the *russ* go too far is present, but is rarely

9   Sande (2000) tells us that the tradition in fact developed from matriculation at the University of Copenhagen, where the Norwegian bourgeoisie sent their children to be educated until the founding of a University in Oslo in the 19th century. Over the years in Norway it became associated with the celebration of completing the Å-levels equivalent, rather than celebrating beginning university life.

10   In Britain, exam-time is a time when newspapers are filled with articles about the stress of revision, when radio stations (eg, Capital Radio, Radio 1) set up revision 'help-lines' with experts available to advise worried students. This is matched at results time by overviews of national results, interviews with proudly glowing students, and musings about the intellectual health of the nation and whether the exams are getting too easy. Such dialogue is absent from the Norwegian media.

discussed in relation to exams; in general, the issue is whether they create too much chaos and whether they cause too much disturbance to others (*Aftenposten* 15 May 1999, and 13, 15, 16 and 18 May 2000).

In my interpretation, through their uniforms *russ* display the importance of sameness, and through their subjugation of the body in the name of partying they (potentially) sacrifice their individual health, reputation and examination results on the altar of collectivity. To put it crudely, taking part is more important than doing well.

Norwegian society in general tolerates such behaviour (although they may not like the extreme dangers involved), through which the vast majority of children go.[11] There is little challenge to the rest of society. Symbolically (at times literally?) they purge themselves of knowledge and position their bodies (through uniforms, alcohol poisoning[12] and sex) as social beings valuing sameness and equality rather than knowledge and education, ready for adulthood.

Discussion

I suggest that the *im*morality of the *russ* is a riotous participation *in* the moral field which makes explicit a moral and immoral sphere of sociality (Strathern 1997). This moral/social sphere in Norway can be conceptualised as dominated by an axis of good and bad vs same and different in Figure 3 below (Skodbo 2003c, Chapter 8). The ambiguous term '*likhet*' (sameness/equality) carries with it its cultural opposites – hierarchy, difference, multiplicity and inequality (Gullestad 2001: 36). Relationships between people and things, systems of knowledge, work, are all judged against this measure.

It is my contention that when people or things display values or demand practices that are truly 'not same' – when their differences are simply too great along the horizontal axis – they cannot be contained within the moral/social sphere at all. Practices that cannot be understood within the given terms are excluded. Without suggesting any real rigidity here, this places them somewhere on the left-hand side of the diagram: outside of the sphere of 'Norwegian' sociality.

---

11 I met only two people who had not been *russ*. They had taken a year out during A-levels to go abroad and study. When they returned they went into the year below, and were therefore not with the same cohort of companions. It is hard to know which comes first, the desire to withdraw because they felt different or whether they experienced themselves as different for having gone abroad.

12 Garvey (1999) shows how drunkenness in Norway is an important aspect of reaffirming the linkage and blurring of self and collectivity. Rather than being introspective in nature (aimed at the individual's experience of the drugged state), Garvey argues that drunkenness is undertaken in relation to the audience/social context within which it occurs. Drunkenness in the current context is also performed in this way; it subsumes the individual's identity, brain, exam-prospects, into the social collectively. *Russ*-celebrations are a socially-oriented experience that can be interpreted as an 'oath of allegiance', an expression of core values. In such an interpretation the appearance of the *russ* at the centre of the celebrations suggests their proximity to the central norms.

Figure 3 Representation of Norwegian moral/social sphere

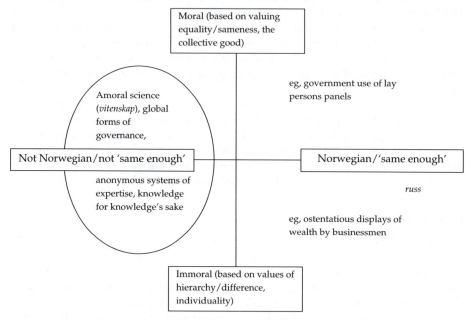

It is this sphere that the biotechnologists are excluded from, and which regulators are ambivalently trying to include them within. The *a*morality espoused by – or embedded in – biotechnologists and genetic technologies cannot be easily judged in reference to the dominant axis of moral values; they are too different, confusing, neither 'good' nor 'bad'. Like 'pure' scientific knowledge, biotechnology is external, and threatening, to the social (see Sirnes 1996 for further discussion of the asocial role of scientific knowledge in Norway).

Biotechnologists are thus associated with pursuing something amoral, external to Norwegian values (science, genetic technology, expert-based knowledge systems, knowledge-based aspirations). These actors have their own agency and that of the technology conflated. Though they may desire strongly to be part of society they are not easily accepted. Biotechnologists, like their technologies, are outsiders. They are simply too different, and become amoral beings who wish to redesign the basis of sociality by including amoral expertise and anonymous governance as a form of relationality (Skodbo 2003a, 2003b). Biotechnologists are unable to pursue their relations with other people and institutions in the field in traditional moral/immoral terms; instead they become isolated and slightly ostracised, and remain excluded from 'good society'. In part they exclude themselves in irritation or through a critical stance; in part they are expelled by others for being associated with something difficult and disruptive.

The agency of the genetic technology is thus twofold in this context. On the one hand genetics places the scientists outside of any state of 'knowing sociality' associated with moral reasoning (Howell 1997, Strathern 1997), unable to represent their actions in relation to the moral/immoral axis. This makes adherence to the Norwegian project of sociality impossible for actors closely associated with it. They are excluded by the mainstream, as their desire to be included in the social realm on their own amoral terms is extremely problematic. Such scientific amorality and expertise contradicts Norwegian traditions of face-to-face interaction and trust.

On the other hand, when existing traditions of Norwegian governance, equality and sameness try to operate in the vicinity of genetics, fundamental contradictions emerge. Genetics demands that regulators treat them fairly. In order for regulation to be fair towards genetics, fundamental changes in the regulatory process have to take place. Consensus decision-making processes and the personal integrity of the political leadership are no longer sufficient. Instead, expert scientific knowledge must be given higher precedence than other knowledge forms. As a result, regulators are left wondering what to do. The values of sameness as equality which underlie governance and selfhood are fundamentally disturbed by genetics and no longer function.

CONCLUSION

In this context, genetic technology as a technology or knowledge is perhaps best understood as a kind of *wulya* poisoning (Strathern 1997). The *wulya* poisoning of the Hagen people of Papua New Guinea is thought to make people unable to make sensible judgements about their social relations; they become vulnerable and easy targets for feuding rivals. Once the substance has been imbibed, the victim cannot pursue a 'knowing sociality' (ie, a moral relation with the world). Instead they make poor judgments about their actions, expose themselves to danger and die at the hands of enemies. It is a substance or thing that puts people outside of the 'knowing sociality' that makes up the social-moral sphere in Norway. Like *wulya* (although not necessarily leading to death) genetic technology causes severe distress and disempowerment to those that are closely associated with it. They are ultimately made vulnerable; the terms of their power and position are threatened, and they suffer varying degrees of personal and professional distress.

Thus, both biotechnologists and regulators are set outside of normal processes of Norwegian sociality. Biotechnologists are unable to pursue their relations with other people and institutions in the field; they become isolated and ostracised. In part they exclude themselves in irritation or through a critical stance, in part they are expelled by others for being associated with something difficult and disruptive. Regulators struggle with their task of pursuing governance on the basis of sameness and equality, and become unable to pursue their normal social relations of consensus processes.

Examining the agency of genetic technology in the way discussed here has developed a deeper understanding of the clash of morality that genetics has provoked worldwide (Bud 1993, Ho 1998, Reiss and Straughan 1996). Ultimately the moral clash between 'science' and 'nature', 'God' and 'man' that biotechnology represents is a symptom of processes of constituting and redefining the moral boundaries of self and State in Norway's encounter with late modern global culture. Genetic technology disrupts the moral field not in the sense of simply upsetting how we think about right and wrong in relation to 'nature', 'God' or 'human rights'. Instead, biotechnology has associated with it certain modes of thought and modes of praxis that conflict with the underlying building blocks of Norwegian morality and sociality. A morally defined domain of self and nationhood must now negotiate an emerging amoral genetic claim to participation in the social domain.

BIBLIOGRAPHY

Abram, S and Vike, H (2003) 'Introduksion: antropologi, strring og forraltning' ('Introduction: anthropology, regulation and governance') 2–3 *Norsk Antropologisk Tidsskrift* 53–69

Andresen, Ø (1999) *Organisasjonsdeltakelse i Norge fra 1983 til 1997 (Participation in Organisations in Norway 1983 to 1997)*, Oslo and Kongsvinger: Statistics Norway

Badiou, A (2001) *Ethics: An Essay on the Understanding of Evil*, London: Verso

Barnes, JA (1954) 'Class and communities in a Norwegian island parish' 7 *Human Relations* 39–58

Bud, R (1993) *The Uses of Life*, Cambridge: CUP

Callon, M (1986) 'Some elements of a sociology of translation: domestication of the scallops and the fishermen of St Brieuc Bay', in Law, J (ed), *Power, Action and Belief: A New Sociology of Knowledge?*, London: Routledge and Kegan Paul

Carrier, J (1998) 'Abstraction in economic practice', in Carrier, J and Miller, D (eds), *Virtualism: A New Political Economy*, Oxford: Berg

Dahl-Jørgensen, C (1997) 'The social management of difference: employees in a Norwegian municipality and a new wage system', paper presented to Nordisk Etnografi conference *Likhetens Paradokser*, Hadeland, Norway

Elvbakken, K (1996) *Offentlig kontroll av næringsmidler: Institusjonalisering, apparat og tjenestemenn (Public Regulation of Foods: Institutionalisation, Apparatus and Officials)*, Bergen: Institutt for Adm Org/Senter for Samfunnsforskning

Foucault, M (1978/1991) 'Governmentality', in Burchell, G, Gordon, C and Miller, P (eds), *The Foucault Effect*, Chicago: Chicago UP

Garvey, P (1999) 'Conformity through transgression: Norwegian drinking parties in the home', paper presented to the Norwegian Anthropological Association Conference, Hadeland

Gell, A (1998) *Art and Agency*, Oxford: Clarendon

Gopal, K (2000) 'Janteloven, the antipathy to difference, looking at Danish ideas of equality as sameness' 42 *Tidsskriftet Anthropologi* 23–43

Graubard, SR (ed) (1986) *Norden – The Passion for Equality*, Oslo: Norwegian UP

Graves-Brown, PM (ed) (2000) *Matter, Materiality and Modern Culture*, London and New York: Routledge

Gullestad, M (1984) *Kitchen Table Society*, Oslo: Universitetsforlaget

Gullestad, M (1989) *Kultur og Hverdagsliv*, Oslo: Universitetsforlaget

Gullestad, M (1992) *The Art of Social Relations: Essays on Culture, Social Action and Everyday Life in Norway*, Oslo: Scandinavian UP

Gullestad, M (1996) 'From obedience to negotiation: dilemmas in the transmission of values between the generations in Norway' 2(1) *The Journal of the Royal Anthropological Institute* (New Series) 25–42

Gullestad, M (2001) 'Likhetens grenser' ('The limits of equality/sameness'), in Lien, ME, Lidén, H and Vike, H (eds), *Likhetens Paradokser*, Oslo: Universitetsforlaget

Hacking, I (1991) 'How should we do the history of statistics?', in Burchell, G, Gordon, C and Miller, P (eds), *The Foucault Effect: Studies in Governmentality*, Chicago: Chicago UP

Hakken, D (1999) *Cyborgs@Cyberspace? An Ethnographer Looks to the Future*, New York and London: Routledge

Ho, M-W (1998) *Genetic Engineering, Dream or Nightmare? The Brave New World of Bad Science and Big Business*, Bath: Gateway

Howell, S (ed) (1997) *The Ethnography of Moralities*, London: Routledge

Ingold, T (2000) 'Making culture and weaving the world', in Graves-Brown, PM (ed), *Matter, Materiality and Modern Culture*, London and New York: Routledge

Klausen, AM (ed) (1984) *Den Norke Væremåten: Antropologisk Søkelys På Norsk Kultur (The Norwegian Way Of Being: Anthropological Search Light On Norwegian Culture)*, Oslo: Cappelen

Knappett, C (2002) 'Photographs, skeuomorphs and marionettes: some thoughts on mind, agency and object' 7(1) *Journal of Material Culture* 97–117

Latour, B (1987) *Science in Action: How to Follow Scientists and Engineers Through Society*, Cambridge, MA: Harvard UP

Latour, B (1988) *The Pasteurization Of France*, Cambridge, MA: Harvard UP

Latour, B (1996) *Aramis, or The Love of Technology*, Cambridge, MA: Harvard UP

Latour, B (2000) 'The Berlin key, or how to do words with things', in Graves-Brown, PM (ed), *Matter, Materiality and Modern Culture*, New York and London: Routledge

Latour, B and Woolgar, S (1985) *Laboratory Life: The Construction of Scientific Facts*, Princeton, NJ: Princeton UP

Lien, ME, Lidén, H and Vike, H (eds) (2001) *Likhetens Paradokser: Antropologiske Undersøkelser i det Moderne Norge (The Paradox of Sameness: Anthropological Investigations of Modern Norway)*, Oslo: Universitetsforlaget

Miller, D (1998) 'Conclusion: a theory of virtualism', in Carrier, J and Miller, D (eds), *Virtualism: A New Political Economy*, Oxford: Berg

Nelkin, D and Lindee, SM (1995) *The DNA Mystique: The Gene as a Cultural Icon*, New York: WH Freeman and Company

Nielsen, TH, Haug, T, Berg, SF and Monsen, A (2001) 'Norway: biotechnology and sustainability', in Gaskell, G and Bauer, MW (eds), *Biotechnology 1996–2000 – The Years of Controversy*, London: Science Museum

Nielsen, TH, Monsen, A and Tennøe, T (2000) *Livets tre og kodenes kode. Fra genetikk til bioteknologi, Norge 1900–2000 (The Tree of Life and the Code of Codes)*, Oslo: Gyldendal Akademisk

Odner, K (1996) '*Norsk makt, likhet og moral: eksempler fra Hedemarken*', ('Norwegian power, sameness and morality: examples from Hedemark'), in 2 *Norsk Antropologisk Tidsskrift* 149–60

Ommundsen, Y and Aarø, LE (1994) *Folk i Form til OL Kampanjen: En Evaluering Basert på Spørreundersøkelse i Voksenbefolkningen i 1990 og 1994 (Get Fit for the Olympics Campaign: A Survey Evaluation Amongst Adults 1990 and 1994)*, Bergen: HEMIL-senteret

Rabinow, P (1996a) *Essays on the Anthropology of Reason*, Princeton: Princeton UP

Rabinow, P (1996b) *Making PCR: A Story of Biotechnology*, Chicago: Chicago UP

Reiss, MJ and Straughan, R (1996) *Improving Nature? The Science and Ethics of Genetic Engineering*, Cambridge: CUP

Richards, P and Ruivenkamp, G (1996) 'New tools for conviviality: society and biotechnology', in Descola, P and Pálsson, G (eds), *Nature and Society: Anthropological Perspectives*, London: Routledge

Rose, N (1991) 'Governing by numbers: figuring out democracy' 16(7) *Accounting, Organizations and Society* 673–92

Sande, A (2000) '*Den norske russefeiringen: om meningen med rusmiddelbruk sett gjennomrussefeiring som et ritual*' ('The Norwegian *russefeiring*: the use of alcohol as a ritual in the "rite of passage" to adulthood') in 17 *Nordisk Alkohol- & Narkotikatidsskrift* 340–54

Sandemose, A (1933) *En Flyktning Krysser sitt Spor: Fortelling om en Morders Barndom (A Refugee Crosses His Tracks)*, Oslo: Tiden Norsk Forlag

Shapin, S (1994) *A Social History of Truth: Civility and Science in Seventeenth Century England*, Chicago: Chicago UP

Shore, C and Wright, S (1997) 'Policy: a new field of anthropology', in Shore, C and Wright, S (eds), *Anthropology Of Policy*, London: Routledge

Sirnes, T (1996) *Risiko og Meining: Mentale Brot og Meiningsdimensjonar i industri og Politikk. Bidrag til den Sosiale Stadieteorien (Risk and Meaning: Mental Breaks and Dimensions of Meaning in Industry and Politics)*, Report No 53, Department of Administration and Organisation Theory, University of Bergen: Bergen

Skodbo, S (2003a) '*Å få aksept: genteknologiens kamp for en plass i forvaltningsprosesser*' ('To gain acceptance: genetic technology's battle for a place within regulation') 2–3 *Norsk Antropologisk Tidsskrift* 84–98

Skodbo, S (2003b) 'Conflicting rationalities: science, morality and genetic engineering in the Norwegian food industry', paper presented to the 5th Decennial Conference of the Association of Social Anthropologists of the UK and Commonwealth, University of Manchester, 14–18 July

Skodbo, S (2003c) *Consuming Biotechnology: Innovation, Regulation and Resistance in the Food Industry – The Case of Norway*, unpublished PhD thesis, University of London

SNT (nd) *Genmat På Våre Fat (GM Food on Our Plates)*, Oslo: SNT

SNT and Veterinærinstituttet (2001) '*Utvikling av analysemetodikk og påvisning av genmodifisert mais- og soyamateriale i utvalgte næringsmidler på det norske markedet i år 2000*' ('Development of analytical methods and detection of genetically modified corn and soya in selected food products on the Norwegian market in 2000'), SNT Report, Oslo

Strathern, M (1988) *The Gender of the Gift: Problems with Women and Problems with Society in Melanesia*, Berkeley, CA: California UP

Strathern, M (1997) 'Double standards', in Howell, S (ed), *The Ethnography of Moralities*, London: Routledge

Strathern, M (1999) *Property Substance and Effect: Anthropological Essays on People and Things*, London: Athlone

Vabo, SI (2000) 'New organisational solutions in Norwegian local councils: leaving a puzzling role for local politicians?' 23(4) *Scandinavian Political Studies* 343–72

Vike, H (1997) 'Reform and resistance: a Norwegian illustration', in Shore, C and Wright, S (eds), *Anthropology of Policy*, London: Routledge

Vike, H, Lidén, H and Lien, M (2001) *'Likhetens virkeligheter'* ('The realities of equality/sameness'), in Lien, M, Lidén, H and Vike, H (eds), *Likhetens paradokser: antropologiske undersøkelser i det moderne norge (The Paradoxes of Equality/Sameness: Anthropological Investigations in Modern Norway)*, Oslo: Universitetsforlaget

COMMUNITY, THE COMMONS AND COMMERCE: THE OWNERSHIP OF BRCA GENES AND GENETIC TESTING

Sahra Gibbon

This chapter examines the way moral claims to community, and rights to and responsibilities for the 'commons' (Strathern 2004), were negotiated and contested in relation to the prospect of commercial genetic testing in the UK. It contributes to recent work in anthropology and sociology which has begun to make ethics an 'object' of inquiry (Massé 2000). In the context of recent developments in genetics, this research has focused on how different kinds of social relations, and their attendant moralities, are being deployed to reproduce and sustain new knowledges and technologies (Franklin 2001, Høyer 2002, Hayden 2003a, 2003b, Rabinow 1999). As Rose and Novas point out, social scientists need to examine the new 'ethical technologies being assembled' in the domain of genetics (2004) and their 'world building affects' (Franklin 2001).

One such 'ethical technology' is the way that different conceptions of community and ideas about 'the commons' are used as a form of social legitimacy in the different social spaces of the new genetics. For Strathern, debates around gene patenting and intellectual property rights provide an opportunity for theoretical and conceptual purchase on questions of community because of the way 'ownership' is simultaneously a matter of 'property' and 'belonging' (1996, 2001). She points out that those who make or oppose proprietary claims on genes engage in a form of boundary making which serves to define what is inside and outside nature, so that for critics the immorality of laying claim to that which is 'naturally' or freely available to all reproduces a notion of 'enclosing the commons' (2004). At the same time Hayden's work on the negotiations that take place in relation to bio-prospecting practices highlights a more flexible deployment of ideas of inclusion and exclusion in the social processes associated with claims to ownership (2003a, 2003b). She demonstrates how the apparent dualism of market and community are not always aligned or deployed in simple binary ways, a mutability that, as she points out, 'helps to manage the political liabilities of corporate extraction, accountability and legitimacy' (2003a: 368). In this sense the analyses of Hayden and Strathern demonstrate how community is 'consumed *and* produced' precisely in and through capitalism and commerce (see also Joseph 2002). Drawing from this conceptualisation of community, this chapter takes a particular moment in a cascade of events in relation to the patenting and public/private provision of testing for the 'BRCA' or so-called 'breast cancer genes' in the UK.[1] It examines how the boundaries of different ethical communities, the constituting features and rights of the commons, and the scope and limits of 'commerce' were defined, claimed and contested as those with different stakes in the debate over ownership and its consequences sought to delineate the political and ethical validity of their positions.[2]

In spring 2000 a public meeting was convened between a group of NHS professionals, a 'patient representative' and a representative of a UK pharmaceutical company, to discuss the impact on the NHS of licensing a private genetic test for the two BRCA genes offered by an American company, Myriad Inc (Meek 2000). At the time of this meeting, much media coverage of developments in genetics was associated with the hype and hope of the imminent announcement of the first draft of the human genome (King 2000). The prospect of the completion of this endeavour had generated some interest in the issue of 'ownership' of human genes, precipitated by the 'competition' between different public and private ventures to sequence the human genome, but explicit concerns about the patenting of genes had not yet reached the levels of exposure that they were to receive by the end of the summer 2000. By the beginning of September it seemed as if the public debate over the ethics of patenting could not be divorced from Myriad's patent claims on the two BRCA genes, where then and subsequently this issue was widely cited in the UK media in terms of 'patents on life' and seen as a negative portent for the future of health care and research (McDonald 2000). Although questions over patents, and even awareness of commercial interests such as Myriad, had not yet exploded into the UK public domain, for those within the NHS genetics community a number of issues had been cause for concern. In America the US patent Myriad had secured on the BRCA genes had led to a monopoly on genetic testing services for breast cancer (Williams-Jones 1999). The sense of uncertainty this generated for clinicians and scientists in the UK was compounded when, in January 2000, Myriad granted exclusive licences to Rosgen, a UK biotechnology company, to market the Myriad test in the UK. At the time of the meeting Rosgen was on the cusp of launching Myriad's 'fast turnaround/full sequence' *BRACAnalysis®* test in the UK. Although heated and complex negotiations were underway between relevant parties as to terms and scope of this licensing agreement, no statement or policy directive had yet been issued about this.[3] For those at the meeting these developments contributed to a climate of uncertainty about what this might mean for the future of the UK's rapidly growing, yet somewhat fledgling cancer genetic services.

---

1 These 'inherited susceptibility' genes were identified in the mid-1990s and are thought to be involved in 5–10% of all cases of breast cancer occurrence. Since this time genetic testing has become available for those at 'high risk' of developing the disease in specialist clinics across the UK where risk assessment for breast cancer is at the vanguard of an expanding field of genetics (Wonderling 2001)

2 This research was carried out as part of my PhD looking at the social and cultural context of developments in BRCA genetics for which I undertook fieldwork in the UK from 1999 to 2001 with clinicians, scientists and a range of publics including patients and fundraisers for a breast cancer research charity. The research was funded by a three year ESRC award.

3 A growing sense of underlying unease about these developments was reinforced by the fact that a British cancer charity, the Cancer Research Campaign, had filed a legal writ contesting the patent that Myriad held on the BRCA2, gene claiming prior ownership rights (see Williams-Jones 1999).

Following Heath (1998), this chapter analyses this meeting as a 'performance' setting which provides a unique vantage point from which to examine the 'public' interface and interaction between those with a stake in the licensing and private provisioning of genetic testing for the BRCA genes in the UK. Organised around the perspective and practice of three key players at the meeting – patient representatives, commercial interests and key members of the NHS – it explores how their responses engaged and articulated notions of community *and* the commons as they sought to position claims to ethical and moral legitimacy.

THE RIGHTS OF BRCA FAMILIES: A GENDERED COMMONS

Over the last decade breast cancer has become increasingly culturally prominent in Euro-American societies. This is testimony in part to the 'activism' of a broad and diverse range of 'patient' and lay organisations which have helped highlight the scale of the disease, inform a discourse about risk and the need for awareness (Anglin 1997, Kaufert 1998, Lantz and Booth 1998, McPherson 2001). These particular modes of breast cancer activism have drawn from, and at the same time somewhat transformed, the rhetoric of 'visibility and voice', which were so much a part of the consciousness raising feminist movement of an earlier era and the identity politics of the 1980s. At the same time, the last few years has witnessed moves to establish more so-called 'patient centred' care (Calman 1995), or the recognition of the 'expert' patient (Donaldson 2001), such that public inclusion and engagement is an obligatory passage point in formulating objectives for health policy and practice. Given this coalescing of breast cancer 'activism' and new policies of deliberative democracy in the health care arena, it is perhaps not surprising that the first speaker to talk at the meeting was a so-called 'patient' representative. Nevertheless the claim to speak as a patient was situated by the speaker and those attending the meeting in particular ways.

A woman in her early 40s from Canada was introduced at the start of the meeting as offering a 'patient's perspective'. Those in the audience were also made aware that she had been invited to the meeting in part because of her unique experience as the first person to single-handedly win a test case establishing a right to have a Myriad predictive test, paid for by her health authority. Her presentation at the start of the discussion was powerful and compelling. Telling the first hand account of her experiences, and eloquently recalling the shock and trauma of life events, lent a very personal edge to meetings which are normally imbued with a very different 'second hand' or even statistically informed version of the 'patient's perspective'.

Narrating what she calls 'her story', she explained how first one of her sisters developed cancer before she was 30, how her mother was then diagnosed with the same cancer, and then very shortly after this another sister was diagnosed with breast cancer. She told the audience how both sisters subsequently died. Her story was peppered with details about the pressure these experiences, and her subsequent decision to pursue genetic testing, had on personal relations in the family. She explained what 'her dilemma' was at that time:

Having had three members of the family develop cancer and seen two members die
from it I needed to know if I was carrying one of the two BRCA genes.

She told the meeting how, at that time, the predictive test offered in Canada was
only available within a research framework which could have taken up two years
to get a result. After her second sister went down with breast cancer, she described
how she felt 'like a patient' with an impending diagnosis of cancer 'hanging over'
her. The choice was from her perspective fairly stark, 'either risk breast cancer or
have a prophylactic mastectomy'.[4]

In order to 'try and be there' for her children, she explained how she was
preparing to go through with this procedure without waiting the two years
necessary for the results of a state test when she learnt of the 'more accurate and
fast turn around' testing service available from the American company Myriad
Inc. However, her health authority would not pay for this test and as a single
mother she could not afford it. She told the meeting how, after receiving a
substantial amount of publicity in her local press, an anonymous benefactor
agreed to pay for the Myriad test which subsequently revealed that she was not
carrying the gene mutation that had been affecting the family and so did not have
to go ahead with the surgery she had planned. She concluded by outlining how a
lawyer, who took up her case for free, helped her pursue in the courts the right for
the state to pay for her and 'other women in a similar position' to have a Myriad
test, which she subsequently won.

Her presentation suggested that the circumstances which had led her to contest
and secure the legal right to have a Myriad test paid for by her regional health
authority, and subsequently lobby for a more freely available Myriad test, rested
on her identification and right to be identified with various different yet
interconnecting communities of 'deserving' patients. In fact the moral imperative
and urgency of her claims relied on a fairly ambiguous definition of patienthood,
where there was productive and enabling slippage between the health dangers
posed to oneself and those posed to others, both related kin and larger gendered
communities of patients or persons at risk of being patients.

For the speaker at this meeting the experience of cancer in her family had led
her to think of *herself* as a patient with 'urgent' rights and needs. This was evident
not only in the way she talked of her feeling of *imminent* patient status following
her sister's death, but also in the way she described the history of illness and
death in her family in terms of '*her* cancer journey'. This expression has now
become common parlance not only among some cancer patients but also
enlightened health professionals and managers as a way of describing the
different stages a cancer patient goes through as they are diagnosed or treated. For
the woman talking at the meeting, who had not had cancer and was in fact
ultimately not carrying a pre-disposing gene, it enabled her to frame her
experiences as that of a patient, and blur the boundary between being a cancer
patient or being at risk of being a cancer patient, an ambiguity which is inimical to
the newly emerging arena of predictive medicine.

---

4   A surgical intervention to remove one of both breasts in order to decrease the risk of
     developing breast cancer.

By drawing connections between her own personal tragedy or sense of risk and the common experiences of other families who had lost relatives to breast cancer, she was able to foreground the rights of a particular group of deserving patients. She talked of herself and others in terms of 'these BRCA families',[5] pointing out that 'whether they are carriers of the gene or not these families are so permanently affected by the deaths of other family members they deserve all they can get'. The moral imperative of imminent, possible or yet to be proved patienthood for this 'community' of individuals was also supported by the 'patient's' lawyer who also spoke at the meeting. He used it to underline the urgency of his client's and others' situation. Making full use of the slippage inherent in the definition of patienthood in predictive medicine, he pointed out how his client, 'given her age and the age at which her other sisters had died from breast cancer', had a 'window of opportunity available to her, suggesting that 'for the BRCA *patient in waiting* timescale is paramount' (emphasis added).

If, as Diprose argues, technology constitutes a social category of people rather than simply mending a body part (1994), predictive technologies clearly bring an expansive criteria set of criteria and scope to definitions of possible, imminent or yet to be known patient status. This powerful mobilisation of the rights of those at risk or potentially at risk within the family was also enabled by contextualising such demands within a broader collectivity and linking the morality of such rights to a naturalised and normalised cultural value long associated with female gender identity.

The 'patient' representative at the meeting talked about her rationale for seeking a Myriad test not only in terms of the sense of responsibility to her family and children, but was quoted in a copy of a Canadian newspaper article (that had been handed out to the audience) as saying that she felt 'a genuine responsibility to women to fight for this that came from my mother getting breast cancer and watching my two sisters die from it' (Abraham 1999). There was therefore an enabling and productive elision, not only between the rights of patients or at-risk individuals who are kin, but between the sense of responsibility some women might feel towards their own family in seeking a genetic test and the argument that a more collective set of gendered rights were at stake. In this instance, the value of female nurturance is naturalised and normalised. As Saywell *et al* point out in their examination of the way this ethic of care, long associated with female gender identity, is embedded in media representations of the disease, 'what is at stake fits neatly into the moral order' (2000: 49). At the same time as the right to have a Myriad test echoed a personal and collective gendered ethic of nurturance, care and responsibility towards related others, it could also be set against a shadowy but nevertheless present 'enemy'; the paternalism of the state and/or medical establishment who might seek to curb the freedom of women's rights to choice. In this way, by linking it to naturalised notions of female nurturance, the question of patient rights was couched in more universal terms.

---

5   A description often used by health professionals to refer to families where a gene is suspected or has been identified.

These modes of patient identification might be seen as one variant of a form of 'biological citizenship' where increasingly, as Rose and Novas point out, 'the vital damage and suffering of ["lay" or "patient"] individuals and groups' are becoming integral to claims being made and pressures being exerted (2004: 441, see also Rose 2001). I would argue that such claims must also be situated in relation to broader shifts surrounding gender in which intimacy, suffering and trauma are becoming increasingly common modes of, particularly female, identification and citizenship (Berlant 1998).

THE DANGER OF 'CONSUMER' CHOICE AND PATIENT ACTIVISM

The audience at the meeting were clearly unnerved by the demands brought to bear on them and the fledgling NHS cancer genetic services by the these new articulations of individual and collective patienthood and citizenship. Despite a closing re-assurance from the lawyer, that a more legally entrenched hierarchical system of UK governance would prevent a successful legal challenge from any one individual, the discussion which ensued was one of increasing unease among the audience, which reflected certain misgivings about the kind of rights that greater consumer choice might precipitate. This was powerfully vocalised by one consultant who was concerned about being 'pushed' into an agreement with Myriad, 'if patients in the UK want it badly enough and are prepared to take it to court'.

There was also an effort to counter the morality of patient choice by re-asserting professional definitions of risk, thus undermining the particular lay definition (and or perception) of danger that had been articulated by the previous speaker and was central to her claim to rights as a 'patient'. One genetic specialist at the meeting did concede that there were situations where there was an urgent need to know the result of a genetic test. She told of how, faced with this situation, she had sent five cases to Myriad. However, by emphasising that these were all young women with 'suspected cases of breast cancer', she implied a more qualified and normative 'professional' definition of what constituted deserving patienthood and the right or need for technological intervention or care.

These discussions following the 'patient's' presentation therefore reveal some of the underlying tensions among a group of health professionals. They indicate their responses to recent government health policy and rhetoric that seeks to include patients as active participants in the planning, delivery and evaluation of health services. In this social arena where the impact of patenting and private licensing was being contested, the collective rights of a particular community of patients were seen more as a threat to professionally defined expertise and care than they were regarded as a moral standard to adhere to.[6] Such responses must

6   Interestingly the rights of a particular 'deserving' group of patients was mobilised by a London hospital in their effort to publicise the controversy over Myriad's actions. St George's Hospital's public website contained a news item which outlined how much of the work in identifying the BRCA genes was done 'on families in London as part of charitable work'. They concluded that 'it therefore seems ironic that relatives of those individuals who gave samples to improve medical services for all should potentially have their testing prejudiced by this commercial interest'. Here therefore it was the morality of collective patient altruism rather than the urgency of patient choice that was being used to contest Myriad's claims. See www.genetics-swt.org/oldnews.htm.

also be seen in relation to newly emerging specialist services, such as breast cancer genetics in the UK, which operate within a system that is responsive to finite resources and not just the self-assessed needs or anxieties of patients. At the same time that this specialism benefits from having no shortage of willing, if anxious, women seeking a referral, it also currently has to negotiate the discharge of some of the very many women referred to a specialist at the clinic who are at moderate, low or not substantially increased risk.

SACRIFICING PROFIT AND BEHAVING ALTRUISTICALLY: THE OPPORTUNITIES OF 'ETHICAL' COMMERCE

In her examination of the kind of questions about ownership precipitated by recent claims and legal debates over intellectual property rights, Strathern (2001) points out that patents both produce private property and compel the owners of this property to 'yield information to the world' because 'the philosophy [behind patent law] is that inventions should in the long run contribute to the general good' (2001: 8–9). As Hayden says in her examination of bio-prospecting agreements, there is a 'need to inject the right kind of publics' into new forms of commerce associated with genetic knowledge and technology (2003a). As well as attempting to circumvent the de-naturalising effect of proprietary claims that arise from the practices of gene patenting, it was nevertheless a particular kind of 'public good' that the next speaker, a spokesperson for the UK biotechnology company Rosgen, attempted to foreground.

It is striking that in marketing the *BRACAnalysis*® test in the US, Myriad have drawn on a discourse of female empowerment, choice and rights (Paratharsarathy 2003). By contrast, outlining the 'opportunities' and possible terms and scope of private testing at this meeting was situated not in terms of consumer choice and rights but in relation to an image of community in which the values of altruism, care and public health held sway.

Despite having the apparent support of the one 'patient representative' at the meeting, consumer endorsement is something of a hindrance, rather than a help, in this instance. To circumvent the growing sense of anxiety among the audience about the kind of patient-led demand that might arise in the wake of private licensing of testing, the spokesperson for Rosgen started by downplaying the kind of issues raised by the 'ownership' of genes. He stressed that he didn't want to discuss Myriad's 'legal claims' and patenting rights to the BRCA genes, given, he said, 'that the patent has been upheld by the European patenting office', but to focus more on the 'opportunities' generated by a public/private 'partnership'. This strategy seems as much about circumventing the uneasy and difficult questions about the circumstances which have led to the patenting of genes as it does about highlighting the new types of alliances between commerce and state made possible by ownership claims on genes.

At the centre of this set of opportunities is what he termed the 'fast turnaround gold standard testing' that Myriad offers to UK patients through private testing from Rosgen. He pointed out how Rosgen was set up in 1997 with the explicit aim of providing 'high quality' DNA testing with an emphasis on technical capabilities, where he noted it had a good track record. Nevertheless, most of his presentation was constituted not by a specific discussion of this expertise but by different attempts to ground this technological capability and commercial opportunity within the parameters of an ethical community. The speaker emphasised how both Rosgen and Myriad were prepared to 'subsidise the cost of the test' to 'push research forward'. He pointed out that the NHS would have the 'freedom' to continue using the test for research purposes, even though Rosgen had been granted exclusive rights, based on Myriad's patent claims, to offer the test in the UK. He added that although there would be a capped rate on the number of free diagnostic tests undertaken by the NHS for BRCA testing, this would 'rise from year to year'. He also outlined how there would be no 'backcharging', or 'reach through rights', of tests already undertaken by the NHS. This ethical stance was further supported by the speaker's attempt to align commercial sector practices within the regulatory framework of standardised NHS testing procedures. He explained how Rosgen's laboratories were working toward 'clinical accreditation and would very soon be in a position to cover the Data Protection Act'.

In this situation, moral claims were sought and secured less by emphasising the enabling potential of capital in terms of consumer choice, and more by efforts to demonstrate the ability of commercial interests to sacrifice profit, behave altruistically and act ethically. The speaker was astute in deducing that in this social arena, explicating an 'alliance' only with the consumers, or in this case patients, was unlikely to be the only or most significant source of legitimacy.

The possibility of a 'partnership' was mostly met with reluctance from the audience. As well as no explicit engagement or support for the 'opportunities' offered by Rosgen, there were many comments and questions which served to highlight the very issue that the Rosgen representative had hoped to circumvent, the so-called hybrid status and 'unnaturalness' of gene patenting rights.

This was brought centre stage at the meeting in a number of different ways. It was, for instance, alluded to initially through a point of clarification made by a clinician at the meeting. He pointed out that although clearly Myriad could show the necessary industrial application of the gene, in terms of genetic testing, the patent protection does in fact 'cover the gene itself'. He went on to explain that the only reason why MEPs voted for the European Patenting Directive in July 1998, which made this claim possible, was because they were 'duped' into believing that it only applied to technical applications associated with the discovery of genes. Using a number of articles of patenting law displayed on an overhead projector, the speaker made a further, more light-hearted snub that makes this development comparable with another, more readily suspect 'hybrid' development. He indicated that the company should be aware of another aspect of this legislation, which was also visible on the overhead projector. He explained how this forbids the potential patenting of cloned humans. Judging from the ripple of laughter in the audience, many would have been aware of his reference to the connection between Rosgen and the Roslin institute where the work to clone 'Dolly' the sheep had been undertaken.[7] Despite its humorous intent, this

---

7   Rosgen was part of a number of commercial start-up companies that were collaborating with the Roslin Institute.

comment drew an explicit parallel between the ethics of cloning and the patenting of human genes.

These analogies served to highlight the immorality of patenting practices, paralleling the way that other opponents of these practices have framed their critique in terms of 'unnaturalness'. As Strathern puts it, 'to assert that nature is being patented is to draw up political or ethical lines in order to curb the extended agency of human interference and draw attention to the politics of disenchantment' (2001). Such juxtapositions went some way to preventing Rosgen from establishing the new alliances they sought in attempting to align their testing service within public health service provision.

'IMAGINED COMMUNITIES': THE NATURALNESS OF A NATIONAL GENETIC TESTING SERVICE

The response to the Rosgen representative's presentation was further underlined by the last speaker at the meeting. Given by a geneticist working within the NHS, this final presentation articulated more clearly the threat to the 'commons', by drawing, somewhat nostalgically, on the founding vision of the NHS.

The speaker talked initially of the 'fifteen years' commitment to fairness and equality' which characterised clinical genetics and the 'rational' framework in which this aspect of health care has evolved in the NHS. He pointed out that this had ensured that BRCA testing was now available in more than half the labs throughout the UK, constituting a 'comprehensive regional genetics service'. Unlike the disease-specific organisation of genetic testing in other European public health care systems, he said that this institutional framework enabled 'technological integration' and a 'cross fertilisation' of ideas and resources between different disciplinary interests. Left to continue on its present course, he predicted that as the 'cost goes down' and 'more people are included in risk assessment', BRCA testing will be a 'major' area of expanding activity in clinical genetics. This will, he pointed out, stimulate the introduction of new technologies and create pressure for government investment of funds for new staff and equipment across all genetic services.

He compared this situation with an alternative vision of the future that would be made possible by a company who were 'first heard of eighteen months ago' and their insistence on upholding gene patenting rights. He went on to point out that having no, or even limited, BRCA testing available in the NHS would lead to a disincentive to invest in this area and thus damage the service infrastructure of genetic testing 'for all and not just the few'. The commitment by national genetic testing clinics to provide their service within what he terms an 'ethical substructure' would also be challenged, making it difficult to retain what he termed the much valued 'counselling in testing culture'.

By arguing, therefore, that it was the preservation of a 'collective commitment' to longstanding ideals of welfare provision that was at stake, the speaker was able to demarcate a powerful image of community. While this founding image of the NHS enabled and required paternalistic expertise and patient altruism to co-exist, it also excluded the new social relations presaged by the hybridising force of commerce and consumerism.[8] Mobilising the support of those in the room, he was therefore able to argue that resistance was the only possible strategy to the threats that patenting rights and private licensing of testing presented.

There was much support for the speaker's argument that patenting and licensing arrangements challenged the ethos and values of a 'national' health care culture. This was reinforced by comments on the predicted scale and scope of genetic testing. One GP suggested that genetic testing could soon be a very big part of clinical management when pharmacogenetics emerges and 'all breast cancer patients start to be included in testing as part of their clinical management'.[9] Concurring with the speaker, another clinician pointed out that the impact of the EU Patenting Directive would set a precedent that was 'unlike any other licensing agreement in the NHS'. He explained that the US company would be in the unique position of not only 'forcing' the NHS to send them samples, but also getting money for doing so. A cost comparison illustrated the sense of immorality he sought to generate: he observed how the £20,000 that had currently been spent on genetic testing in the NHS, yielding 89 mutations, would, if testing had been sent to Myriad, have only got 11 tests done and identified many fewer mutations.

This was further compounded by the comments of another geneticist who stressed the importance of 'being clear about the kind of genetic test that is being done when discussing the impact of the patenting and licensing agreement on health care practices'. He outlined how two of the three types of test available for breast cancer predisposition testing in the NHS compared quite favourably to the timescale on testing offered by Myriad, and that the gap between the 'sensitivity' of public testing compared with the Myriad testing, although marginally better, is also not that wide. He did concede that in at least one instance, the technology which Myriad possessed meant they were able to provide a service which identified mutations in more coding regions of the gene and in much less time. However, by highlighting one of the circumstances in which this particular type of test might become available to members of the public, he was able to situate the expertise of private testing in a more questionable ethical domain. The geneticist explained how Myriad appeared to be willing to undertake this test, on behalf of the patient, even when the circumstances under which this is normally done cannot or do not apply (in this case the absence of a blood sample from an affected relative). He openly speculated about whether the NHS would want to make this test part of their testing protocol, even if they could, pointing out that the 'validity and medical utility of this kind of test is not clear'. He explained how difficult it was to relate test result obtained in this way to the test results of other family members. More importantly, he suggested that for the NHS this kind of testing raises concerns over 'informed consent', given the circumstances which might

---

8   The essence of the argument put forward by this speaker is reflected in a policy/discussion document produced by the Clinical Molecular Genetics Society (January 1999).

9   There were nevertheless one or two dissenting voices who raised doubts about the significance of this issue for the NHS as a whole, as well as the future utility of genetic knowledge, with one cancer surgeon pointing out that 'currently genetic testing only accounts for a small portion of the management of women with breast cancer'.

have occurred to make this type of test necessary, 'such as family members not being willing to offer samples'.

By suggesting that the Myriad testing could contravene one of the 'sacred' tenets of ethical health care practice,[10] by acceding to patient demands and choices (themselves given greater scope by the advent of patenting and private testing), the speaker highlighted the hybridising effect and hence immorality of patent rights, and to a certain extent *patient* rights also. By contrast, the professionally defined ethical expertise of the NHS genetic testing was preserved and extended.

But the national order can also become synonymous with a natural order, a phenomenon widely documented in anthropology (see for instance Geertz 1983, Shore and Wright 1997, Falk Moore 1993). Rabinow's work draws attention to a more contemporary re-working of this conjunction in his examination of how DNA and genes may come to be identified with national patrimony in ways that makes welfare provision highly contestable (1999) (see also Hayden 2003a). The connection between the ownership of genetic material and national culture of health provision was also brought to the fore in this arena through the concerns raised by a number of European visitors. For instance, a practitioner from Holland spoke about how many countries simply 'don't want to have to send their samples of DNA away to America' and have 'a right to keep them and test them within their own country'. By suggesting a 'natural' right or capability not to accede to foreign or international patenting law, these comments became conflated with the more vocal defence that was being made about the need to preserve the ethical value of community at the heart of a national health care culture.

CONCLUSION

The meeting could therefore be seen as something of a victory in terms of articulating a consensus against the threat of private licensing and patenting. It was clear that the effort to delineate a post-welfare agenda grounded in a consumerist ethos of choice, alongside attempts to contain commerce within an ethical domain, were not well received by this audience of NHS practitioners. This was a sentiment that was partly reflected in the contestations around gene patenting rights that emerged over the following few months in the public arena.[11] Although only one moment in the ongoing negotiations over this issue, among a particularly invested population, the meeting does provide a window into the different ways that community, the commons and commerce were being positioned and re-positioned in debates around patenting and the private licensing of genetic testing.

---

10 See Corrigan (2003) for a discussion of the way that informed consent has become an 'ethical panacea' in health care settings.

11 For instance, Rosgen entered receivership six months after launching their private genetic testing service and there has been further opposition in Europe to Myriad's patenting rights (see Henley 2001).

Most striking were the efforts undertaken at this meeting to delineate and define a number of 'moral communities' marked by specific types of social relations, in which the authority to determine the shape or scope of care was claimed and contested and in which different kinds of natural and naturalised 'commons' were at stake. This included the rights of an emergent consumer agenda, which rested on the moral imperative and common rights of both a particular and more universal 'community' of gendered citizens with collectively identified claims to 'patienthood', or rights to care and health care choices. The ethical value of a threatened mode of welfare provision was also foregrounded. This was predicated on a rational and fair national health service, and a definition of the commons in which the sanctity of a particular type of care relationship, marked by practitioner expertise and patient altruism, was preserved and in which health care provision, sovereignty and national DNA were elided. A new kind of ethical community was also sought by the commercial interests represented at this meeting, less through an alliance with 'patients' or promoting a consumer ethic of choice, and more by identifying continuities with public health service provision. As Hayden points out, where new forms of genetic knowledge and property are at stake, the market may be less an undoing of community than a search to articulate it in new ways (2003b). Nevertheless, such attempts were overshadowed by the continuing emphasis on the 'unnaturalness' of rights in genes and the suggestion that a particular image of national (and for some naturalised) welfare provision might be transformed by such novel alliances. For those at this meeting, it was the sanctity of this particular image of community and the commons which it was seen to protect which was at stake. Its constituting social relations risked being transformed and reified, turning patients into customers, and 'expert' members of the NHS into sub-contractors to a commercial venture. The different idioms, rights and values mobilised during this meeting draw attention therefore to the paradoxical nature of community in capitalist societies, where even as it seeks an image of a 'lost romantic Other' it is at the same time productive of neo-liberal values and economies (Joseph 2002).

At the same time, despite the power of testimony, 'patients' were less a source of social legitimacy in this instance than a hindrance and threat to preserving and attempts at claiming 'ethical legitimacy'. By making comparable the impropriety of patenting rights in genes and consumerism in the NHS, it was possible to bring both into question. However, I want to conclude by recounting one startling interchange that took place during the course of the meeting which raised questions about the long-term sustainability of such alignments in containing the demands, hopes and expectations of patients.

At the end of a wide-ranging and heated discussion there seemed to be a general sense that many of those in the audience not only opposed the right to patent but saw it essentially as an 'immoral' activity. A visiting doctor from Sweden argued that gene patenting rights should be tackled head-on, stating that 'we should take advantage of the fact that most patients are with us on this and pursue legal actions against the patenting of life'. At this point the Canadian woman, silent for most of the subsequent presentations and discussions, spoke out. She explained that one of the reasons why she opted out of a national programme of testing was because this would mean going through what she saw as a time-consuming and invasive process of 'psychological tests and screens'.

In bringing this rationale to light, the representative patient at the meeting cast doubt on the suggestion that 'most' patients would be behind an effort to oppose patenting. More importantly, she cast aspersions on one of the crucial ethical arguments for those in the room who opposed patenting and private licensing: that it would damage the ethical infrastructure which had thus far ensured that psychological support and counselling continued to be part of the NHS testing service. However, in refusing what many saw as the key value of a national programme of testing and upholding her right to choose the means by which testing might be undertaken, there is a sense in which she implicitly supported the legal and market situation (as instantiated in, for example, the patenting of genes) that makes this choice possible.

Although the representative patient was in this instance Canadian, the quite literal silence of the audience in response to these comments seemed to reflect their surprise and shock. Despite its successful strategic deployment in the context of the meeting examined in this chapter, it was an interchange that raised new and troubling questions for them about the extent to which the culture and value of welfarism would continue to define public health care provision in the NHS. This suggests that in an era in which there is a growing, yet shape-shifting, co-mingling of science and society (Nowotny *et al* 2001) it is not necessarily clear that the communities and commons perceived to be at stake in the face of new kinds of genetic ownership and health care provision will always be a shared one for patients and practitioners in the NHS.

BIBLIOGRAPHY

Abraham, C (1999) 'Tenacious woman scores medical victory: Fiona Webster's fight opens access to genetic breast-cancer test' *The Globe and Mail* (Toronto), 27 August

Anglin, MK (1997) 'Working from the inside out: implications of breast cancer activism for bio-medical policies and practices' 44(9) *Social Science and Medicine* 1043–1415

Berlant, L (1998) (ed) 'Intimacy: a special issue' *Critical Inquiry*, Winter

Calman, K (1995) *A Policy Framework for Community Cancer Services*, Report by the Expert Advisory Group on Cancer to the Chief Medical Officers of England and Wales, London: Department of Health and the Welsh Office

Clinical and Molecular Genetics Society (1999) 'Gene patents and clinical molecular testing in the UK: threats, weaknesses, opportunities and strengths', available at www.cmgs.org/patents.htm

Corrigan, OP (2003) 'Empty ethics: the problem with informed consent' 25(7) *Sociology of Health and Illness* 768–92

Diprose, R (1994) *The Bodies of Women: Ethics, Embodiment and Sexual Difference*, London: Routledge

Donaldson, L (2001) *The Expert Patient: A New Approach to Chronic Disease Management in the 21st Century*, Report by the Chief Medical Officer, London: Department of Health

Falk Moore, S (1993) *Moralising States and the Ethnography of the Present, Arlington,* VA: American Anthropological Association

Franklin, S (2001) 'Culturing biology: cell lines for the second millennium' 5(3) Health 335–54

Geertz, C (1983) *Local Knowledge: Further Essays in Interpretative Anthropology,* New York: Basic Books

Hayden, C (2003a) 'From market to market: bioprospecting's idioms of inclusion' 30(3) *American Ethnologist* 359–71

Hayden, C (2003b) *When Nature Goes Public: The Making and Unmaking of Bioprospecting in Mexico,* Ewing, New Jersey: Princeton UP

Heath, D (1998) 'Locating genetic knowledge: picturing Marfan Syndrome and its travelling constituencies' 23(1) *Science, Technology and Human Values* 519–39

Henley, J (2001) 'Cancer unit fights US gene patent' *The Guardian,* 8 September

Høyer, K (2002) 'Conflicting notions of personhood in genetic research' 18(5) Anthropology Today 9–13

Joseph, M (2002) *Against the Romance of Community,* Minneapolis: Minnesota UP

Kaufert, P (1998) 'Women, resistance and the breast cancer movement', in Lock, M and Kaufert, P (eds), *Pragmatic Women and Body Politics,* Cambridge: CUP, pp 287–309

King, D (2000) 'De-coding life' *The Guardian,* 21 June

Lantz, P and Booth, K (1998) 'The social construction of the breast cancer epidemic' 46(7) *Social Science and Medicine* 907–18

Massé, R (ed) (2000) 'Anthropology, ethical relativism and health' 23(2) Anthropologie et Sociétés

McDonald, V (2000) 'Paying for your genes, special report, Channel 4 News, 24 July

McPherson, K, (2001) 'A descriptive study of UK Cancer genetics services: an emerging clinical response to the new genetics' 85(2) *British Journal of Cancer* 166–70

Meek, J (2000) 'US firm in cancer check deal' *The Guardian,* 9 March

Nowotny, H, Scott, P and Gibbons, M (2001) *Re-thinking Science: Knowledge and the Public in an Age of Uncertainty,* Cambridge: Polity

Parthasarathy, S (2003) 'Knowledge is power: constructing the user of genetic testing in the US and Britain', in Oudshoorn, N and Pinch, T (eds), *How Users Matter,* Cambridge, MA: MIT Press

Rabinow, P (1999) *French DNA: Trouble in Purgatory,* Chicago and London: Chicago UP

Rose, N (2001) 'The politics of life itself' 18(6) *Theory, Culture and Society* 1–30

Rose, N and Novas, C (2004) 'Biological citizenship', in Ong, A and Collier, S (eds), *Global Assemblages: Technology, Politics and Ethics as Anthropological Problems,* Oxford: Blackwell, pp 439–64

Saywell, C, Beattie, L and Henderson, L (2000) 'Sexualised illness: the newsworthy body in media representations of breast cancer', in Potts, L (ed), *Ideologies of Breast Cancer,* London: Macmillan, pp 37–62

Shore, C and Wright, S (eds) (1997) *The Anthropology of Policy: Critical Perspectives on Governance and Power,* London: Routledge

Strathern, M (1996) 'Cutting the network' 2 *Journal of the Royal Anthropological Institute* 517–35

Strathern, M (2001) 'The patent and the Malanggan' 18(4) *Theory, Culture and Society* 1–26

Strathern, M (2004) *Commons and Borderlands: Working Papers on Interdisciplinarity, Accountability and the Flow of Knowledge*, Oxford: Sean Kingston Publishing

Williams-Jones, B, (1999) 'History of a gene patent: tracing the development and application of commercial BRCA testing' 10 *Health Law Journal* 121–44

Wonderling, D, Hopwood, P, Cull, A, Douglas, F, Watson, M, Burn, J and McPherson, K (2001) 'A descriptive study of UK cancer genetics services: an emerging clinical response to the new genetics' 85(2) *British Journal of Cancer* 166–70

CHAPTER 3

MORALITY, RISK AND INFORMED CONSENT IN CLINICAL DRUG TRIALS

Oonagh Corrigan

Biomedical research involving human subjects cannot legitimately be carried out unless the importance of the objective is in proportion to the inherent risk to the subject. Every biomedical research project involving human subjects should be preceded by careful assessment of predictable risks in comparison with foreseeable benefits to the subjects or to others (World Medical Association 2000).

INTRODUCTION[1]

It might appear that risk/benefit calculation is more akin to the world of business and insurance than biomedical ethics. Yet, if we think about risk as a strategy for governing conduct, both of others and ourselves then its use as an ethical tool does not seem so strange (O'Malley 1996, 2000).[2] Indeed, as any scholar of moral philosophy will know, Bentham's calculus is the cornerstone of Utilitarian ethics and Utilitarianism in turn is the basis of contemporary bioethical theory.[3] Determination and management of risk have become major strategies in bioethical discourses and regimes designed to govern practice in biomedical research involving the use of human subjects. How does this strategy work in practice? Using the case of clinical drug trials, this chapter will examine the ethical regulatory discourse of risk, the expert assessment and management of risk as

---

1   The data for this chapter is drawn from research undertaken as part of my PhD, *Trial and Error: A Sociology of Clinical Drug Trials and Bioethics*. My research included participant observational research of research ethics committees, interviews with patients, 'healthy volunteer' subjects, nurses and doctors involved in seven different drug trials that took place in five different clinical settings. In total, 28 trial subjects and seven doctors and nurses involved in the consent process were interviewed. In addition, documentation given to subjects prior to consent, such as written information sheets and consent forms were studied and analysed. Although subjects' health varied along a continuum from healthy through to critical, none were suffering from conditions associated with mental impairment. This chapter draws primarily from interview data with patients and healthy volunteer subjects. I would like to express my thanks to Nikolas Rose, Ann Robertson and members of UCL's Genetics, Anthropology and Technology Group for their helpful comments.

2   The relationship between risk calculation and technologies of governance directed at the prudent neo-liberal subject is central to studies in 'governmentality'.

3   Utilitarianism was originally formulated in the writings of Bentham (1748–1832) and developed by Mill (1806–1873). It is a teleological ethical theory that holds an action as morally right if it brings about good consequences, or if the action were of a kind which, if everyone did it, would have good consequences.

conducted by research ethics committees, the information that is given to research subjects about potential risk and how this is interpreted and understood by them. In particular, this chapter explores the way this domain of risk is governed by regulatory guidelines applied by 'experts' and contrasts this with the extent to which those on whom the risk impacts directly, the research subjects, engage with and manage their own risk. The chapter suggests that very different moral spaces are occupied by those experts who administer the field and those who ultimately bear the risk. First, let us briefly look at the context within which a plethora of ethical guidelines and an explosion of strategies designed to manage such risk has emerged.

REGULATORY CODES IN BIOMEDICAL RESEARCH

Practices involved in clinical drug trials are governed by systems of control based on adherence to certain key international, national and professional guidelines. These are overseen by independent review and regulatory bodies aimed at governing biomedical research more generally. Conventionally, the emergence of these guidelines and regulatory practices that have steadily flourished in the West during the past 50 years are understood as a result of growing public concern about the kind of abuses to research subjects that have taken place since the second world war. Revelations of horrific experiments that took place at Nuremberg, subsequent events such as the Tuskegee syphilis experiments and cases highlighted by Beecher (1970) and Pappworth (1967) are presented in historical accounts as the main catalysts for the contemporary bioethical framework (Annas and Grodin 1992, Beauchamp and Childress 1989, Faden and Beauchamp 1986, Gray 1975, Katz 1992).[4] Many of these experiments were conducted without the subject's knowledge or consent and experiments often resulted in suffering and sometimes death. While I am not disputing the significance of these factors in the production of the current framework, I think it is important to also look beyond these cases at the broader medical and scientific historical context within which 'experiments' involving humans and particularly those in the pursuit of new drugs have taken place.

Although it is likely that the use of humans as research subjects is as ancient as medicine itself, it seems that until the middle of the 19th century the practice of medicine was generally conducted in accord with the ancient Hippocratic Oath. The Oath has nothing specific to say about experiments in medicine but obliges the physician to do whatever he thinks is best for the patient according to his ability and judgment. So, although anatomists had cut up bodies from the fifteenth century, these practices were based on case-oriented medicine and physicians were working within the Hippocratic tradition (Porter 1997). With the

---

4   Moral philosophers and bioethicists who write on the historical emergence and development of ethics in clinical research point to a number of significant events occurring between the second world war and the 1970s, which, they claim, have raised concern among those within the medical field and beyond. They claim that public and medical concern with these issues is responsible for provoking the implementation of many of the policies, guidelines, and the general proliferation of bioethical material that now exists to ensure ethical practice in clinical research involving humans.

advent of modern medicine, moral codes were originally, for the most part, written by practising physicians concentrating on professional codes of conduct. These writings articulated a series of obligations that required physicians to act responsibly, virtuously, often heroically and to avoid causing harm. Adherence to these principles implied that non-therapeutic research should never be conducted. This fitted within the tradition of medical experiments carried out on humans that consisted in the main of the trial of innovative treatments and practices to help benefit the patient. However, the nature of medical experimentation began to alter radically during the latter half of the 19th century:

> The pursuit of medical knowledge was increasingly carried out by teams in institutions, in a planned and organised way which obeyed the division of scientific labour ... The virtues of the new order were thoroughness and efficiency; the methods of discovery had been discovered, innovativeness made routine. 'The future belongs to science,' declared William Osler (Porter 1997: 526).

There was a shift away from dissection and the study of anatomy to new forms of scientific and technology based on experimentation. Referring to the changes he witnessed as a medical student during the first decades of the 20th century, Carl Binger wrote:

> No longer were anatomists content with describing bones, muscles, and nerves, or pathologists with describing the gross and microscopic appearances of tissues. Experiment entered all these domains as it did the domain of medicine and surgery ... The ancient, fixed, traditional academic borders were breaking down (Porter 1997: 528).

SCIENTIFIC RESEARCH

New disciplines within medicine such as neurophysiology and organic chemistry began to emerge and flourish. Major laboratories were built and developed, research establishments such as the Medical Research Council (MRC) in the UK were founded. It was also from the mid-19th century that the first important synthetic drugs made their appearance. Anaesthetics such as nitrous oxide, ether, and chloroform were produced and a number of drugs to control pain were manufactured. The changing nature of experimentation and development of new drugs prompted debate about the wider moral ramifications. In 1865, Claude Bernard, a French professor of physiology, wrote a classic text in which he claimed that physicians should never conduct an experiment on a person that may be harmful to that person, no matter how beneficial the resulting knowledge might be to society (Bernard 1957). Increasingly, however, large-scale experiments involving large numbers of human subjects were conducted to gain knowledge that might prove beneficial to future patients rather than those subjected to the experiment. By the late 1930s and early 1940s, the success of the two new drugs, sulfanilamide and penicillin heralded a new era of drug therapy and production. Experimental procedures for the clinical testing of new drugs became increasingly formalised and the rapid expansion of the pharmaceutical industry began to standardise clinical drug trial procedures. In 1946, the first Randomised Control

Trial (RCT) was set up by the MRC to test the efficacy of a new drug for the treatment of tuberculosis.[5] Randomised control trials where subjects are randomly allocated to the experimental therapy, a placebo (an inert substance) or a comparative treatment have since become the optimal standard with which to claim scientific validity. Since the 1950s, the number of research subjects involved in medical research in general, and clinical drug testing in particular, has increased dramatically. In the 1950s randomised controlled drug trials included tens of patients, by the 1960s it was hundreds, in the 1970s thousands and in the 1980s tens of thousands. Today, millions of patients worldwide take part in clinical drug trials. Since the late 1950s research for new therapies has increasingly moved away from what Renée Fox describes as 'patient oriented research' (Fox 1996) – research that is flexible, allowing the needs of individual patients to influence experimental design – towards highly organised drug trials conducted according to procedures that fulfil the scientific requirement of an 'objective', empirical, evidence-based approach to the development of new medicines. Many of these trials take the form of large international pharmaceutical company sponsored studies. These are highly bureaucratised, designed in accordance with strict protocol requirements and subject to relatively standard formal codes of practice and ethical regulations.

REGULATORY DEFINITIONS OF RISK

Developments in modern scientific medical practice have brought with them new kinds of moral problems. Given that in clinical trials research subjects are treated as 'objects' of research, which may or may not be in the best interests of these individuals, this presents a particular problem insofar as the clinical encounter obliges doctors to treat patients according to their individual needs. The main moral conflict in biomedical research centres on the fact that those taking part in research are not necessarily being 'treated' according to the likelihood of receiving the best possible therapy, but rather their participation is necessary to fulfil the requirements of the experimental study. Management of risk is articulated around the danger of the objectification of the patient; of research subjects being treated as 'objects' and means to an end, rather than as 'subjects' in their own right. The solution for this problem that has emerged in contemporary guidelines is to manage risk, first and foremost, through the establishment of a system of informed consent, thus ensuring that subjects are free to decide whether or not to participate. By implication, in obtaining the subject's informed consent, the autonomy and personhood of the patient as subject is maintained. Since the emergence of the Nuremberg Code (1947) that stipulated, 'The voluntary consent of the human subject is absolutely essential' (Annas and Grodin 1992), this principle has been of paramount significance in contemporary guidelines and systems of governance.

---

5   RCTs involve the random allocation of patients/subjects to either the new therapy under investigation, or one of a number of different therapies or placebo. Most RCTs are double blind; that is, neither the patient nor the clinician knows which arm of the trial the patient/subject is on.

As drugs are powerful, potentially dangerous substances and trials are used to discover the efficacy and safety of a new drug treatment, subjects in clinical drug trials are being exposed to substances the effects of which are only partially known. Adverse drug reactions generally occur with considerable frequency presenting significant, common and at times, potentially lethal clinical problems. In the UK they are believed to account for 5% of all hospital admissions, occur in 10–20% of hospital inpatients, and cause deaths in 0.1% of all medical inpatients (Pirmohamed *et al* 1998). Furthermore, a recent study (Lazarou, Pomeranz and Corey 1998) in the US suggests they could be the fourth leading cause of death after heart disease, cancer and stroke. As such, guidelines also address the potential physical, psychological and legal harm to the subject. Such guidelines promote the anticipation, calculation and weighing of potential harm against the anticipated benefit of the trial. Although this assessment is seen as an 'inexact science', it is frequently presented as a mathematical type of objective and empirical-based strategy that is relatively unproblematic.[6] Risk is to be calculated in terms of a sliding scale, from minimal through to high. The following extract illustrates the ambiguity of such concepts. The Royal College of Physicians (1990) defines minimal risk as follows:

> The term 'minimal risk' is used to cover two types of situation. The first is where the level of psychological or physical distress is negligible though there may be a small chance of a reaction which is itself trivial, eg a mild headache or feeling of lethargy. The second is where there is a very remote chance of serious injury or death comparable to the risk of flying as a passenger on a scheduled aircraft .

The terms *negligible, small* and *mild* are not 'objective' in the empirical sense, but rather contain implicit subjective and value-laden judgements. The analogy of the risk of serious injury or death to a passenger flying on a scheduled aircraft is not quantified, nor is it possible to compare these risks. Historical data on death and serious injury caused by aircraft travel may exist, but similar data on the dangers of a particular drug trial do not. More recent guidelines (Royal College of Physicians 1996) attempt to aid this task by quantifying risk. For example, 'minimal risk' is defined as a risk of death less than one per million, and 'low risk' as the risk of one to 100 per million for death and 10 to 1,000 per million for major adverse events. Further considerations of risk focus on other procedures involved in the drug trial process. The British Paediatric Association (1992), for example, defines procedures such as the collection of urine samples as 'minimal', injections and the taking of blood samples as 'low' and more invasive procedures, such as biopsies and arterial punctures, as 'high'.

The main problems with such forms of risk/benefit assessment are that they involve the calculation and comparison of incommensurable phenomena and that such decisions rely on the ability to predict consequences. In clinical drug trials, risks in terms of efficacy and safety are, to a large extent, unknowable. A clinical drug trial, most obviously, is an attempt to gain information and assess the relative efficacy (benefit) and safety (risk) of a particular compound. Adverse drug reactions are recorded as part of the trial data, but their detection is a very complex and contingent business (Corrigan 2002). Although data is accumulated

---

6   The Royal College of Physicians states: 'The assessment of risk is an inexact science even when applied to conventional investigations and well established treatments' (1990: 5.16).

and examined throughout the various phases of clinical trial, there remains a great deal of uncertainty about the risk profile of a drug until it has been on the market for some time and further data is gathered. Furthermore, although this form of risk assessment purports to be objective and value-neutral, because the very nature of risk implies that what is known is very little in comparison with what is unknown, the decisions that risk assessors make in terms of 'educated guesses' inevitably involve value judgments. As Douglas and Wildavsky (1982) claim, risk analysis can never be 'objective' as it always involves a social judgment. Perceptions of risk and benefit are not morally neutral, nor based on 'objective' facts of value-free science, but rather what emerges as 'facts' are premised on value judgments, and uncertainty about causal mechanisms.

As I have already stated, most guidelines place paramount importance on the obligation to obtain the subject's informed consent. For example, the World Health Organisation's initial guideline states that 'informed consent is based on the principle that competent individuals are entitled to choose freely whether to participate in research. Informed consent is designed to protect the individual's freedom of choice and respects the individual's autonomy' (Council for International Organizations of Medical Sciences 1993: 13). Furthermore, guidelines 2 to 9 give explicit instructions on informed consent and the others make references to it. In addition, the European legal directive (International Conference on Harmonisation 1998), an industry-led initiative which regulates a broad range of practices relating to pharmaceutical research, specifies that the clinical investigator must obtain written consent from the subject before commencement of the study, and this must be based on the prior submission and approval of the standard information to be given to the subject by the appropriate research ethics committee. Written information to be given to the prospective research subject must include explanations of 20 different aspects relating to the subject's involvement in the trial. These include explanations of the 'purpose of the trial', the trial procedures to be followed, the 'reasonably foreseeable risks' or inconvenience to the subject, and responsibilities the subject undertakes as a result of his or her involvement in the trial. Guidelines suggest that risk assessment should be conducted by a variety of agents involved in the clinical drug process. The scientists who design the protocol, the clinicians who conduct the trial, the research ethics committees that review the trial, and the patient or healthy volunteer subject are all involved in the implementation of informed consent and are required to play their role in assessing the relative risks and benefits.

RESEARCH ETHICS COMMITTEES

In the UK during the 1970s, steps were taken to regulate ethical practice in research with the establishment of Local Research Ethics Committees (LRECs) which followed the formation of Independent Review Boards (IRBs) in the US. Also in the UK, centralised ethics committees known as Multi Research Ethics Committees (MRECs) were established in 1996. The principal mandate for these committees was, and continues to be, the review of proposals to carry out research on patients or healthy volunteer participants within the medical environment. It is now mandatory for all biomedical research involving patients to be subject to the ethical review of such committees. It is important to realise that such institutions generally act as gatekeepers rather than policing bodies *per se*. In the UK, ethical review of proposed research is based almost entirely on documentation submitted by the clinical investigator conducting the trial. The key task for ethics committees is to assess the risks and benefits associated with a proposed piece of research and decide whether to give approval for the trial to be conducted. Ethics committees are advised that, as far as possible, the risk to the research subject should be minimised. But how is this 'risk' understood and measured?

Guidelines tend to differentiate the population into those that have the capacity to act autonomously and others whose capacity to make rational and autonomous decisions are compromised. A clear distinction is made between competent and incompetent subjects. Competency is defined as ability to comprehend and make rational choices with regard to consent. 'Some research proposals will draw their subjects from groups of people who may find it difficult or impossible to give their consent, for example the unconscious, the very elderly or some other vulnerable group' (Department of Health 1991). Further, they specify that ethics committees should give special consideration to research on children, prisoners, and 'mentally disordered people'. In instances where research is conducted on these 'vulnerable groups', definitions of risk tends to alter in favour of patient protection. Although guidelines place emphasis on the duty for committees to ensure that subjects are not exposed to undue harm, and specific guidelines are designed to ensure the protection of particular vulnerable patient groups, the protection of individual autonomy and the implementation of informed consent is given main priority. Pharmaceutical industry guidelines to researchers conducting clinical trials list 20 items related to general information that should be imparted and understood by the research subject about the proposed study. These include information relating to 'the trials treatments(s) and the probability for random assignment to each treatment … the subject's responsibilities' and research 'the reasonably foreseeable risks or inconveniences to the subject' (International Conference on Harmonisation 1998). Therefore, the principal risk management strategy encouraged by those conducting research and deployed by research ethics committees is to facilitate the process of informed consent. Ethics committees spend much of their time ensuring that sufficient written information given to the patient or healthy volunteer subject includes details of the anticipated risks and benefits so that he or she may assess the risk and choose whether or not to participate. A recent survey of 58 members belonging to six LRECs from the Sheffield area reveals that LREC members rated their duty 'to ensure prospective subjects understand the implication of taking part in the study as the most important aspect of their work' (Kent 1997). This was given priority over and above the duty to protect subjects from harm.

INFORMATION ON RISK

It is a regulatory requirement that patient information sheets, given to subjects prior to consent, give details of the possible side-effects and risks that could be incurred while as a result of participation in the trial. In the study I conducted, I examined seven different drug trial information and consent forms and found that such information was presented under headings such as, 'What are the risks involved in taking part?' and 'Possible side-effects'. As ethical guidelines require that subjects are given information on *all* known foreseeable potential risk, information about relatively minor risks were often listed alongside more serious possible effects. For example, on one of the trials, information about the potential risk 'for some bruising or inflammation at the needle site' resulting from blood sampling immediately preceded information that the study drug may induce crystals in the urine. The information sheets usually attempted to relay some information about the likelihood of these risks occurring. However, in most cases, such information was referred to in general terms such as 'a small number', 'few, if any' and 'common side-effects'. Only one of the information sheets included a rough quantification of the risk. It was presented as follows:

> Serious bleeding that is likely to require a blood transfusion in patients receiving either heparin or enoxaparin and asprin is expected to occur in about 3–4% of patients.

Although there is a problem in assessing the likelihood of certain adverse drug reactions occurring, as well as the problem of identifying their profile at the clinical trial stage, the risk of as yet unknown reactions was rarely mentioned. Of the seven information sheets I examined, only two even hinted at this uncertainty as a component of the risk involved. The first of these states that 'all medicines may cause side-effects', while the most explicit example states:

> The side effects of Nolvadex therapy include gastro-intestinal disturbance, vaginal dryness, hot flushes and weight gain. Extremely rare side effects of Nolvadex include overgrowth of the lining of the womb and a very slight increase in the likelihood of womb cancer, eye problems and an increased incidence of blood clots
> ...
>
> The side effects of Arimidex include fluid retention, gastro-intestinal disturbances, hot flushes and vaginal dryness. We would like to find out how these two drugs compare in terms of side effects and to see what side effects the two drugs together might cause. You will, therefore, be carefully monitored and asked about side effects.

Although this information implies that there are possible as yet unknown side-effects when the two drugs are taken together, it does not state this clearly. It is implied rather than explicitly conveyed.

CONSENTING TO RISK

> When a patient gives consent to participate in a piece of research he [*sic*] should have been given enough information to make his [*sic*] own choice. The concept of risk/benefit analysis should be conveyed to patients as part of the procedure of seeking consent. The patient's own assessment of risk and harm is sometimes more relevant to himself that that of the expert (Royal College of Physicians 1990).

Whether trial subjects realise it or not, in giving 'informed consent' they are in effect taking partial responsibility for any potential harm that they may incur while on the trial. The trial subject is agreeing to the potential risk as outlined in the patient information text and thus he or she becomes major-bearer of the risk. By signing the consent form, the subject attests that he/she has been accurately informed about the trial and has understood this information.[7]

Although both patients and healthy volunteers are governed by many of the same guidelines, especially with regard to informed consent, evidently these are two distinct groups of research subjects and there are separate kinds of moral issues to be considered. Patients recruited to clinical trials are generally under the care and consultation of a physician who invites them to consent. For the majority of patients involved in clinical drug trials, such trials are therapeutic and of potential direct benefit to the patient. Although ethical guidelines refer to altruism as a morally justifiable reason for participation, great emphasis is placed upon the potential benefit of therapeutic treatment, albeit that the predicted trial outcome is as yet unknown. As such, the risk of trial participation is measured against potential therapeutic benefit.

In contrast, healthy volunteers are initially recruited through advertising campaigns and are financially rewarded for their participation. However, the amount made payable to the volunteer is not permitted to be 'such as to persuade people to volunteer against their better judgement, nor induce them to volunteer more frequently than is advisable for their own good'; furthermore, the payment should be related to the nature and degree of inconvenience and discomfort involved and 'should never be offered for undergoing risk' (Royal College of Physicians 1986). In the case of healthy volunteers, although the benefit is financial and is to be offset against the risk of harm from the study drug or procedure, there is no direct, commensurable relationship between the two.

In interviews I conducted with both healthy volunteers and patient subjects taking part in clinical drug trials, I found that their attitudes concerning potential risks were somewhat ambivalent. In general, their responses fell into three categories: denial of risk; the 'halo effect' – a general rather than a personal acceptance of risk; and 'bravado' – a heroic response to risk.

Denial of risk

Among patients in particular, I found that most did not seem concerned about the possibility of drug-induced side-effects or other risks occurring. This seemingly general lack of concern is supported with evidence from other studies which indicates that, after giving consent, patients were unable to subsequently recall any side-effects listed (Bergler *et al* 1980, Cassileth *et al* 1980, Estey *et al* 1994). Given the fact that my interviewees had indeed all consented, perhaps their lack of concern about possible side-effects was hardly surprising.[8] Although many of

---

7   This is in accordance with ICH GCP (1998) guidelines 4.8.9.

8   A study of patients attitudes to participation in clinical trials (Bevan *et al* 1993) revealed that, of those that consented to trials, 25% of respondents disliked the thought of potential side-effects, whereas this figure was 58% for those who declined participation. Nevertheless, caution must be used with these findings insofar as they are based on 66 patients who consented and only 12 who declined.

them acknowledged the possibility of side-effects and other unknown risks occurring, it was common for patients with potentially serious or life-threatening conditions to be more concerned about further threats brought about by their illnesses, or associated procedures such as surgery, or radiotherapy, than the trial medication. For example, when I asked a patient on a post-operative breast cancer trial whether she was bothered by the information about the occurrence of possible side-effects, she replied:

> Not especially, no I wasn't. I was thinking more about whether I would have any side-effects from the radiotherapy, so I wasn't bothered.

Also, a patient on a trial for a new hypertension drug trial told me:

> I know the conditions that can lead from high blood pressure can be a lot worse than suffering from drug side-effects.

Nevertheless, it must be acknowledged that, for some patients, the inability to recall information about side-effects may not be so much due to their lack of concern about them, but rather due to suppression as a coping mechanism for their fears about the possibility of these occurring. For example, Annie, who had breast cancer and was taking part in a post-operative breast cancer trial revealed how she tried to obliterate the thought of side-effects occurring:

> OC: When you took the information leaflet home with you did you read it again afterwards?
>
> Annie: I can't remember. Let me see if I can find it.
>
> OC: It is OK, I have a copy. Does that look familiar to you … [I show her the information sheets] Did you get a copy of an information leaflet like this?
>
> Annie: Oh, I probably did, but I don't actually remember. Oh, but I must have done because I knew all about the side-effects, you see. I read all about that, yes, must have done. Yes, I did definitely.
>
> OC: Do you remember reading the form again at anytime?
>
> Annie: No, you see, because I try and blot things like that out.

However, a few patients did express concern about the possibility of experiencing side-effects. One of the patients on the pre-operative breast cancer trial told me that initially she spent a lot of time worrying about and looking out for them. 'I was looking for all those side-effects. That was terrible! I wouldn't like to go through all that again.' Also, one of the patients on a trial for a hypertension drug told me how he had asked for reassurance from the trial doctor that the trial drug was not linked to a class of drugs from which he had experienced very bad side-effects in the past.

The halo effect

In 'healthy volunteer' subjects, this ambivalence towards risk is evident in what I call the 'halo' effect. Their general awareness about potential risk may reflect the fact that, unlike patients, the 'healthy volunteer' subjects cannot offset the risk against the possible benefits of treatment. Many healthy volunteers saw themselves as paid workers and regularly took part in trials for the extra income. All but one of the healthy volunteers cited financial reward as the primary motivation for their participation. Among many of the healthy volunteer subjects there was a general awareness of risks but some saw these dangers pertaining to others or to circumstances from which they were excluded. For example, when I asked Jack whether he had any concerns about the potential risks, he replied:

> Not for this drug because it is for stomach ulcers and it has been on the market for quite a while … though if it was something totally new they were testing out I might be a bit more apprehensive.

Jack also though it could be risky to be involved in too many trials: 'there is a person here who has done about eight studies in the last couple of years and that is risking it a bit.' Dave, another 'healthy volunteer' told me he was only willing to take part in the trial because he was not planning to father more children:

> I think that because my wife has been sterilised we won't have any more children and so that would be the only thing I would consider. If we were going to have more children then maybe I wouldn't have done the study because you know it's in the back of your mind what I am taking would affect a baby.

In both of the healthy volunteer trials, subjects were informed to refrain from unprotected sexual intercourse for a three-month period:

> We will require you not to attempt to conceive a child during the study and in the 3 months following the end of the study and that adequate contraceptive measures be used during this 3 month period.

This instruction was presented in the information sheets under the heading of 'study restrictions' and listed alongside a number of other study prohibitions such as alcohol, caffeine, strenuous physical exercise, and 'over-the-counter medicines'. No explanation was given about why these restrictions were necessary, so subjects were left to draw their own inferences. However, when I questioned Dave further about whether he thought there was any risk in his participation he, like the majority of other 'healthy volunteer' subjects, replied emphatically 'no'. Frank, another one of the 'healthy volunteer' subjects who worked as a scientist within the pharmaceutical company where the trials where being conducted, told me that because of his pharmaceutical knowledge he was quite happy to take part in drug trials, but he would draw the line at in trials for psychotropic drugs as he believed they could adversely effect mental capacity. Although the 'halo effect' was far more evidently a feature of 'healthy volunteer' subjects, occasionally patients too exhibited this effect. For example, an elderly patient in a blood thinning compound trial told me he would probably not have consented to go on the trial if he had been a younger man as he would have had to consider the long-term side-effects. In other words, he perceived the potential for risk in terms of long-term effects from which, because of his age, he would be excluded.

Bravado

There was also a sense of bravado running through the accounts of the 'healthy volunteer' subjects. For example, the following extract reveals how Ed was aware that others saw his participation in the trial as potentially dangerous, and this made him feel somewhat heroic:

> My wife thought more about them [the side-effects] you know. She said you are obviously going to have to ask them about the side-effects. She said they might give you something to turn you into a complete nutter, and I said 'no' [he laughs] … It's like being an unsung hero really.

Dave made similar comments:

> I work with 400 men and it's a bit like working with 400 women really. You know the normal banter like 'you are going to grow another head' and 'all your hair might fall out', just the normal banter … A friend I work with just can't bear needles and so he says 'I don't know how you can do it' but the needles and things don't bother me you know.

Although this form of bravado did not emerge as an issue for patients, many of them explained that they knew research for new drugs was important and realised that 'somebody has to do it'. Simon, one of healthy volunteer trial subjects, told me his primary motivation for volunteering to take part in trials was because he wanted to help others. He informed me that his father and a number of other family members had died from cancer and he felt he had a responsibility and obligation to do something to help. Although Simon was the only trial subject I interviewed who cited altruism as their primary reason for participation, many other trial subjects told me that their decision to participate was in part based on an ethical stance to help others or in gratitude to doctors and medicine in general. For example, one of the hypertension trial subjects told me:

> I was very grateful to Dr Patel [patient's GP] because he stopped me from having a stroke and I thought if I can be of help to other people later on, then fair enough.

TRUST

In consenting to participation, trial subjects are placing their trust either consciously or unconsciously in medical scientific expertise, pharmaceutical drug development and the government regulatory bodies that oversee them. One of the patients on the hypertension trial told me how, in choosing to take part in the trial, he felt safe placing his trust in the progress of medical science:

> I am sure they are not going to give me anything that will do me any lasting damage, and somebody has to it otherwise there were never be progress will there?

And, as one of the healthy volunteer subjects told me:

> I thought if there was anything wrong or anything that could be allowed to happen that would cause long-term injury or anything, then they wouldn't be allowed to do these sorts of studies. I though it has got to be pretty safe for them to be allowed to do it.

While some social commentators suggest that trust in scientific and medical expertise is breaking down, my interviews reveal very little conscious challenge to expert opinion on drug safety. My data suggests that subjects' explicit or implicit trust in expert systems remains intact. As one of the interviewees told me, 'I shouldn't think they would let you have some drug they don't know anything about'. Even when subjects expressed misgivings or apprehension about potential risk, they were still willing to trust the system. As one of the healthy volunteer subjects said:

> I remember him talking about crystals developing inside you which I wasn't very clear about. It sounded like it could possibly be dangerous if it occurred but it didn't seem to be very likely … I would have preferred if you had some statistical information.

Despite his misgivings, Keith said he trusted that this was generally a safe thing to do and he had not heard of 'any kind of danger involved in all this'. One of the patients on a trial for a new hypertension drug told me:

> While I understand that pharmaceutical companies are motivated by profit, nevertheless they do appear to be serving the public as well.

The following extract from an interview with James, a patient participating in the hypertension trial, also reveals the sense in which he knew that he was an object of research and yet at the same time he has an implicit trust that he will not be harmed:

OC: What do you think about this being a new drug?

James: I should think it has been fairly well tested before they give it to us guinea pigs.

OC: Are you relieved you are not the first guinea pig?

James: Well they wouldn't give me anything that was going to cause me problems afterwards.

Another healthy volunteer subject told me he felt reassured because 'all the animal data has been reviewed by the authorities, the ethics committees and the various review boards'. Also Ed, a healthy volunteer, told me how he was reassured by the doctor's consent talk:

> He [the trial doctor] talked about what we were going to take and about the side-effects and just basically put my mind at ease. He said 'you shouldn't really experience anything'. That was good enough for me.

Rather ironically, Ed, who had just been given a dose of the trial drug prior to the interview, complained of a headache and by the end of the interview had developed a distinct rash on his face and neck.

CONCLUSION

Risk, as a technique through which problems are made calculable and thus manageable, is increasingly a feature of Western liberalism more generally. Also, as Carlos Novas illustrates in Chapter 4, moral discourses relating to the development of predictive genetic testing for Huntington's disease construct the identity of those 'at risk'. Nevertheless, in the case of clinical drug trials, despite a discourse that highlights risk as an inherent feature of such research, it would seem that healthy volunteers and patients do not make decisions upon consideration of risk benefit calculations, at least in terms of the information given to them about the potential risks. There appears to be a disjuncture, then, between a moral framework that primarily manages risk through the informed consent of the individual research subject, and the common refusal or reluctance of research subjects to fully engage with this process. This is not to suggest that subjects felt that they were somehow coerced or duped into trial participation, but rather their decisions to participate are based to a large extent on other considerations such as the desire for therapy, financial reward, and trust in scientific and medical expertise.

Sociology and anthropology frequently draw attention to significant and often overlooked local lay forms of knowledge as equally valid and a counterpoint to 'expert' knowledge. Matthew Weinstein (2001) notes the recent emergence of a 'guinea pigging culture' in which healthy volunteers who regularly take part in clinical drug trials form alliances with each other, exchange information and generally try to 'extract as much as possible out of adverse circumstances without either embracing or directly challenging expertise' (Weinstein 2001: 196). Steven Epstein also examines the activities of AIDS activist patient groups and their success in altering the design of drug trials. The search for a cure for AIDS has often resulted in patients willing to take high-risk strategies, in terms of their willingness to endure burdensome drug regimes, serious adverse reactions and uncertainty about whether these regimes will be effective. Nevertheless, such activism makes onerous demands upon citizens and I would argue that for most patients and healthy volunteer subjects these demands seem unreasonable. Indeed, this highlights the problems of moral citizenship more generally. Citizenship as a new social contract is based on a complex relationship of rights and responsibilities between the State and individual members within a bounded, specific realm. Membership of a scientific or technological citizenship implies the right to be given accurate information as well as the obligation actively engage with this information. In support of such an approach Philip Frankenfeld states:

> Valid public acceptance affirms human autonomy. Valid public acceptance must be deep and informed, subjective, voluntary, rigorous, and rich. Invalid acceptance involves thoughtless deference and blind trust (Frankenfield 1992: 460).

It seems the right to be informed has become an obligation be informed, and a process designed primarily to protect subjects from harm makes it incumbent upon them to make such an assessment. Such an emphasis on autonomy and 'empowered decision-making' is at the core of contemporary liberalism. Nevertheless evidence here and in a number of other studies reveal that those who consent to take part in clinical trials frequently do so without fully engaging in the consent process. As has been shown, after giving consent, subjects are often unable to recall the information they were given about side-effects and a number of further studies show that those who take part in clinical trials do not understand the process of randomisation (Cassileth *et al* 1980, Jan and DeMets 1981, Snowdon *et al* 1997). Do subjects have a right to opt out of such decision-making, and can society provide safeguards to give adequate protection?

It was in part because of the inability of medicine to guarantee that biomedical research would necessarily be in the individual's patient best interest that ethical guidelines first began to emerge. The increasing emphasis on informed consent largely leaves the subject responsible for his or her own welfare. What happens then when patients or research subjects are harmed as a result of their participation on a trial? Are they simply to be told that as they were given information on such risk prior to giving their 'informed consent' they had been adequately warned? If so, the current risk management strategy appears to do more to protect the medical and pharmaceutical establishment than patient and healthy volunteer research subjects. Nevertheless, as I suggest in the introduction of this chapter, the proliferation of ethics has as much to do with facilitating new form of scientific and medical experimentation as it has with looking after the welfare of research subjects.

BIBLIOGRAPHY

Annas, G and Grodin, M (1992) *The Nazi Doctors and the Nuremberg Code*, Oxford: OUP

Beauchamp, T and Childress, J (1989) *Principles of Biomedical Ethics*, Oxford: OUP

Beecher, H (1970) *Research and the Individual: Human Studies*, Boston: Little, Brown

Bergler, J, Pennington, A, Metcalf, M and Freis, E (1980) 'Informed consent: how much does the patient understand?' 27(4) *Clinical Pharmacology and Therapeutics* 435–40

Bernard, C (1957) *An Introduction to the Study of Experimental Medicine*, New York: Dover

Bevan, EG, Chee, LC, McGhee, SM and McInnes, GT (1993) 'Patients' attitudes to participation in clinical trials' 35 *British Journal of Clinical Pharmocology* 204–07

British Paediatric Association (1992) *Guidelines for the Ethical Conduct of Medical Research Involving Children*, London: Ethics Advisory Committee for the British Paediatric Association

Cassileth, B, Zupkiss, R and Sutton-Smith, K (1980) 'Informed consent – why are its goals imperfectly realized?' 302(16) *New England Journal of Medicine* 896–900

Corrigan, O (2002) 'A risky business: the detection of adverse drug reactions in clinical trials and post-marketing exercises' 55(3) *Social Science and Medicine* 497–507

Council for International Organizations of Medical Sciences (1993), *International Ethical Guidelines for Biomedical Research Involving Human Subjects*, Geneva: World Health Organization (WHO)

Department of Health (1991) 'Local Research Ethics Committees' Health Services Guidelines (91)5 Heywood: Department of Health

Douglas, M and Wildavsky, A (1982) *Risk and Culture: Essays on the Selection of Technological and Environmental Dangers*, Berkeley: University of California Press

Estey, A, Wilkin, G and Dossetor, J (1994) 'Are research subjects able to retain the information they are given during the consent process?' 3 *Health Law Review* 37–41

Faden, R and Beauchamp, T (1986) *A History and Theory of Informed Consent*, New York: OUP

Fox, R (1996) 'Experiment perilous: forty-five years as a participant observer of patient oriented clinical research' 39 *Perspectives in Biology and Medicine* 206–26

Frankenfield, PJ (1992) 'Technological citizenship: a normative framework for risk studies' 17(4) *Science, Technology and Human Values* 459–84

Gabe, J and Bury, M (1996) 'Halcyon nights: a sociological account of a medical controversy' 30 Sociology 447–69

Giddens, A (1990) *The Consequences of Modernity*, Cambridge: Polity

Giddens, A (1992) *Modernity and Self-Identity*, Cambridge: Polity

Gray, BH (1975) *Human Subjects in Medical Experimentation*, New York, London, Sydney and Toronto: John Wiley and Sons

International Conference on Harmonisation (1998) 'Guidance for trials of medicinal products in the European community', in Foster, C (ed), *Manual For Research Ethics Committees*, London: Centre of Medical Ethics and Law

Jan, H and DeMets, D (1981) 'How informed is informed consent?' 2 *Controlled Clinical Trials* 287–303

Katz, J (1992) 'The consent principle of the Nuremberg Code: its significance then and now', in Annas, G and Grodin, M (eds), *The Nazi Doctors and the Nuremberg Code*, Oxford: OUP

Kent, G (1997) 'The views of members of local research ethics committees, researchers and members of the public towards the roles and functions of LRECs' 23 *Journal of Medical Ethics* 186–90

Lazarou, J, Pomeranz, BH and Corey, PN (1998) 'Incidence of adverse drug reactions in hospitalized patients: a meta-analysis of prospective studies' 279 *Journal of the American Medical Association* 1200–05

O'Malley, P (1996) 'Risk and responsibility', in Barry, A, Osborne, T and Rose, N (eds), *Foucault and Political Reason*, London: Chicago UP and UCL Press

O'Malley, P (2000) 'Uncertain subjects: risks, liberalism and contract' 29(4) *Economy and Society* 460–84

Pappworth, M (1967) *Human Guinea Pigs*, Harmondsworth: Penguin

Pirmohamed, M, Breckenridge, AM, Kitteringham, NR and Park, BK (1998) 'Adverse drug reactions' 316(7140) *British Medical Journal* 1295–98

Porter, R (1997) *The Greatest Benefit to Mankind*, London: HarperCollins

Royal College of Physicians (1986) *Research on Healthy Volunteers*, London: Royal College of Physicians

Royal College of Physicians (1990) *Research Involving Patients*, London: Royal College of Physicians

Royal College of Physicians (1996) *Guidelines on the Practice of Ethics Committees in Medical Research Involving Human Subjects*, London: Royal College of Physicians

Snowdon, C, Garcia, J and Elbourne, D (1997) 'Making sense of randomization: responses of parents of critically ill babies to random allocation of treatment in clinical trials' 45(9) *Social Science and Medicine* 1137–55

Weinstein, M (2001) 'A public culture for guinea pigs: US human research subjects after the Tuskegee study' 10(2) *Science as Culture* 195–223

World Medical Association (2000) 'Declaration of Helsinki', Edinburgh

ETHICS AS PASTORAL PRACTICE: IMPLEMENTING PREDICTIVE GENETIC TESTING IN THE MEDICAL GENETICS CLINIC[1]

Carlos Novas

INTRODUCTION

Over the course of the last three decades, the experience of illness and health has been transformed with the introduction of new technologies into the practice of medicine. These technological developments transform our conceptions of normality and pathology, the ways we think and act in relation to our bodies and selves, the ways we deliver our sufferings to the secular hopes and promises of science. Accompanying this movement is the widespread belief that the authority and conduct of the physician has to be organised along an ethic that promotes the autonomy of the subject, supports the choices they make in deciding the course of their health and illness, obtains their voluntary and informed consent to submit to a programme of medical intervention, and seeks to avoid harm to all those who enter into relations of medical care. While these values and principles carry significant weight, they should not be taken at face value, as the realities of the negotiation and resolution of ethical dilemmas in medicine take place in a plural and contested field. Furthermore, the translation of these principles into medical practice involves a technical labour that blends together heterogeneous forms of knowing, modes of perception, types of judgment, practices of calculation, specialist vocabularies, conceptions of persons, ways of speaking and acting, the mobilisation of skills, capacities and dispositions. This technical labour works upon and shapes the conduct of medical practitioners and the subjects who fall under their authority to achieve certain outcomes that are considered desirable and to avoid untoward events. This labour can comprise efforts to provide the best quality of medical care in relation to new developments in medical science, attempts to improve the capacities of individuals to enhance the quality of their lives in the realisation of a programme of medical care, programmes that enable individuals to take responsibility for their health or illness in alliance with the medical profession, and efforts to minimise the instances in which individuals may bring harm to themselves, such as those provoking severe depression or

---

1 I gratefully acknowledge the support of the ESRC Postdoctoral Fellowship Programme for financial assistance. Many thanks to Nikolas Rose, Nanneke Redclift, Oonagh Corrigan, Sahra Gibbon, Adam Hedgecoe and Sara Skodbo whose comments have greatly improved this chapter.

suicide, as is thought possible when individuals decide to learn their biological fate for late onset genetic diseases.

Through a case study of the development and implementation of ethical guidelines relating to a predictive genetic test for Huntington's disease (HD – previously known as Huntington's chorea), this chapter examines how genetic counsellors, in alliance with a number of other professions, have helped at-risk individuals decide if they wish to learn their biological destiny, in addition to helping them assimilate and cope with this information. Based on the discursive analysis of the statements and texts produced by genetic counsellors, medical geneticists, psychologists, psychiatrists, neurologists, commissions of inquiry, and patients' organisations over the past 30 years in countries such as the US, the UK and Canada, an attempt will be made to show how the formulation of ethical guidelines relating to the use of this test is a practical and technical endeavour. A key theme that will be elaborated in this chapter is how the ethical discourses relating to the development and implementation of this technology construct the identity of those likely to use this test as a 'person genetically at risk' and as an 'uncertain subject'. It will be shown how the mobilisation of these conceptions of personhood formed part of the justification for the development of predictive tests and subsequently informed the interventions of genetic counsellors and psychologists to minimise the harms that may come to these individuals in the process of revealing their genetic fate.

This chapter further tries to draw out how the formulation of ethical guidelines relating to predictive testing for HD acts as a conduit for the growing scientific rationalisation of ethics. The harms and benefits of offering this test as a clinical service were not be found exclusively in the principled reason of philosophical bioethics, alternatively, it was predominantly grounded in a criterion of truthfulness achieved through a process of empirical psychological experimentation. It will be demonstrated how the knowledge produced through this process of experimentation is practical: it has enabled the subject genetically at risk to be produced as a calculable entity, an entity whose reactions and ability to cope with the results of a genetic test can be predicted in advance, an entity that can be intervened upon to minimise the potential for untoward outcomes such as severe depression or suicide. It will be further proposed that this scientific rationalisation of ethics has certain public qualities. The knowledge and experience gained in providing predictive genetic testing for HD was not confined to this illness alone, rather it has served as an exemplar of how these types of tests ought and should be offered for other late onset genetic diseases.

Through focusing on this particular case study, a key concern is to draw attention to how the development and application of ethical guidelines is not a predominantly philosophical enterprise, but rather a practical and technical endeavour that is integrally related to how power is exercised in our contemporary present. While the bioethics precepts of autonomy, informed consent, beneficence and non-maleficence constitute an important grid of intelligibility, an axis through which the negotiation of the ethical dilemmas of offering predictive genetic testing were discursively charted, I wish to suggest that they form part of a broader morality of how individuals should be governed in their relations with figures of authority, medical or otherwise. These principles are consistent with a form of exercising power in advanced liberal democracies that seeks to govern individuals through their very freedom, make use of their self-activating capacities, and shape their conduct in desirable directions (Rose 1992, 1999). I suggest that the practical and technical resolution of the ethical dilemmas of predictive genetic testing constitute a pathway through which it has become possible to exert an individualising form of power over these individuals which Michel Foucault terms 'pastoral' (Foucault 2001a, 2001b).

The concept of pastoral power introduces a new problematic into the bioethics literature. Unlike principles-based bioethics (Beauchamp and Childress 1989), which seeks to provide both a grid of intelligibility through which the ethical dilemmas in medicine can be interpreted, and at the same time restrain medicine from exercising undue power over individuals, pastoral power suggests a different avenue for interrogating the relations that transpire between medical professionals and the individuals who seek such counsel. Pastoral power proposes that we pay attention to the different modes in our culture through which human beings are turned into subjects (Foucault 2001a, 2001b). The bioethics precepts of autonomy, informed consent, beneficence and non-maleficence can thus be considered as one specific rationality, amongst many, that assemble the medical professional and the individuals to whom they provide care or guidance, as specific kinds of subjects. Hence, in considering this form of power, attention needs to be paid to the multiple sites and forms of knowledge that act upon and shape the conduct of those who exercise a form of pastoral power, and the effects of this knowledge in creating particular kinds of medical subjects. Pastoral power is thus plural. It is not necessarily organised or administered by the State; rather, it can be exercised by a multitude of agents such as medical geneticists, genetic counsellors, neurologists, commissions of inquiry, and patients' organisations.

What, can it be said, is specific to this form of power? Why draw on a concept that Foucault discussed in relation to the development of early Christianity and propose that it has some relevance to contemporary medicine? The answer, I would argue, is that pastoral power provides a way of looking at how individuals are integrated into the modern matrix of medicine in a manner that is concerned with promoting individual and collective wellbeing. Pastoral power thus has moments of individualisation and collectivisation. It is individualising in that it seeks to gain knowledge of each and every individual who can be said to form part of a collective, to anticipate and provide for their needs, to assure their wellbeing, to provide an account of all the harms that may come to them, to provide them with the techniques by which to examine their souls and realise their aspirations through the exercise of choice. It is also a totalising form of power in which the wellbeing of each and every member of a particular collective is not only at stake, but the wellbeing of the collective as a whole also has to be provided for and taken into account. The specificity of this dimension of pastoral power rests in gaining knowledge about particular subjects in order to shape individual and collective conduct in directions that are considered desirable.

Pastoral power is integrally related to the accumulation and deployment of knowledge in order to provide individual and collective guidance. The specificity of this form of power consists of its reliance upon subjects to reveal, disclose or confess some truths about themselves to a range of contemporary pastoral professionals such as genetic counsellors or psychologists. Unlike Christian forms of pastoral power, in which confession was oriented towards ensuring salvation, contemporary practices of disclosure are more therapeutic, oriented towards shaping some aspects of conduct or behaviour in socially desirable directions. These practices of self-disclosure, open to analysis personal circumstances and needs, providing the very foundation for working upon subjectivity. As such, this form of power can only ever be effected by working through the freedom and the willingness of a subject to disclose salient aspects about themselves. Resistance, then, to this form of power can simply involve the refusal to speak the truth about oneself or to fully co-operate with pastoral professionals. This form of power, requires, at the very minimum, compliance with pastoral professionals so that individuals can be assisted in understanding their experiences and their conduct guided in socially desirable directions.

The provision of pastoral forms of care can further entail the aggregation of individual experience to produce quantitative accounts of the attributes and characteristics of specific populations. Through the acquisition of individual and collective knowledge, a range of pastoral interventions can be designed to provide highly specific guidance and care to each and every person within a specific population. Furthermore, knowledge of individuals and collectives feed into the training and conduct of pastors so that they can best meet the needs of each and all whom they serve (Rose 2001). In analysing this form of power, attention needs to be paid to the range of techniques through which individuals are incited to reveal the truth about themselves and the how this individualised knowledge is used to produce generalisable statements about particular social groups or technological practices. Central to pastoral power is the development of particular understandings of subjects so that guidance and care can be provided to each and all.

UNCERTAIN SUBJECTS: CONSTRUCTING THE PERSON 'GENETICALLY AT RISK'

In examining the history of the development of a test capable of predicting carriers of the gene for HD, it is apparent that the life of the person likely to inherit this disorder gradually became characterised by persistent and unrelenting uncertainty (Novas 2003). How has this movement come about? It will be suggested that the division of persons into different kinds of beings is central to the practical ethical rationalities developed in contemporary medical genetics. Through this labour of division it becomes possible to formulate guidelines for the conduct of medical practitioners, design appropriate interventions, and consider the medical technologies that should be made available to such persons. It will be shown that the construction of the person genetically at risk as an uncertain subject takes place at the intersection of several modes of thought and practice. What I want to suggest as being central to pastoral forms of power is the development of certain conceptions of individuals, and methods of attaining knowledge about them, in order to shape a range of pastoral interventions.

Our contemporary understanding of the person genetically at risk as an uncertain subject has been achieved through a variety of forms of thought and practice which divide and classify individuals into particular categories. One of these modalities consists of clinical genetics. Carriers of the gene for HD have not always understood to be subjects at genetic risk. Their lives have been questioned since the inception of genetics, in terms of its dominant mode of transmission in which each offspring has a 50:50 chance of developing the disease, and its late onset which means that many will have reproduced by the time the illness makes its presence (Davenport and Muncey 1916). Through this clinical problematic, the search for a reliable method of distinguishing between those who carry the gene and those that do not had its inception. In the eugenic age from the early 1910s to the late 1940s, the problematisation of the lives of potential 'choreics' took place in the context of a threat to nation and race. The disease was thought to pose a drain on the nation's coffers through the need to institutionalise affected individuals in asylums, and to the quality of the race through its 'degeneration' by the unwitting transmission of this disease onto subsequent generations. From the 1950s to the 1970s, the problematisation of the lives of 'choreics' for the most part lost its eugenic overtones and became couched in a preventative and epidemiological mentality. This gaze sought to measure the incidence of the disease in the population and reduce the burden that it imposed on affected families through the provision of genetic counselling. From the 1970s onwards, the lives of potential carriers of the gene started to be described in the language of risk. This subtle mutation in thought transformed genetic risk into something personal, an ever-present factor creating uncertainty in decisions concerning marriage, childbearing, education, career decisions and so forth. With this personalisation of risk, the uncertain probability of developing the illness became not only a threat to subsequent generations, but to one's sense of self and ability to plan for a future. Through the language and calculus of risk, the problematisation of HD was mapped onto a new social and interpersonal space (Armstrong 1983, 1993).

Another avenue through which the person genetically at risk was constructed as an uncertain subject was through the formation of a Congressional Committee in the United States. This committee investigated the social impact of this disease and made recommendations for research funding. The Report of the Congressional Committee to Combat Huntington's Disease and its Consequences[2] contributed to the articulation of this conception of personhood with the following type of statement:

> Individuals at risk live in a state of uncertainty which imposes a heavy psychological burden. Not only must they bear witness to the painful decline of a parent; they must carry the burden of fear and anxiety that some day the same thing may happen to them. They are unable to plan ahead, to prepare for college, careers, or for love, marriage, and parenthood without apprehension and doubt. They are unable to pass each day without the constant watching for symptoms ...
> (US Department of Health, Education and Welfare 1977: 2)

---

2   This congressional committee was set up through the active lobbying of the Committee to Combat Huntington's Disease. It was designed to give an assessment of the implications of the disease in the US, assess current research, and propose potential avenues of research to fund (see Wexler 1996: 137–43).

Furthermore, the Commission used this conception of personhood to provide justification to the US Congress to finance the search for a predictive test. The value of a predictive test was to be found in:

> The removal of the gnawing uncertainty for both those found to be free of the gene as well as those receiving positive diagnosis, permitting them to plan their lives in light of their destiny; and

> The ability of those at risk to act responsibly in light of this knowledge, and in so acting, to increase their humanity and moral status, because to act responsibly is to act in a human fashion (US Department of Health Education and Welfare 1977: 305).

Through the mediation of technology, the life of the subject genetically at risk could be delivered from a state of uncertainty and ambiguity to a life that could be planned and realised through the exercise of a series of choices in the light of one's biological destiny. This formulation can be seen as a constituent element of a new ethics of human responsibility, whereby objective knowledge of one's body is seen to augment the moral status and humanity of the individual at genetic risk (Novas and Rose 2000). The search for a presymptomatic test can be seen to fit into a broader project for the valorisation of health in our present, which seeks to secure the health and wellbeing of each and all through the transformation of human vitality into a multiplicity of factors of risk and, by extension, the creation of the new set of ethical responsibilities for the management of biological fate (Castel 1991, Cox and McKellin 1999, Gifford 1986, Hallowell 1999, Kenen 1996, Lupton 1993, Nettleton 1997, Petersen 1997, 1998, Petersen and Bunton 2002). Through the 'making up' of this particular 'kind' of person (Hacking 1986, 1992, 1995), the genetically at risk, predictive genetic testing emerges as a technology that claims to be able to resolve many of the uncertainties of such a life and way of being.

Lastly, I want to point out how psychology assisted in the construction of the person genetically at risk as an uncertain subject. Through the language of psychology, genetic risk became interiorised within the self (Hans and Gilmore 1968, Kessler 1988, Lynch, Harlan and Dyhrberg 1972, Smith, Holloway and Emery 1971, Weijer and Emanuel 2000, Wexler 1979, 1984). Nancy Wexler,[3] the foremost psychologist on HD, based on 35 interviews with persons at risk, claims that 'The experience of being at risk is a separate and distinct state, with its own unique psychology ... Their lot is one of chronic, unremitting ambiguity – neither healthy nor sick, neither confident that health will continue nor certain that illness will intervene' (Wexler 1985: 280). Through this formulation, the person genetically at risk is constructed as an individual who wants to plan for the future, a possibility that is obstructed when 'all decisions must be made in the context of uncertainty' (Wexler 1985: 281). This planning for the future and concern over their personal wellbeing extends not only to the self, but to others such as potential children, their parents and siblings, as well as prospective marriage partners. This person is also active in relation to the disease through the constant

---

3   Nancy Wexler is a person whose family is at risk of developing HD. Apart for her work on the psychology of being at genetic risk and on genetic counselling, she has also played an instrumental role through the Heredity Disease Foundation (which her father Milton Wexler founded) in contributing to scientific research on HD.

exercise of vigilance and scrutiny over mind and body for the manifestation of any symptoms of the disease. Through the language of psychology, the person genetically at risk is constructed as a self-realising subject, who with a risky identity wants to exercise control over their life through the enactment of a series of choices and decisions. The words of Nancy Wexler highlight the operation of a modality of health that has come to characterise our present, where the personalisation of factors of risk create a new state of health, where individuals are 'neither healthy nor sick'. Personalised risk introduces a state of uncertainty and ambiguity concerning one's being and health, where health becomes no longer, as for Leriche, 'life lived in the silence of the organs' (quoted in Canguilhem 1991: 91), but the quiet murmur of the calculation of so many factors of risk. In the case of genetics, the resolution of this uncertainty is sought through a technological solution, a predictive test that is able to precisely forecast those who will develop the illness in opposition to those who will not.

MORAL EXPERIMENTS: CREATING RATIONAL ETHICS

In 1983, following the discovery of marker genetically linked to HD (Gusella *et al* 1983) which created the possibility for predictive testing based on linkage analysis, within the medical genetics community there was widespread consensus that ethical guidelines needed to be developed prior to the introduction of this technology. On writing about the responsibilities of professionals at a moment when a new technology was being introduced, Craufurd and Harris (1986: 249) declare that 'Ethical guidelines should be established, but these require greater knowledge of the potential benefits and hazards of this powerful new technology'. They further suggest that 'Controlled clinical trials are urgently needed'. The evidence to be produced in these clinical trials were considered to be not only of relevance for HD, but could act as 'a paradigm for similar problems that will surely arise after the application of new predictive methods to other and perhaps more common diseases' (1986: 251). The clinical trial was a key technique used to determine the ethical validity of offering predictive genetic testing to the HD population. It can be said that as a result of these clinical trials, the practical questions of how we should act, what should we do, and what the consequences of our actions are became subject to a process of empirical rationalisation. This process of ethical rationalisation should be viewed in the light of its positivity: it provided a means of quantifying and qualifying the various outcomes and individual responses to predictive genetic testing in a way that fed into the pastoral responsibilities of avoiding harm to the subjects at risk for HD, and to the broader public of the medical genetics community. The clinical trial as a form of gathering knowledge facilitates pastoral power by being both individualising and totalising. Clinical trials provide a means of analysing how particular individuals cope with predictive genetic testing, but also enable the production of quantitative accounts of the aggregate benefits and harms of this new technology.

This process of the rationalisation of ethics should not be considered as another instance of the insidious penetration of science into everyday life – rather, it can be considered as facilitating pastoral power by determining the forms and limits of how one should act at a moment where the outcomes and consequences of so acting are uncertain and potentially grave. The positivity of this knowledge should not solely be considered in terms of its truth claims, but also on how it acted upon the conduct of genetic counselling teams and the subjects undergoing predictive genetic testing, in order to produce certain kinds of ethical effects. The normative, practical and pedagogical nature of this research is evident in a widely cited paper by Nancy Wexler and colleagues (1985: 21) who suggested that:

> One aim of this research would be to develop the optimally supportive approach by which to deliver presymptomatic diagnostic information. Another would be to discover the impact of positive, negative, and non-informative outcomes when test results are given under (presumably) optimally supportive conditions. Clinical investigators should try to determine the physical, psychological, demographic, and sociological variables that predict a good or poor adjustment to the testing procedure and associated counseling. Interventions should be designed to reduce the factors associated with adverse outcomes and both enhance and teach ways of constructive coping.

The knowledge to be produced in this experimental research phase was not only oriented towards the production of truth, but also to a range of practical, ethical objectives. It was concerned with acting upon the conduct of the genetic counselling team so that it would optimally support and meet the needs of those who came to learn their genetic fate. This research phase was also designed to produce knowledge of the subjects undergoing predictive genetic testing so that they could be made calculable, so that predictions could be made as to their capacities to deal with a new genetic destiny, so that interventions could be designed to prevent any harms from coming their way. This process of experimental knowledge generation further entailed a commitment to monitor, report and record the singularities of the individuals undergoing predictive genetic testing so that their experiences could be made comparable, analysable, and rendered into practicable thought. These interventions are both preventative and pedagogical: they not only seek to avoid harm, but to teach ways in which harm can be avoided. It is at this junction that biomedicine intersects with a whole range of technologies of the self. In this particular instance, work upon the self is seen to foster the ability to integrate the results of predictive genetic test into everyday life, in relations with spouses and children, other siblings and family members at risk, potential marriage partners, employers, insurance companies and the like.

The concern with evaluating the long-term psychosocial consequences of predictive genetic testing for HD has led to the institutionalisation of this process of ethical verification through the formation of collaborative projects amongst a number of genetic counselling centres.[4] The general objectives of these projects can be found in the Canadian Collaborative Study of Predictive Testing established in 1988 amongst 14 centres to 'describe the baseline attributes of

---

4   The collaborative projects consist of the UK Huntington's Disease Prediction Consortium, the Baltimore Huntington's Disease Project, and the European Collaborative Study Group on HD Predictive Testing. Important centres which conduct research on HD testing consist of the University of British Columbia, the Johns Hopkins University School of Medicine, Boston University Medical School and Massachusetts General Hospital, the University College of Medicine in Cardiff, and the Aberdeen Royal Hospital (Wexler 1996: Afterword).

candidates for predictive testing and to compare the short-term and long-term psychological effects of such testing' (Wiggins *et al* 1992: 1,402).[5] The establishment of these collaborative projects acts upon the conduct of the genetic counselling teams at diverse centres through the standardisation of counselling protocols for the provision of the test, and the methods employed to gather psychosocial data on these individuals. Through this process of standardisation, of enabling comparison, and the magnification of the numbers of persons amenable to observation, the capacity for statistical generalisation and correlation is thereby augmented, enhancing the validity of these veridical practices. Through this process of the institutionalisation of the methods used to determine the benefits and harms of predictive testing, it acts as a further conduit for the rationalisation of ethical practices along scientific lines. What is significant about these practices is that from this moment forward, the ethical validity of offering predictive genetic tests for HD, and many other genetic disorders, would have to employ or make reference to a process of empirical psychological verification.

The validation of predictive genetic testing for HD through a 'program of empirical psychological research' (Brandt 1994: 47) constitutes a key technique through which the morality of offering predictive genetic tests was negotiated. This form of morality is technical, in that the evaluation of the harms and benefits of predictive genetic testing made reference to the baseline psychological characteristics of the individuals undergoing such tests prior to the disclosure of results and at regular intervals thereafter. This morality is statistical, through the aggregation of individual experience in a format that is amenable to quantifiable representation in a chart, that is combinable and comparable with the observations produced at other centres, that can be co-related with a range of personal, demographic and sociological variables. This morality is interventionist, as it sought to identify characteristics that predispose individuals to suffer an adverse psychological reaction and to develop practical ways in which counselling could be provided to mitigate against these occurrences. It is normative, in that individuals are judged through a psychologically mediated criterion of normality and pathology, of wellbeing and illness, of positive and negative adjustments relating to the integration of test results into their everyday lives. This morality is public, in that the clinical experiences of offering predictive testing and the experiences of those undergoing this procedure were thought to provide an exemplar for other late onset genetic diseases. As I will now attempt to show, this programme of experimental research was not only discursive, it has a materiality that is manifest in the practices of providing such a service.

MAKING ETHICS PRACTICAL

One of the central objectives of the clinical research phase was to develop the optimal approach by which to provide predictive genetic testing for HD. This

---

5   The goals of these collaborative projects are not limited to Canada alone. The UK's Huntington's Disease Prediction Consortium was established to promote 'good standards of service provision', 'agree a common protocol' and to 'collect data to evaluate the testing programme' (Tyler, Bull and Craufurd 1992: 1,593).

empirical research provided a venue through which past ethical concerns and experience could be translated into a minute series of practices for organising and shaping the conduct of genetic counselling teams who subsequently were to offer presymptomatic genetic testing. A paper by Robin L Bennett and colleagues (1993) is illustrative, as it draws upon their experiences during the experimental research phase to suggest ways in which predictive genetic testing for HD can be offered in the medical genetics clinic in a manner that is both conscientious and cost effective.

In their paper, Bennett and colleagues begin by describing the process of establishing a predictive testing programme. Attention is drawn to the forms of expertise required to staff the clinic: this includes professionals such as a board certified genetic counsellor, a medical geneticist, and access on a consultative basis to a neurologist and a psychologist. These professionals are not brought together solely for the purposes of clinical care, but the consultation of expertise 'from a panel of laboratory, medical and ethical experts' is seen as helpful 'when psychosocial, ethical, and legal problems arise' (1993: 124). This process of ethical review can form part of the habitual workings of the medical genetics clinic, as Bennett and co-workers state that in their own practice, 'After each client's visit, the case is anonymously discussed from the laboratory, medical, counseling and ethical standpoints as part of our regularly scheduled medical genetics clinic conference' (1993: 125). In making a process of ethical review part of the habitual operation of the clinic, each individual case becomes a pedagogical tool that can be used to constantly improve the working of the clinic, and a little experiment by which to generate more knowledge about predictive testing and the subjects who come for it.

Another facet of establishing a predictive testing programme relates to determining the eligibility of clients to participate in such a clinical service. In the clinic of Bennett and colleagues, the 'eligibility requirements are that the person be at 50% risk to develop HD (25% if the at-risk parent is deceased) and of legal age to be able to make an informed decision about testing' (1993: 125). The eligibility requirements further take into consideration the pastoral concern of being able to provide adequate psychosocial care, as individuals who live more than 300 miles away are not considered eligible to enter the programme, although exceptions are made if a local professional counsellor is available. The pastoral function of the eligibility criteria further includes evaluations as to the psychological competence of the subject to undergo predictive testing. Individuals in a state of psychological crisis, due, for example, to divorce or substance abuse, are encouraged to postpone their plans for being tested (1993: 125). The client is also required to bring a support person to each visit, preferably an individual who is not an at-risk family member as they may not be able to provide relevant support.

Another practical pastoral matter relates to the number and duration of the genetic counselling sessions believed appropriate for the competent provision of predictive genetic testing. Based on the experience of the authors, 'four visits seems to be the minimum for a person given a decreased risk and five for a person given an increased risk' (1993: 126). These sessions are divided into the pre-counselling stage, which takes place prior to the disclosure of the results, and the post-counselling phase, which seeks to help the client adjust to the results of a genetic test. In the pre-counselling phase, they suggest it is important to evaluate the motivations of the client for requesting predictive testing and to explore how clients expect to react to the possible outcomes of this procedure. They provide a list of questions they use in their own clinical practice that may be of relevance to others offering this service. Such questions include: 'What will you do the day you are given your results if you are given an increased risk? A decreased risk? An uninformative result? What will you do the next week? The next month? The next year?' (1993: 128). Through this line of approach, individuals are asked to work upon themselves, to examine their lives and the meaning that a predictive genetic test will have upon it. They also suggest that persons considering testing view a videotape produced by the Canadian Predictive Testing Program, which consists of 'testimonials from four individuals who have pursued presymptomatic testing and discussion of the impact the results had on their lives' (1993: 127). The talk of the genetic counselling team does not stand alone, it is supplemented through the aid of a visual device that seeks to incite the client considering predictive testing to perform a certain work upon themselves in the light of the experiences of others. These combined elements are constitutive of a pedagogy of genetic counselling that seeks to encourage the formation of certain prudential relation to the self: caution, circumspection and foreknowledge are to be encouraged in the process of learning one's genetic fate.

The provision of competent genetic counselling for predictive genetic testing further requires that the counselling team pay close attention to the ways in which they conduct themselves and how the routines of the clinic are organised. Both of these aspects need to be carefully micromanaged in order to achieve desirable affects – a process that can take into consideration time, space and language (Silverman 1997). One aspect of the experience of predictive genetic testing which Bennett and colleagues suggest should be carefully conducted is the disclosure session, in which test results are delivered to the client. They begin by suggesting that the timing of the disclosure of laboratory results to the genetic counsellor is significant in relation to future pastoral concerns. It is suggested that the genetic counsellor may choose not to know the test results until immediately before the disclosure session since a 'client may decline to know his or her results at the last moment and if the counseling staff already has test information, unbiased counseling in the future will be virtually impossible' (1993: 133–34). To diminish the anxiety and stress of the client, the timing and organisation of the disclosure session receives special consideration. In the practice of Bennett and colleagues, 'The client is scheduled early in the day and escorted to the room quickly'. As the disclosure session is considered to be a highly stressful experience, the genetic counselling team needs to be especially vigilant towards their behaviour as the 'client may interpret every movement to be indicative of the test results' (1993: 134). The timing of the delivery of results and the language employed by the genetic counselling team constitute further actions that need to be closely regulated. In this particular practice, the results are delivered 'immediately, without preamble. Results are not modified with adjectives such as "good" or "bad", "high" or "low" since only the client can interpret the positive and negative impact the results will have' (1993: 134). The kinds of practices being described here entail the micromanagement of conduct in a way that enfolds normative, pastoral, spatio-temporal and linguistic aspects of being.

The paper written by Robin L Bennett, Thomas D Bird and Linda Teri (1993) provides a very different reading of how ethics can become part of the routine operation of medical genetics clinics offering presymptomatic genetic testing for HD. Their account presents an engagement with the bioethics precepts of autonomy, informed consent, confidentiality, beneficence and non-maleficence; however, the universal qualities of these principles are rendered into a practical form – a form that works upon the conduct of the genetic counselling team. In the alchemic process of translation from the universal to the local, a qualitatively new property seems to have been added to the experience of providing predictive genetic tests – an elixir that enfolds experience, space, time and language within the orbit of a highly managed encounter. Ethical principles and the results of the experimental research phase seem to have been transmuted into a whole range of minute conducts for organising the practices of the clinic and the comportment of the counselling staff, so that the chances of harm being encountered are minimised and the opportunities for promoting individual wellbeing are realised. In this admixture, judgments and evaluations are made that draw on the principles of bioethics and empirical research in order to realise a range of pastoral objectives – practices that in part involve assessments regarding the competence of the subject to take part in a process that provides them with a vision of their genetic destiny.

CONCLUSION

By concentrating on the implementation of a predictive genetic test for HD in the medical genetics clinic, this chapter has attempted to highlight how the development of ethical guidelines is a practical and technical endeavour. In the process of developing a predictive test for HD and negotiating its ethical dilemmas, the life of the person genetically at risk for this disease has come to be characterised by persistent and unrelenting uncertainty. The case of HD emphasises how particular conceptions of personhood have been central to the development of genetic counselling over time, and how they shape the kinds of medical technologies and interventions designed to assist these persons act upon their risk status and assimilate it into their everyday lives. Here we can begin to see how the accumulation of knowledge about this population through a programme of empirical psychological research and individual observation feeds into the pastoral role of genetic counselling to promote wellbeing and to avoid harm from coming in the way of each and every person at genetic risk who wishes to learn their biological future. In considering ethics as a form of pastoral practice, this chapter has tried to show how the conduct of the genetic counselling team providing predictive testing needs to be carefully micromanaged in order to maximise the chances by which individuals will successfully adapt to a new genetic risk status. In this process, genetic counsellors mobilise a range of techniques of the self which enable persons at genetic risk to develop a prudential relation to themselves.

Through the analysis of the diverse materials presented in the chapter, ethics is considered as a form of pastoral practice. As a way of considering how ethics forms part of the contemporary enterprise of medicine, Michel Foucault's concept of pastoral power was drawn upon as a means of developing an alternative way to that of bioethics for interrogating the relations that transpire between medical professionals and the persons who come to them for counsel. This is in contrast to bioethics' assertion that its key principles of autonomy and informed consent help to restrain medicine from exercising undue power over the persons who fall under its care. Pastoral power, by suggesting that we pay attention to the diverse modes in our culture through which human beings are turned into subjects, explores how power relations pervade medical encounters by acting upon the conduct and subjectivity of medical professional and client alike so as to achieve a number of socially and ethically desirable objectives. Rather than conceptualising persons as rational actors who autonomously make decisions, as is commonly held in the bioethics literature, pastoral power suggests that we take notice of the specific conceptions of personhood that are employed in the field of biomedicine and the forms of truth through which knowledge is produced about each and every subject who falls within its ambit. We can begin to see how knowledge is central to the operations of pastoral power in the empirically grounded programme of psychological research that was used to negotiate the ethical dilemmas surrounding predictive testing, which did not make extensive reference to the universalising principles of bioethics. This programme of empirical psychological research not only determined the ethical validity of offering predictive testing but, in the process, produced a composite image of these subjects. As such, their experiences could be made calculable so that interventions could be designed in order to minimise harm and promote the wellbeing of each and every person who wishes to learn their genetic fate. The findings produced in this empirically grounded research programme have not been limited to HD; they are used as a general model for how these tests should and ought to be offered for other late onset genetic diseases.

BIBLIOGRAPHY

Armstrong, D (1983) *Political Anatomy of the Body: Medical Knowledge in Britain in the Twentieth Century*, Cambridge: CUP

Armstrong, D (1993) 'Public health spaces and the fabrication of identity' 27(3) *Sociology* 393–410

Beauchamp, TL and Childress, JF (1989) *Principles of Biomedical Ethics*, 3rd edn, Oxford: OUP

Bennett, RL, Bird, TD and Teri, L (1993) 'Offering predictive testing for Huntington disease in a medical genetics clinic: practical applications' 2(3) *Journal of Genetic Counseling* 123–37

Brandt, J (1994) 'Ethical considerations in genetic testing: an empirical study of presymptomatic diagnosis of Huntington's disease', in Fulford, KWM, Gillett, GR and Soskice, JM (eds), *Medicine and Moral Reasoning*, Cambridge: CUP

Canguilhem, G (1991) *The Normal and the Pathological*, New York: Zone Books

Castel, R (1991) 'From dangerousness to risk', in Burchell, G, Gordon, C and Miller, P (eds), *The Foucault Effect: Studies in Governmentality*, London: Harvester Wheatsheaf

Cox, SM and McKellin, W (1999) '"There's this thing in our family": predictive testing and the construction of risk for Huntington disease' 21(5) *Sociology of Health & Illness* 622–46

Craufurd, D and Harris, R (1986) 'Ethics of predictive testing for Huntington's chorea: the need for more information' 293 *British Journal of Psychiatry* 249–51

Davenport, CB and Muncey, EB (1916) 'Huntington's chorea in relation to heredity and eugenics' 73 *American Journal of Insanity* 195–222

Foucault, M (2001a) '"*Omnes et singulatim*": toward a critique of political reason', in Faubion, JD (ed), *Power: Essential Works of Foucault, 1954–1984*, London: Allen Lane

Foucault, M (2001b) 'The subject and power', in Faubion, JD (ed), *Power: Essential Works of Foucault, 1954–1984*, London: Allen Lane

Gifford, SM (1986) 'The meaning of lumps: a case study of the ambiguities of risk', in Janes, CR, Stall, R and Gifford, SM (eds), *Anthropology and Epidemiology: Interdisciplinary Approaches to the Study of Health and Diseases*, Boston, MA: Kluwer Academic Publishers

Gusella, JF, Wexler, NS, Conneally, PM, Naylor, SL, Anderson, MA, Tanzi, RE, Watkins, PC, Ottina, K, Wallace, MR, Sakaguchi, AY, Young, AB, Shoulson, I, Bonilla, E and Martin, JB (1983) 'A polymorphic DNA marker genetically linked to Huntington's disease' 306 *Nature* 234–38

Hacking, I (1986) 'Making up people', in Heller, TC, Sosna, M and Wellbery, DE (eds), *Reconstructing Individualism: Autonomy, Individuality and the Self in Western Thought*, Stanford, CA: Stanford UP

Hacking, I (1992) 'World-making by kind-making: child abuse for example', in Douglas, M and Hull, D (eds), *How Classification Works: Nelson Goodman Among the Social Sciences*, Edinburgh: Edinburgh UP

Hacking, I (1995) 'The looping effects of human kinds', in Sperber, D, Premack, D and Premack, AJ (eds), *Causal Cognition: A Multi-Disciplinary Approach*, Oxford: Clarendon

Hallowell, N (1999) 'Doing the right thing: genetic risk and responsibility' 21(5) *Sociology of Health & Illness* 597–621

Hans, MB and Gilmore, T (1968) 'Social aspects of Huntington's chorea' 114 *British Journal of Psychiatry* 93–98

Kenen, RH (1996) 'The at-risk health status and technology: a diagnostic invitation and the "gift" of knowing' 42(11) *Social Science & Medicine* 1,545–53

Kessler, S (1988) 'Invited essay on the psychological aspects of genetic counseling v preselection: a family coping strategy in Huntington disease' 31(3) *American Journal of Medical Genetics* 617–21

Lupton, D (1993) 'Risk as moral danger: the social and political functions of risk discourse in public health' 23(3) *International Journal of Health Services* 425–35

Lynch, HT, Harlan, WL and Dyhrberg, JS (1972) 'Subjective perspective of a family with Huntington's chorea: implications for genetic counselling' 27(1) *Archives of General Psychiatry* 67–72

Nettleton, S (1997) 'Governing the risky self: how to become healthy, wealthy and wise', in Petersen, A and Bunton, R (eds), *Foucault, Health and Medicine*, London: Routledge

Novas, C (2003) *Governing 'Risky' Genes: Predictive Genetics, Counselling Expertise and the Care of the Self*, unpublished PhD thesis, Goldsmiths College, University of London

Novas, C and Rose, N (2000) 'Genetic risk and the birth of the somatic individual' 29(4) *Economy and Society* 485–513

Petersen, A (1997) 'Risk, governance and the new public health', in Petersen, A and Bunton, R (eds), *Foucault, Health and Medicine*, London: Routledge

Petersen, A (1998) 'The new genetics and the politics of public health' 8(1) *Critical Public Health* 59–71

Petersen, A and Bunton, R (2002) *The New Genetics and the Public's Health*, London: Routledge

Rose, N (1992) 'Towards a critical sociology of freedom', Inaugural Lecture given on 5 May 1992, Goldsmiths College, University of London

Rose, N (1999) *Powers of Freedom: Reframing Political Thought*, Cambridge: CUP

Rose, N (2001) 'The politics of life itself' 18(6) *Theory, Culture & Society* 1–30

Silverman, D (1997) *Discourses of Counselling: HIV Counselling as Social Interaction*, London: Sage

Smith, C, Holloway, S and Emery, AEH (1971) 'Individuals at risk in families with genetic disease' 8(4) *Journal of Medical Genetics* 453–59

Tyler, A, Bull, D and Craufurd, D (1992) 'Presymptomatic testing for Huntington's disease in the United Kingdom' 304 *British Medical Journal* 1,593–96

US Department of Health, Education and Welfare (1977) *Report of the Commission to Control Huntington's Disease and its Consequences*, Betheseda, MA: US Department of Health, Education and Welfare

Weijer, C and Emanuel, EJ (2000) 'Protecting communities in biomedical research' 289 *Science* 1,142–44

Wexler, A (1996) *Mapping Fate: A Memoir of Family, Risk and Genetic Research*, Berkeley, CA: California UP

Wexler, NS (1979) 'Genetic "Russian Roulette": the experience of being "at risk" for Huntington's disease', in Kessler, S (ed), *Genetic Counseling: Psychological Dimensions*, New York: Academic Press

Wexler, NS (1984) 'Huntington's disease and other late onset disorders', in Emery, AEH and Pullen, IM (eds), *Psychological Aspects of Genetic Counselling*, London: Academic Press

Wexler, NS (1985) 'Genetic jeopardy and the new clairvoyance', in Bearn, AG, Motulsky, AG and Childs, B (eds), *Progress in Medical Genetics*, New York: Praeger Scientific

Wexler, NS, Conneally, PM, Housman, D and Gusella, JF (1985) 'A DNA polymorphism for Huntington's disease marks the future' 42(1) *Archives of Neurology* 20–24

Wiggins, S, Whyte, P, Huggins, M, Adam, S, Theilman, J, Bloch, M, Sheps, SB, Schechter, MT and Hayden, MR (1992) 'The psychological consequences of predictive testing for Huntington's disease' 327(20) *New England Journal of Medicine* 1,401–05

PART 2

MORAL BOUNDARIES: CREATING DIFFERENCE THROUGH ETHICAL CLAIMS

CHAPTER 5

RESPECTABILITY, RISK AND SEXUAL PRACTICES: HIV/AIDS IN PEUBLA, MEXICO

Sara Corben de Romero

INTRODUCTION[1]

The emergence of HIV/AIDS highlighted the lack of understanding we have of cultural variations in ideas about sexual practice and identity. Although public health policy normally side-steps the moral universe in the delivery of education/prevention programmes, local ideas about sex, and the values surrounding sexuality and gender, in conjunction with understandings and approaches to health, affect perceptions of HIV and the risk of infection and should be considered in the formulation of local health education programmes.

Appadurai argues that cultures make local what is global (1990), a perception which must be extended to the experience of epidemics. The HIV/AIDS pandemic has been described as several local epidemics, each with their own geographies, affected populations, and types and frequencies of transmission (Mertens *et al*: 1994). This chapter discusses local knowledge of HIV in the context of understandings of sexual behaviour, homosexuality and bisexuality in southern Mexico; it also discusses the value of applying a universal understanding of risk in different moral environments. Education about sexually transmitted disease, whether using locally produced or imported information, remains an extremely difficult and problematic area. Mexico imported an international AIDS education model produced in Anglo-Saxon cultures that privileges use of condoms, monogamy and an idea of 'homosexual identity'. Analysing the local discourses surrounding this problem contributes to our understanding of the processes of globalisation, as new information is differentially incorporated, resisted and rejected, and medical beliefs and practices are affected. Qualitative ethnographic studies contribute an understanding of how individuals use ideas in practice to the medicalised, quantitative discussions of sex and disease that have hitherto dominated the debate.

---

1   This chapter is based on fieldwork carried out in Puebla, Mexico. The material was gathered through semi-structured interviewing and participant observation with 43 people over a two-year period from 1995 to 1996. All names have been changed.

RISK AND SOCIAL SCIENCE

A discourse that developed initially around identity rather than sexual practices separated 'risk' groups from the general population. That the 'risk' groups in northern developed countries might be different from those in the south is obscured by the fact that most medical and academic research is carried out in the north, and those discourses hold a privileged place in the production of knowledge. Risk, as a theoretical concept, has become increasingly important in studies of HIV/AIDS because of the difficulties associated with the continued adoption of 'safer sex' techniques in relation to a perceived risk of infection. Sociologists and anthropologists have argued that epidemiologists and public health educators should look to social theory, where risk has been analysed as a culturally constructed concept, for answers to the questions about the difficulties associated with behaviour change.

Public health models of risk presume underlying models of the body, environment, health, illness and normality that may not coincide with local models (Kendall 1995). Hart and Boulton (1995) investigated AIDS from the sociology of risk perspective, and produced further criteria that have to be considered when a change of behaviour fails, not least of which are the social and material constraints on people's ability to change – access to condoms is one such case in point. Additionally, risky sexual behaviour is frequently 'constructed as social action' (1995: 64) both operating within and generating the form of that behaviour. *Machismo*, a quintessential Mexican concept of 'manliness', carries within it an idea of risk, the element of danger that a man continually lives with, and that determine him as a man. Hart and Boulton, and Patton (1994) also point to the balance of power, particularly gender inequality, in any sexual relationship, that also needs to be negotiated in order to instigate behaviour change.

Whereas risk has been fully discussed in relation to HIV and, through the assumption of social norms, continues to be used as a label for individuals and practices, the question of trust remains under-discussed, and is surely more relevant. The assumption of implicit trust that is often made in formal long-term sexual relationships, and which is articulated through diffuse moral codes and values, has lead to infection amongst groups widely believed to be 'low-risk'. The significance of 'respectability', and implied trust emerged in my conversations with Mexican women about HIV/AIDS.

WOMEN'S UNDERSTANDING OF HIV

HIV/AIDS (*SIDA*) has a high profile in Mexico. Although there is no sense of this health problem as widely publicised and open for discussion, it was not unknown to any of the people I interviewed. What they know, however, is extremely variable, as is their response, or ability to respond. SIDA is understood as a disease of the blood, and sex as the primary route of infection. Intravenous drug use was not generally mentioned as a possible source of infection, but blood transfusions, and mother-child infection were occasionally referred to. Television was cited as the source of knowledge in most cases. Given the lack of information on television during the fieldwork year, this was either said with reference to earlier television campaigns, evidence that the government's campaigns over the years have created a layer of understanding, or cited as a modern and ostensibly reliable/'true' source of information. Radio and newspapers were not mentioned as sources of information, although these media do generally give fuller and more accurate accounts.

Most lower income women treated this topic of conversation with some embarrassment, particularly when discussed in the presence of older children. However there was a certain matter of fact-ness to the conversations that suggested that a connection between the problem and the self might not have been made. A popular idea expressed was that sons should not marry women who 'get around'.

Augustina's husband Benjamin, a self-employed plumber, was present the first time I went to speak with her. When I asked them together if they had ever heard of an illness called AIDS, he replied:

> AIDS is fatal, and a slow death. You get it if you have sex with prostitutes – they give it to men. You use a condom, and you don't get it, and you don't go with those women.

Middle class women were just as unlikely to openly relate HIV to themselves:

> You get it through sexual contact and blood transfusions. I have never known anyone who got it. I think people who mess around get it. I don't think homosexuals can avoid it. I think heterosexuals can use condoms. (Alejandra)

Patti, a younger woman of 15, demonstrates the vagueness with which she understands sexual matters, with her following comments:

> AIDS is a sexually transmitted disease, which you can get if you don't look after yourself.[2] Also, you can get it from malnutrition.[3]

The problem was not unknown to any of the women I spoke too, although there was little sense of a differentiation between a virus, and a complicated medical syndrome. Most of the middle class women receive US cable television in their homes, giving them access to wider information. As the poorer women do not have access to cable TV, local television programmes, especially ever-popular soap operas that might include a character with HIV, may account for the reason why HIV had been located in the world of female sex workers and 'homosexuals'. Popular ideas about sex workers as unclean has emphasised the connection between HIV and 'bad' women or promiscuity. The male character in the soap *Cuna De Lobos*, who contracted HIV, had previously been evil towards the female protagonist. Infection and a rapid demise were his punishment.

Class differences did not appear to be very significant in the sense that this information, held with varying degrees of accuracy, is not directly applied to women's own personal lives. Eliza was one of the few to make the link between her husband's potential behaviour and cultural license to do as he pleased sexually, and her own position of not-knowing, and not being able to control her risk of exposure to HIV:

---

2   *Ciudarse* – take care of oneself. A euphemism more commonly used for prevention of pregnancy.

3   *Mala alimentacion.*

We used to think that only gays got AIDS [*entre el maricon, el SIDA*], but now we know that anyone can get it, like cancer. I suppose it might be a threat to me because of a blood transfusion – but they check all the blood now. Maybe through my husband, because of the way he is, his way of thinking. It's very rare to discuss these sorts of things with one's husband.

The women who discuss their perceptions of risk above may be far more aware of the potential effect of infection on their lives than they demonstrate in discussion, but they may also simultaneously recognise the difficulties of modifying their own or their partner's behaviour. It is one thing to be aware of and discuss condoms with a foreign researcher, it is quite another to introduce them into a marriage. When a young woman is admonished to 'take care', mystifying as this can be, the practical means and ability to do so are often lacking. When a woman does 'take care', her aim will normally be the avoidance of pregnancy, rather than a STD. It cannot be presumed, therefore, that even when an understanding of risk of infection is present, that behaviour change will automatically follow, or will even be possible. A universal model of risk is therefore unhelpful, as it ignores the reality of differential gender access to knowledge/information and how different layers of knowledge are played out in practice.

HIV/AIDS has been located in a separate space from the family and the expectation of monogamy in a long-term relationship such as marriage or consensual union. It therefore does not encroach upon the expectations of women who behave 'respectably', indicating that the 'general population' has been constructed as separate domain from that occupied by 'risk groups'. The risk group is largely assumed to be bounded from the 'normal' population, being composed of female prostitutes, or of prostitutes and 'homosexuals'.

FEMALE SEX WORKERS

As female prostitutes are popularly thought to be sources of infection, it is important to examine how sex workers themselves respond to this perception. Dania, who works in a small market town outside the city, relies on a system of luck and home remedies to avoid pregnancy in her private life, but her attitude towards her working life is more careful. I met her at COESIDA,[4] when she came to take her six monthly test. Dania is very conscious of HIV as a problem, particularly as she has to provide a certificate of HIV negativity every six months to her place of work. Her attitude towards infection in her private life is that it simply will not happen. Dania's current boyfriend is a former client. The difference between client and partner then, concurs with research into safer sex and gay men, that finds that increasing familiarity with a partner leads to increasing perception of safeness (Schiltz and Adam 1995). As a paying client, Dania perceives a man as unsafe, whilst as a lover the same man becomes safe. This dangerous transition is based in the idea of romantic love and mutual trust as a safety net, and is very much inscribed in female cultural discourses, not only in Mexico. When I asked Dania about her trust in her partner, she replied: 'He is faithful to me.'[5]

---

4   The AIDS clinic.
5   *Me es fiel.*

She perceives risk only in terms of her professional life, which to some extent indicates that she too believes the popular ideas about herself, that is, that prostitution makes her polluted. An understanding of 'risk' as straightforward and rational, therefore, is contradictory. Despite her active decisions and use of contraception in her professional lives, in her personal life she conforms to prevailing gender values, and accepts her partner's decisions about contraception. Drawing a line between personal and professional life may be a crucial part of her own understanding of herself as an individual, differentiating professional sex from romantic sex.

Female sex workers are not at the centre of the problem in Mexico, although, perceived as such, both by themselves and others, they have had to accommodate the problem, and thus now bear the additional work expenses of condoms and tests. Dania and her friends' ability to do so is a reflection of her own autonomy in her business. This is often not the case for street prostitutes, and those controlled by boyfriends/pimps (Fonseca 1996). Their access to information however appears to be patchy, and, since prostitution is illegal and subject to moral censure in Mexico, it is difficult to encourage educational contacts between women and government health institutions.

MEN WHO HAVE SEX WITH MEN

As the other category of individuals popularly perceived of as at risk of infection, I also asked self-identified homosexual men to describe their experiences, knowledge and understandings of their personal risk. The men discussed below are to some extent 'out', by which I mean that even if they have not disclosed their sexual preference to their family, they quite openly participate in gay events in Puebla, attending discos, gay parties and some visiting gay public baths. This association with gay sub-culture indicates that their knowledge should be good.

Attitudes amongst this group range across the spectrum, from fear-driven regular testing to the occasional, 'unsafe' fling, to a certain indifference and recklessness. Despite the range of responses, HIV is an important and contemporary issue for them, and one that all feel has made inroads into their lives:

> AIDS is my number one health fear, because it is incurable. First it was homosexuals equals degeneration equals AIDS. Then it was Rock Hudson. All that memory lingers on, it doesn't go away. My aunts, for example, they still think it is a gay disease. Then it comes close and someone else you know has got it, then all the gossip – so and so has got it, so and so is dead. It's finishing everyone off, and there is a sort of mass hysteria. HIV is very easy to get, and I am overloaded with information. There are no treatments – although I think AZT slows it down a bit. Two years ago there was a fad for a treatment called *agua de tlacote* – it was water from a spring on this man's land. Everyone rushed to take it. There was one woman who tried it, believed in it, but she is dead now. People will try anything. (Enrique, 23)

I don't know how many sex partners I have had. More than 50, less than 100, I think. Some were just oral sex, some were a lot more. By the third grade of secondary school (15) I used to go cruising in the *zocalo* (main square) in Tampico. I went to gay parties, the baths – I was very promiscuous. I had heard nothing about AIDS in those days, there was no news of it here. Men don't get pregnant, so there is nothing to worry about. There is no virginity to be lost, nothing to be insecure about, and we don't worry like the *machos* about women comparing us to other men. HIV is a worry, but in the gay world we don't care about Hepatitis B, for instance. I have had herpes, and one other STD, but I can't remember the name of it. (Memo, 24)

Although the men felt there was a lack of information about AIDS, self-identifying (middle class) gay men in Puebla are well informed and aware that it presents a problem for themselves. The close links between the Mexican and US gay worlds partially account for this. Three of the men I interviewed have all visited the United States on holiday and (legal) working trips, and one had been twice on all expenses paid trips to the US, in response to the small ads in the Mexican gay press.[6] Information is also available to a limited extent at gay discos and clubs. All the men admitted casual, non-safe relationships, and also made comments about the extreme promiscuity of the gay world.

Such men are operating from a very different position to the women: whilst they may or may not consider that their own behaviour puts them at risk, they are more commonly in circles where there is infection, and information, and like the female sex workers, believe to some extent that they are amongst the polluted/polluting. Some men claim that other facets of their lives de-prioritise this knowledge, emphasising desire, and loss of self-control in sexual encounters, and thus removing their individual responsibility from the equation. Their newly self-declared gay identity, and the greater sexual freedom they have acquired with greater maturity, is in some ways more valuable than a possible future health crisis. The moral codes that underpin their approach to sex are very different from those expressed by women as respectable and appropriate conduct.

HOW WOMEN UNDERSTAND HOMOSEXUALITIY

HIV/AIDS is thus popularly understood to be associated with prostitution and with homosexuality. What became evident from the comments made by many female interviewees however was that homosexuality and femininity/ transvestitism were considered to be one and the same:

Sylvia: I don't know much about homosexuality. I have seen them in town on 6th street.

SCR: How do you know they are homosexuals?

Sylvia: Because when they talk they have men's voices, and they have the slim hips of a man.

---

6   The Mexican gay press carry small advertisements from men in the US who provide all-expenses paid holidays in the US for Mexican, male 'companions'.

SCR: Oh, you mean they are dressed as women?

Sylvia: Yes.

Well, it's difficult to know if it's natural or not. I don't know – some of them are so female, they even operate themselves, almost as if they reject the sex they were born with. I think it's natural, it's from birth. Some of them, they are degenerate. But I don't think they are guilty for it (Maria).

A masculine homosexual? I have never thought about it. I suppose it is possible, but I think gays are only those who dress and act like females. I think so. But then, there are those *'artistas'* like Rock Hudson, who are surrounded by beautiful women, from the nature of the work they do, and they get bored of women and look for something else, some new experience ... and that lead singer of *Cafe Tacuba*, with the long hair, he is *'un loco'*. (Lucia)

Whilst middle class women expressed tolerance on the subject of homosexuality, they tended to see it as something removed from their experience, and as a deviation, or an illness, and often as a sin. There is a common view that while some men are born homosexual, others become so because older men 'get involved' with them. Again, the idea that a man is homosexual only if he is visibly feminine, and the idea that a man who in any way contravenes male stereotypes – by being delicate, or somehow interested in non-manly things – is of suspect sexuality, was expressed here.

In light of the way in which homosexuality is presented in and by popular culture in Mexico, it is not surprising to find these attitudes easily expressed, especially as these conversations usually took place in family homes, and in the context of discussions about men, women and family life. Women who were tolerant and open to 'different' ideas on the subject of women's responsibilities, expressed intolerance of homosexuals, mostly through their understanding of the possibility that homosexuals 'influence' young men and boys to become homosexuals. There was also often a combination of contradictory beliefs held in conjunction, specifically, that homosexuality is an illness, that it is also something 'natural' or essential, but that it is also possible to become homosexual, revealing that this deviancy is also somehow contagious.

However, homosexual Mexican men do sometimes become accepted, or get re-accepted into their families. Some of my male interviewees had re-negotiated membership within their families after coming out. Perhaps the view expressed by female interviewees only capture at a superficial level how homosexuality is perceived, reflecting normative ideas and the important representational element of gender discourse. They also perhaps reflect how homosexuality is tolerated and absorbed into the dominant Mexican social institution, the family, by demonstrating the silence which surrounds the subject in the family sphere, and the removal of its discussion, other than as a joke (*alburre*), from the family (see Carrier 1978).

The women I talked to connect homosexuality with femininity, sexual degeneration, illness, sin, and 'otherness'. It is not a topic any of the women talked of with ease, except for the sisters Dominga and Lourdes, who joked about it, even in the context of their own family experiences. There was little easily stated acceptance of the possibility that masculinity and homosexuality might co-exist in one individual. Whereas homosexuality is often considered 'natural', congenital, bisexuality is not. Bisexuality is seen as the result of excess sexual experimentation, and as a 'degradation'.

HOW GAY MEN UNDERSTAND HOMOSEXUALITIY

In common with much of Latin America, Mexican gay discussion of homosexuality divides men into 'active' and 'passive' sexual roles. There is a growing category of 'internacional', a term which refers to a man understood to perform both roles in sex. There is a richly developed lexicon of labels with national and regional variations, and labelling of others shifts with differential access to power.

Enrique is the only son of a very prestigious Puebla family. His uncle was an important local politician, and his family also has high-up connections in the Church. His father is a well-known local figure who is greeted by many friends in the street. As he says, his family is very conscious of the '*que diran*' ('what they will say') and his father has made comments on the lines of, 'Guess who turned out to be gay?', so Enrique has decided not to tell him:

> I think a lot of what goes on in the gay world in Mexico can be classified as active/passive. I think Mexican gays try to reproduce what they see in the straight world – heterosexual coupledom. There are some 'internationals' who are more ambiguous, playing both roles, but the norm is that, in a gay relationship in Mexico, one will be the wife and the other the husband. Maybe it's changing a bit now – and that's probably the influence of the US. Here everyone is looking for the perfect partner. In the US there is more sexual freedom.

Most eloquent and informed about being gay in Mexico compared to the same experience in the US, was Juan, aged 42. He had been brought up between San Francisco and Puebla after his parents divorced, and his story reflects aspects of Puebla life as well as a more global gay/AIDS experience:

> I think it's true that gay men are divided into active and passive. A passive man has sex with other men, while an active gay man can have sex with a woman too … I am active and passive – I enjoy being passive. In Latin America we are all a lot more feminine – all looking for the macho, the husband, to order us about. Gays don't like each other in Latin America. In the US we stick together a lot more. There is a distinctly feminine side to gays here – we play it up. In America we look for a stereotype gay male – here we look for a macho … Maybe we aren't looking for the macho type so much now – maybe we realise the macho exists inside all of us.

Juan's comments raise the issue of why gay men perpetuate role separation modelled on that of the heterosexual world. Men who assume the 'male' role do not jeopardise their status as men, whilst for those who live as passive, feminised men, the answer is a little more difficult. Adopting a totally feminine self-presentation, including dress, may satisfy inner feelings about correct gender. Becoming 'female' may also afford protection in a hostile environment. For those who do not dress as women, yet who live as the female half of a couple, there may equally be a form of protection in the form of economic security. Juan's comments reflect the importance of the model of the family and household for gay relationships in provincial Mexico, and that homosexual relationships have been modelled along heterosexual lines.

These men who have sex with men, and who could all be described in biomedical/pathological terminology as 'homosexual', use many different forms of self-identification, and labelling for other men. Their self-identification reflects not only their class values, but other life experiences including foreign travel, and contact with other gay men, as well as their own perceptions about sexual roles and acts. The confusion we experienced in trying to pin down the 'correct' labels for themselves and for other men follows from the multiple meanings and interpretations available within the Mexican gay lexicon. US/global labels used straightforwardly in HIV/AIDS discussion, without consideration of their multiple meanings, may be understood in very different ways to their original intention.

BISEXUALITY

Men who have sex with men have been seen as pivotal in the growth of HIV infection. A man who has sex with both men and women is seen as a key transmission agent between a disease that made early inroads into the gay community, and spread latterly into the heterosexual community. Studies of sexual role separation – whether homo, bi or heterosexual – and an estimate of the proportion of bisexually behaving men in a given population, have been used by epidemiologists to make mathematical models of viral patterns, and for predicting case numbers. (Trichopoulos, Sparos and Petridou 1988). Problems arise however, because this strict labelling of human sexual practices and behaviours, based on a broad, recent, Anglo-Saxon model, rarely reflects the reality of other local models of sexual behaviour.

Many (male) interviewees stated that they had had sexual relationships with married men, but it was harder to find married men willing to talk about this. 'Bisexual' was used as a self-description by four of the men I spoke to – some married and some single. Adolfo was the most willing of all the men who claimed 'bisexuality' to talk frankly about it. This was probably because he, like me, was an outsider in Mexico, and therefore not so integrated into the society he currently lives in. The family ties he had in Puebla were not blood ties, a point that he emphasised. Adolfo married a Mexican woman in order to be able to leave Cuba, and has never revealed his homosexual practices to her. As he said of his wife: 'Why should she suspect me of having sex with other men? She knows nothing of that world.'

The implications of this for discussion of HIV infection in the context of the family are manifold: male same sex practice is removed and not discussed. They may tacitly be acknowledged, but if a husband has sexual relations with other men, rarely will it be mentioned. This implies complicity, to a certain extent, on the part of female members of the family, and some men are convinced that this is the case. With the space men have in Puebla to live a single life both before and after marriage, leading a double life (with other women) is known, and to an extent tolerated.

Alfonso, 34, and his wife Teresa were unusual in speaking openly about their marriage. Whilst he totally denied any auto-definition of homosexuality, when I asked him if he was perhaps 'bisexual', he vacillated. Teresa, his wife, is much more open about his homosexual life, including when speaking in front of him. He said:

> We got married because we love each other. She knew all about me for ages. I think it's quite common, married men going with other men, but I don't think it's normal that their wife accepts it, or even knows about it. People here in Puebla are so straight, but you see those same people living it up in Mexico City, with other women. It's like knowing two completely different individuals.

In these conversations I understood bisexual practice to be a considerably suppressed category. In the Latin American context, the idea that there is a large bisexual practising population is often used in literature about HIV in a vague way, with little referencing or interview material. This reflects the problems of researching an intimate topic, but great care is also needed to avoid assigning exotic sexual practices as part of the ongoing racist/sexist discourse of otherness that has also helped to underpin the idea that all Mexican men are 'machos', as Gutmann has argued (Gutmann 1996). Examples of this practice in the literature are given below (Carrier 1995,[7] Rapkin and Erickson 1990,[8] Valdespino-Gomez *et al* 1992[9]). There are reasons however why bisexual practices might be more prevalent. In a social world in which men and women live largely in separate spaces, there is difficulty of access to the other sex, whilst there is plenty of opportunity for same sex access. This is a simplistic argument however, that acknowledges neither desire nor love. Perhaps more pertinently, the strict gender hierarchy of active/passive that until very recently has been maintained and monitored within and by the gay world has made it easy for men who have sex with both men and women to conceal their activities. By assuming a masculine identity, not developing a personal 'identity' narrative, and living beyond words, the bisexually behaving male remains invisible. This discussion of non-normative sexualities has gone some way to clarify the inadequacy of the categories homosexual, bisexual and heterosexual in HIV/AIDS discourse, in places where these categories are not in common use. However, thinking in terms of active/passive/international does not broaden our understanding very much either. They are to a certain extent a different set of labels that assign assumed, static sexualities to gender categories, and as such are inadequate for a deeper understanding of human sexual practice.

---

7   '[A]s far as I know, no one has made a detailed study of Mexican male bisexuality anywhere in Mexico … In my judgement, at any given point in time the largest portion of the bisexually behaving subset of Mexican men who have sex with men … are probably single men at the peak of their sexual needs' (1995: 199).

8   '[S]ame sex activity has been estimated to be more common among minority (hispanic) than non-minority men' (1990: 898). References given in text, US study.

9   'It is known that nearly half homosexual men in Mexico also have heterosexual practices. Although there are no studies of the prevalence of male bisexuality it is estimated to be more frequent here than in countries like the United States, which is a factor in the greater heterosexual transmission of HIV in Mexico' (1992: 34). No references or statistics given.

CONCLUSION: SEXUALITY, MORALITY AND LOCAL KNOWLEDGE

HIV/AIDS education and prevention is complex because it touches on an arena which is largely unexpressed, but where people make so much meaning. Foucault's suggestion that sex is over-reified in Western culture captures the reality in which sexually transmitted disease has to be considered. Whilst sex is regulated through its sites of construction, the larger social formations of economy, education, criminality and public health (Foucault 1986), Vance (1984) suggests that *sexuality* is an unpromising domain for regulation. The environment we grow up in, and parental mores and values, create a sense of belonging, constitute our world, and often become our own values, even if constantly refashioned, rarely articulated, and sometimes rejected. We create imaginary worlds and myths to deal with the unknown and unknowable, and sexuality is a central part of this. Reproduction, creation, existence and desire are fragile arenas. The mechanics of the sexual act may often be separated from these symbolic worlds, and a heavy-handed approach to sexual education that fails to recognise this will not succeed.

Micro level studies of individual contexts demonstrate how new, global ideas are incorporated into local knowledge in a differentiated way, resulting in understandings of cause and solution that may vary greatly from the original. New information has to find space in complex lives that weigh information according to social, cultural and personal priorities. Scientific discourse is hegemonic in the north, but we make our own moral and personal meanings from it, so that 'even if we could all magically be made to know ... the process of our coming to know these facts would entail embedding them in the diverse social, political, moral and metaphysical meanings with which we construct our daily lives' (Cleason *et al* 1996). While science may be considered truth by many, equally it is frequently held as version (Cohen 1993). This finds echoes in the field of HIV virological knowledge. Biomedicine is the dominant healing system in Mexico, but its limitations are recognised, and other medical systems are legitimised by both government and public. This pragmatic approach to medicine must be considered within yet another well-worn circle of discourse that simultaneously acknowledges northern (US) knowledge as desirable and modern, and yet, as a foreign construction, does not allow it to go unchallenged.

The Mexican government reacted swiftly to the new problem posed by AIDS by establishing an education/advice structure to address the problem. This has always been, as Wilson (1995) stressed, an attempt to contain the *idea* of AIDS, rather than a real effort to get to the root of the problem. Whilst this discussion and other recent survey work (Izazola Licea *et al* 1988) indicate a high level of public awareness about HIV/AIDS, they show that there is neither a real understanding of potential health problems, nor evidence of ability to modify behaviour.

The women and men I talked to know about HIV/AIDS. For the majority of the women, including those popularly perceived to be a source of infection, there are certain types of person who become infected. Open acknowledgment that their own or partner's patterns of behaviour might put them at risk was usually not made. Other women do not make a connection at all, whilst for yet others, the idea might be there, but they would not or could not express it. For most of them, other priorities and aspects of their life need more protection – the basic economic needs of their family, and their own wellbeing, including their sense of propriety and decentness, respectability and belonging. This means that they cannot usually prioritise a negotiation, or challenge to their sexual partner(s) on the use of contraception. The gay men I spoke to were more knowledgeable and in a better position to control their exposure to the virus, but in many cases they also gave more priority to other aspects of their life. Individual 'risk' of infection, therefore, is assimilated within prevailing personal conditions.

Understandings of HIV/AIDS as a blood disease, as sexual and as located with the polluted may have been imported from the north, yet there is enough in common between these 'other' and local understandings of gender, homosexuality and prostitution to make this possible. However, the government, the medical community and the 'general population' have absorbed these understandings without examination of smaller, but extremely important differences in local constructions of sexuality.

Women largely connected homosexuality with femininity. The idea of masculine appearing or behaving homosexual men was not readily acknowledged. Gay men divide their world into active and passive roles and connect personal identity to these categories. The majority of women found the idea of bisexually behaving men extreme and barely plausible, whilst gay men used this term to describe a variety of kinds of sexual activity, from sex with men and women to sex with men alone. The idea of a bisexually behaving man and the category of 'international' within the gay world introduces both the possibility of change in the understandings of sexuality as static and inflexible, as well as an element of disruption of a carefully controlled and gender structured social world. The emergence of these concepts challenges norms both with and outside of the gay world. However, equating bisexual 'identity' with bisexual practice, and using it as the key to resolving the spread of sexually transmitted HIV can over-simplify the issue. Of the men who claimed bisexuality as a label for their own sexual preference, two have never had sex with a woman. The possibilities contained within this one label are various, problematic, and cannot be considered a simple answer to a complex problem.

Public information is essential in order to attempt to combat communicable disease, yet less easily definable types of experience can undermine the effectiveness of public health education. Discussion of prevention in terms of perceptions of risk relies on a model of the world that assumes that people make choices based on an idea of what is rational, and that rationality is universal. Norms and expectations, underpinned by moral codes, and an 'othering' of those who are seen as different, are crucial in forming subjective understandings, our sense of self and appropriate reciprocal behaviour, not least in the delicate arena of sexuality. They provide a self-defence, a reference point, and are central to both an individual's and a society's ideas of itself and how to live. The material presented in this chapter suggests that the analysis of risk which has dominated debates about sexual health and education may be unduly limited by its cultural specificity. An exploration of local discourses of trust, respectability, 'normality' and expectations of sexual loyalty, provides fruitful ground for a broader understanding of sexual practice.

BIBLIOGRAPHY

Appadurai, A (1990) 'Disjuncture and difference in the global cultural economy' 7 *Theory, Culture and Society* 295–310

Carrier, J (1978) 'Family attitudes and Mexican male homosexuality', in Warren, C (ed), *Sexuality, Encounters, Identities and Relationships*, London: Sage, Contemporary Social Science Series, No 35

Carrier, J (1995) *De Los Otros: Intimacy and Homosexuality Among Mexican Males*, New York: Columbia UP

Cleason, B, Martin, E, Richardson, W, Scoch-Spana, M and Taussig, KS (1996) 'Scientific literacy, what is it, why it's important and why scientists don't think we have it', in Nader, L (ed), *Naked Science*, London: Routledge

Cohen, A (1993) 'Segmentary knowledge: a Whalsay sketch', in Hobart, M (ed), *An Anthropological Critique of Development: The Growth of Ignorance*, London: Routledge

Fonseca, A (1996) *'La prostitucion no es un problema, sino un complejo fenomeno social que no acabara con las moralinas'* 6(3) *La Jornada del Oriente* 96, Puebla, Mexico

Foucault, M (1986) (first published 1984) *The Use of Pleasure*, London: Vintage

Gutmann, M (1996) *The Meanings of Macho: Being a Man in Mexico City*, Berkeley, CA: California UP

Hart, G and Boulton, M (1995) 'Sexual behaviour in gay men: towards a sociology of risk', in Aggleton *et al* (eds), *AIDS: Safety, Sexuality and Risk*, London: Taylor & Francis

Izazola Licea, JA *et al* (1988) *'Factores de riesgo asociados a infeccion por VIH en hombres homosexuals y bisexuales'* 30 *Salud Publica de Mexico* 555–66

Kendall, C (1995) 'The construction of risk in AIDS control programs: theoretical bases and popular responses', in Parker, RG and Gagnon, J (eds), *Conceiving Sexuality: Approaches to Sex Research in a Post-Modern World*, London: Routledge

Mertens, TE *et al* (1994) 'An epidemiological overview' 8 *AIDS*

Patton, C (1994) *Last Served? Gendering the HIV Pandemic*, London: Taylor & Francis

Rapkin, AJ and Erickson, PI (1990) 'Differences in knowledge of and risk factors for AIDS between Hispanic and non-Hispanic women attending an urban family planning clinic' 4 *AIDS* 889–99

Schiltz, MA and Adam, P (1995) 'Reputedly effective risk reduction strategies and gay men', in Aggleton, P, Davies, P and Hart, G (eds), *AIDS: Safety, Sexuality and Risk*, London: Taylor & Francis

Trichopolous, D, Sparos, L and Petridou, E (1988) 'Homosexual role separation and spread of AIDS' *The Lancet*, 22 October, pp 965–66

Valdespino-Gomez, JL *et al* (1992) *'Mujer y Sida en Mexico: epidemiologia'*, in *Mujer y Sida: Programa Interdisciplinario de Estudios de la Muje* 121 Jornadas, Mexico DF: El Colegio de Mexico

Vance, C (ed) (1984) *Pleasure and Danger*, London: Routledge & Kegan Paul

Wilson, C (1995) *Hidden in the Blood: A Personal Investigation of AIDS in the Yucatan*, New York: Columbia UP

CHAPTER 6

'BREAD IS FIRST BEFORE EVERYTHING!': MORAL ECONOMY IN HOUSEHOLDS AND STATES[1]

Kathryn Tomlinson

The Meskhetian Turks are a small Muslim group, numbering approximately 300,000, spread across the former Soviet Union, but residing primarily in Azerbaijan, Kazakhstan and the Russian Federation. Until 1944, when they were deported to Central Asia, they lived along the Turkish border of Georgia. In 1989, many were again displaced, this time as a result of conflicts in Ferghana, Uzbekistan. Describing her flight, with her husband, Zemira said:

> I had two-storey house. First we had a one-storey house, then with credit we bought a two-storey house, in Tashkent, in a different village [from his parents]. We lived there only two months. Then the Uzbeks started against us. One day, I made dough, you know, for bread. He came home and said we should go to his parents. So we took everything and left. I took the dough in the car. Then we all went to Baku.

That Zemira mentioned the bread in her narrative is, I argue, particularly significant. Amongst the Meskhetian Turks one is called to eat with the imperatives *Etmek ye!* or *Çai iç!*, 'Eat bread!' or 'Drink tea!'. Bread and tea are never served alone, although both are present at every meal, and whenever guests visit. But etmek ye may equally refer to the main meal, usually potato soup, or to a rare treat of smoked fish. That is, the call to eat bread is an invitation to eat in general.[2]

The use of 'bread' as a shorthand for all foods hints at its wider significance amongst the Meskhetian Turks. Whilst the bread-making process is not perceived as the integration of male and female aspects of the household, as it is for Anatolian Turks and Portuguese Minho peasants, nor is the hearth central to concepts of the household (Delaney 1991: 243, Pina-Cabral 1986: 44), bread *does* play an immensely important symbolic role in Meskhetian Turkish practice. I argue that practices and discourses concerning bread highlight otherwise implicit discourses regarding relationships with within and between households, with relatives, God, and the State. Bread's role as an agent of morality is rooted in, but extends far beyond, its primacy as a subsistence foodstuff.

---

1   The research upon which this chapter is based was generously supported by University College London Graduate School and the University of London Central Research Fund. Thanks to Michael Stewart, Frances Pine and Sahra Gibbon for comments on an earlier version of this paper.

2   Similarly, bread has the same generic meaning in Anatolian Turkish villages, and amongst the Malays of Langkawi, 'cooked rice' means 'food' (Delaney 1991: 243, Carsten 1989: 122).

BREAD AND THE HOUSEHOLD

Meskhetian Turkish bread, *etmek*, is a round, slightly-risen loaf, the size of a large plate. While there are slight variations in the size of loaves made, or the pattern stamped on the loaf down before baking, all Meskhetian Turkish bread is remarkably similar. Most women bake 15 to 20 loaves every two or three days. However, while in the winter the stove is already lit for warmth, in the summer the heat makes baking almost unbearable. Additionally, during this period the *ogorod*, allotment, requires considerable attention, reducing the time available for baking. Therefore in the summer months, many households buy factory-baked loaves. Some households purchase bread throughout the year, but generally home-baked bread is preferred. Cost cannot fully explain this preference;[3] nor can a particular preference Meskhetian Turkish bread's flavour. The explanation for baking practices must be found elsewhere.

Bread is treated with considerable respect. It must stand right way up; if noticed upside down it will be turned: 'Would you like to be put on your head?' Bread must not be wasted. It is stored wrapped in a cloth, in a metal bin, and stays fresh for two days and edible for at least three.[4] Even if unfit for human consumption, it must be fed to a living creature, usually the dogs that guard the house or sheds. The tiny crumbs of bread swept up following a meal are separated from the dirt that goes into the stove, and added to the dog's basin. If bread is found on the road, even when pulverised by traffic, it is taken home for the dogs, as 'it is forbidden to throw out bread'. And bread certainly must not be trodden upon.[5]

The centrality of bread, and its importance beyond its role as basic foodstuff, is illustrated in the following incident. Hadeca, hosting a visit of her daughter's future in-laws, prepared an impressive variety of special foods, including *khinkali*, boiled dumplings of meat and onion. The *khinkali* were very white, and the fine quality of the flour (and hence its price) was noted, but at the last moment Hadeca realised that she had forgotten to make bread. Sultan, Hadeca's husband's paternal aunt, later summarised the neighbours' thoughts: *Etmek her bir şey'dan birinci!*, 'Bread is first before everything!' The primacy of bread in this statement touches something deeper than the fact that bread is eaten at every meal.

A disagreement between brothers' wives over the baking of bread gives some insight into the meaning of bread for the Meskhetian Turks. Ruveida talked about her married home in Uzbekistan:

> Nobody else made bread. There were two other brides, and they didn't make bread. I lived there ten years, and I made bread for ten years. I was pregnant with my son, and about to go into labour; I waited to take out the last bread [from the

---

3   Although in some areas it is cheaper to buy flour, yeast and salt than the factory loaves, in Krasnodar there was little difference in the price in late 1999. By mid-2000 the price of flour had risen so considerably that it certainly cost more to buy two sacks of flour a month needed to feed a family of six, than to purchase bread at 2.30r a loaf.

4   Shop-bought loaves dry out within a day.

5   Very similar practices occur amongst the descendants of Greek refugees from Turkey, in Anatolian Turkish villages, and in the Polish mountains (Hirschon 1989: 137, Delaney 1991: 243, Frances Pine, personal communication).

oven] before going to hospital. They made soup, that was all; it was me that made dough, for *khinkali* and the like. If I didn't make dough they wouldn't have bothered.

Three weeks later, the issue arose with Halima and Kibria, the other two brides, in a heated discussion over how much bread Halima had made in Uzbekistan. Ruveida said that her daughter does not know how to make *khinkali*. Halima declared that her mother-in-law would teach her; this was how she had learnt to make bread. Halima declared that she had made bread for two or three years, after Ruveida had given it up. Ruveida responded, 'What are you saying? I don't remember'. Ruveida pointed out that Halima had been ill, and that she, Ruveida, had been working hectares[6] and bought Halima a dress with the money. Halima initially said that Ruveida had not worked hectares all that time, at which Ruveida got more annoyed and said, 'Look at my work record!'. Eventually Halima worked out that she had made bread 'a whole summer, half a year'. Ruveida said, several times, 'Maybe three or four times, but not all the time', but Halima denied it. Once Halima had left, Kibria agreed that Halima had not baked bread for that long.

Undeniably, making and baking bread is hot, tiring and time-consuming work. But this discussion concerned more than an attempt to prove who had worked the hardest. She who bakes the bread, feeds the household; she also feeds the guests. When Mirza, her husband's cousin, sought to persuade Ruveida to agree to her daughter's marriage to a neighbour's son, he said to her, 'I can argue with your husband, I can scold him, but I can't with you. I have eaten your bread'.

Baking bread is what women do. When the master-of-ceremonies at a wedding invited the neighbourhood's women to dance, he called for bride's mother's friends, the women 'who bake bread, help out',[7] that is, those who *kýzmet oliyirler*, 'serve'. When a woman marries, as she stands before all the guests in the marquee at her husband's home, her head still covered with a large red scarf, loaves of bread are tied with a scarf around her waist, and rice put in her hands. This is done *kýzmet olsun*, so that there will be service, or, 'so that there is always something to put on the table for guests'. As White reports from her work in the squatter districts of Istanbul, '"to serve" (*hizmet etmek*) in one's home is inextricably bound up with status; "to be served" is an honor. Women serve their husbands, their children, and their guests' (1994: 42).

Thus, a central aspect of a married woman's role in her household is to provide for others, both resident and visiting. This provision is symbolised in bread, both in narrative and in practice. When a Meskhetian Turkish woman bakes bread she reiterates her membership in her household, and in the Meskhetian Turkish community. Mirza reminded Ruveida that, since her marriage, 'what she does' is to serve her household and her guests, and that this has always been symbolised by bread. He appealed to her role as provider, and particularly as provider for guests, a role she plays often and well. The respect due to bread also reflects the

---

6   Planting, weeding and harvesting collective farm land.
7   Wedding bread is usually baked by neighbours; the host household provides all the ingredients and the fuel. The quantities baked, in the hundreds, are a source of pride and muted competition.

respect due to women, as Mirza notes when he declares that he cannot argue with Ruveida because he has eaten her bread.

In the story related at the beginning of this chapter, Zemira's grounding of a traumatic event by reference to an everyday productive activity highlights just how abnormal her move was: it interrupted the baking of bread, a core task in a woman's day, and the feeding of the family. It also demonstrates the Meskhetian Turks' pragmatic approach to crisis: Zemira took the dough with her, and baked the bread at her mother-in-law's house. It reminds us that, while life-changing, displacement does not result in immediate loss of culture, or in chaos. Rather, Zemira responded by doing what she always does; she baked bread.

BREAD AND RELATIVES

Bread has further symbolic, even prophetic, meanings. As guests arrived to visit his new granddaughter, Yusuf declared with a grin: 'I knew you were coming today! At breakfast I took one piece of bread, and bit into it. Then I took another piece without finishing the first. So I knew guests would come!' Yusuf's declaration is a variation on the much more common statement that if one drops bread, it means that guests will come. Bread, then, is also symbolic of wider social relations, witnessed daily in the sharing of bread. One should not eat another's bread; 'if you do, you will be angry with each other'. Thus Meskhetian Turks are careful to check that the torn piece they are about to take has not already been claimed. By extension, bread that has been bitten into has to be eaten, so that no-one else will eat the remains by mistake.

But asking who might come when a piece of bread is dropped is the most common comment made when eating. This reflects the centrality of visiting in Meskhetian Turkish social relations, and in particular those between relatives. Other than chance meetings at the market, or at weddings, kin who do not reside in the same village only meet when one household visits the other. Visiting relatives also provides the only form of leisure activity undertaken outside the home village. While men occasionally drop in on friends to whom they are not, or only very distantly, related, women never do, and thus 'to go as a guest', *misefire gitmekh*, almost invariably means to go as a guest to relatives. Visiting, therefore, builds on existing relationships, and is almost the only means for doing so.

And bread, particular and generic food, plays a significant role in the practices of visiting. Visits are framed by the giving and receiving of 'bread'. Guests never arrive empty-handed, but take wrapped sweets and biscuits, bought in 500g or 1kg bags at the market, and sometimes fruit (apples, pears, oranges) or sweet bread rolls. But if the visit is an important one, in the month preceding and year following a wedding, guests bake a special flaky bread, *katmer*, to take with them. *Katmer*, made of many thin layers of dough, brushed with oil, folded over one another and baked, is one of a few specifically Meskhetian Turkish dishes. It served at weddings, to special guests, and given when visiting, and to those going on journeys.[8] Freshly baked bread is also given to guests as they leave, so that

---

8   Another rich bread, made with oil, cream, and milk, is sometimes prepared for visiting sons in the army.

'they do not leave with empty hands'. If there is no edible bread in the house scraps of dry bread, good only for feeding to dogs, are given.

Such sharing of food also occurs between Meskhetian Turks in the same village, when a rice dish, *aş*, is prepared on a Thursday,[9] and on the night before a holiday; or simply when the women of one household have prepared a special dish. A plateful is sent to neighbouring relatives. Hirschon notes a similar practice in Greece, amongst the descendants of the Greek refugees from Turkey. In her case, the shared 'morsel' is given both in thanks for assistance with its preparation, and as a competitive demonstration of the woman's culinary skill, a significant basis of 'the social evaluation of her competence and worth' (Hirschon 1989: 176). Since the plate must not be returned empty, one's own abilities are demonstrated when sending it back with one's own specially prepared dish. Amongst the Meskhetian Turks, there is no obligation to return the plate with food, nor does culinary skill form the basis of a woman's reputation. Rather, the sharing of food with neighbours and guests serves a function similar, but not identical, to that identified by Carsten amongst the Malay of Langkawi.

Carsten identifies a continuum between rice (food), milk and blood. Food consumed by women becomes milk, which, consumed as food by children, becomes 'blood', substance or flesh. The Malays state that all those who have consumed the same milk have the same blood; and siblings are the closest of relatives. More generally, those who consume food cooked at the same hearth are thought to share substance, to be related (Carsten 1997: 107–28): 'Food becomes blood. And through the day-to-day sharing of meals cooked in the same hearth, those who live together in one house come to have substance in common' (1997: 127). It is for this reason that eating everyday meals in others' houses is strongly disapproved of, and that although guests are always asked to join a household meal if they arrive during its consumption, equally they always refuse (Carsten 1997: 113). To eat (rice) together is to be related.

The Malay connection between food and kin relies in part on the symbolic importance of the hearth, an importance not shared by Meskhetian Turks. Nor is blood or shared substance the basis for relatedness. But co-consumption of 'bread' does play a symbolic role in producing relatedness, as it does for other Mediterranean peoples:

> For the Sarakatsani a meal is a family communion to which unrelated shepherds are never invited. The wedding feast is the family meal writ large with the family of kindred sitting down to eat bread together. For all food is in a generic sense bread. 'Come, let us eat bread', cries the wedding master of ceremonies. (Campbell 1964: 116–17)

The communal eating of bread is constitutive of the related community. Much as in the household, where bread stands for meaning not collectively verbalised, so too in relations between households, bread represents implicit moral discourses on the nature of relatedness, enacted primarily through *misefir gitmeye*, 'going as a guest'.

With the arrival of guests, the household's younger women put water on to boil for tea, and set the table.[10] Bread and tea are accompanied by sweet and salty

---

9   The smell of oily foods, such as *aş*, is said to rise up to feed the ancestors.
10   If the group is large, dishes are placed on a plastic sheet laid out on the floor.

items: cheese; cream; thick jam; pickled tomatoes and cucumbers; sweets and biscuits; watermelon in summer, or thinly sliced oranges during the winter. If men and women eat separately, as they do when many people are present, a greater proportion of special food is placed on the men's table, regardless of the number of people eating. Tea is drunk hot, dark and sweet without milk, and concludes every meal. Only once all have finished drinking is the table cleared away.

Providing food for guests is the focal point of their visit; to fail to offer tea to a visitor is unacceptable. Some visits last for little longer than the time taken to consume a bowl of tea, but it is very unusual for a visitor not to at least drink tea, and refusal to eat causes offence. Guests are repeatedly encouraged to consume; 'When a guest eats well at the table, it brings blessings to the hosts'. But 'guests feel embarrassed and need to be encouraged to eat', which leads to repeated exhortations 'take' more, and 'don't be embarrassed'. As one old woman laughed, 'It is a Muslim law: take, take!'.

However, when a prospective groom's relatives ask for a girl in marriage, they do not eat. Even if the hosts know, or guess, the purpose of this visit, they bring out the table and put water on to boil. But until the girls' relatives have agreed to give her in marriage, the visitors will not eat. Ali explained, 'if they set the table I should not eat anything. If I say I don't need the table they know that I have not simply come'. Unless the parents immediately refuse, a second visit is arranged as elder relatives must be consulted. If they agree, the girl's relatives prepare a special meal, a sign to the future husband's relatives that their suit has been successful.[11] The temporary suspension of the foundation of hospitality and relatedness, co-consumption, highlights the life-changing significance of the visit. Once this difficult period has been concluded, the two parties lay generous tables for one another in the visits preceding and following their now joint venture, the wedding. Also notable is that the first time a newly married couple are ever alone with one another, they eat together. The meal is always the same: chicken, *halva*,[12] and *kalamem*, a special square kind of *katmer* bread. Thus while physical consummation of the marriage does not occur until the following night, the bride and groom now constitute their union through co-consumption of bread.

BREAD AND GOD

On the evening before a wedding, local men gather in the host's house. In the bride's home, after a good meal, the elders pray, while the younger men chop carrots for the *aş* that will be served the following day. While *aş* preparation is notable for the disjuncture it represents with everyday food preparation, in that it is a male activity, it also represents a continuation of the place of food in interactions involving guests and God. Meskhetian Turks make the connection between hospitality and Islam in the phrase, *Misefir geliyir kapi'dan, ruskhi geliyir*

---

11   Compare this with the 'formal denial of commensality amongst Sarakatsani shepherds, for whom the groom's family's separate eating of their own food is an expression of their opposition to the relatives of the bride (Campbell 1964: 133).

12   *Halva* is made from butter and flour fried together, to which *şerbet*, sugared water, is added.

ayna'dan, 'If a guest comes through the door, God will send as much as He has created for you, through the window'. Eating with guests is therefore seen as not only encouraged but provided for by God; hospitality involves the host in a relationship with Allah as well as with his guest. Eating 'bread' (food) with others is, I argue, constitutive of Meskhetian Turks' relationship with God, and stands for an unspoken religious discourse.

While elderly men perform the five-times daily prayer alone,[13] for most Meskhetian Turks, communion with Allah is usually a communal event. At the start of a meal, some people say quietly *Bismillah*, literally, 'In the name of God', but described as a prayer 'that you will quickly eat to your fill'. After eating, thanks are given for the food eaten: *Yarar bişkur alhamdulillah*, 'All praise be to God for the food'. At the end of a meal, one does not rub one's hands together to brush off crumbs, as this 'is like saying that you have not eaten anything, that there was no bread'. Rather, Meskhetian Turks pass their hands over their face, as they do after all prayers, to thank Allah for the food.

The three major events in the Meskhetian Turks' religious calendar are *Ramazan*, the month long fast, and two holidays, *bayramlar*: *Ramazan Bayram*, immediately following the end of the fast, and *Kurban Bayram*, which occurs two months and 10 days later. All three are notable for the importance allocated to consumption or non-consumption of food. As Mintz notes, 'Fasting ... is a dramatic means by which to discover the power of food ... people who fast for some larger good are moved by a moral desire' (1996: 4). By following the fast with a holiday during which sharing food with guests is central, Meskhetian Turks further emphasise the 'power of food' to express morality.

During the 30 days of Ramazan, nothing should enter the mouth during the hours of daylight, thus it is forbidden to eat, drink, smoke, kiss or clean teeth between dawn and dusk. Many do not fast,[14] and since fasting is an individual's decision, 'according to your own conscience', no-one may criticise another for not fasting. It is forbidden to ask why another is not fasting. On the morning of Ramazan Bayram, a man from each household (who need not have himself fasted) joins communal prayer at the local mullah's house. After prayers, the men should visit the households of those whose relatives have died in the past year. The rest of the day is given over to visiting elders. Although large gatherings do occur in elder's households, Ramazan Bayram is also the occasion for visits of young brides and their husbands' relatives to the brides' natal homes.

On the first day of Ramazan Bayram, which lasts three days, it is forbidden *not* to eat, since one has been fasting for a month. In the preceding couple of days, the house is cleaned, and special foods, including pies and cakes, are prepared. As guests arrive, the usual greeting is replaced with a jovial *Bayram mübarek olsun*, 'May the holiday be blessed'. Thereafter, the visit progresses as any other, although with a greater variety of special foods than usual. Sometimes guests stay overnight, in which case the festivities continue the next day.

The second, and to some more important, Muslim holiday is called *Kurban Bayram*, 'Sacrifice Holiday', after the animal that should be slaughtered every year

---

13   Except on Fridays, when they gather in the local mullah's home.
14   Amongst my informants, young men and boys fast infrequently, while many teenage girls do fast. Amongst the adults, women fast more than men.

for seven years. The animal, ideally a calf, must be unwounded, 'as it is when it was born'. The meat is split three ways: a third to be eaten by the household; another to be given to close kin, and the last shared around the neighbourhood. The significance of Kurban Bayram was always described in these terms: as a slaughter, in each of seven years, of an animal whose meat is then shared. Relatively few households can afford to slaughter an animal every year, and many who are presently wealthy may not start the seven-year cycle due to uncertainty over future wealth. Some share the cost of an animal with relatives, but for most the only slaughter is that of poultry for the *aş* prepared the evening before the holiday, and for the soup served to guests.

It is notable that for all three events, explanations of their significance are given in terms of food preparation and the visiting of relatives, rather than through reference to Allah and the theology of Islam. This reflects the absence of theological discourse in daily life. While every household possesses a Qur'an, hung on the wall in velvety bag, very few can read Arabic. And although the gathering of men for special prayers is known as *koran okumaya*, 'reading the Qur'an', in practice many mullahs cannot read Arabic either, and the prayer consists of memorised chants. Given their lack of daily theological discourse, it is through understanding the wider moral values imbued in 'bread' that the centrality of shared consumption as religious practice is comprehensible.

BREAD AND THE SOVIET STATE

The use of bread as a carrier of moral values is more explicit in the relationship of Meskhetian Turks (and other post-Soviet peoples) with the State. In her work on early 1990s Moscow, Ries describes bread as 'the key substance linking the entire *narod* [people], physically and metaphorically' (1997: 136). At its most basic, bread is metaphorically important because it is materially important, as the core foodstuff in Russian and Soviet diets, and hence as the item most sought after in times of famine.[15] Until the 20th century, grain dominated the Russian diet (Smith and Christian 1984). Such was the reliance on bread grain that if the crop failed, peasants sold livestock in order to buy bread, with the consequence that during the 1921 famine in Russia's lower Volga region, meat was cheaper than bread (Chayanov 1966 [1926]: 171, in Scott 1976: 14). Bread was also adulterated. In November 1941, during the siege of Leningrad, 'blockade bread' was being produced from rye flour, chaff, dust from flour sacks, cornflour and edible cellulose (Moskoff 1990: 186, 193). Bread, then, represented the last foodstuff available in times of famine, but also that which prevented hunger.

Given the reliance on grain for subsistence, any human activity that diminished the ability of the people to obtain bread provoked concern if not popular protest. But, as Thompson notes, when such protest occurs, it is usually legitimated by popular moral consensus, based on the right to subsist. This 'moral economy of the poor' is 'a consistent traditional view of social norms and obligations, of the proper economic functions of several parties within the

---

15   As Russian pre-Soviet history influenced the new State, the Russian history of bread has affected the role of bread for Meskhetian Turks, as former Soviets.

community' (1971: 79). Actions in response to perceived threats to this moral economy, while sometimes violent, were more often morally reasoned strategies of self-protection: be that the refusal to pay rent in full following poor harvests; or 'setting the price', the forcible purchase of goods, including bread, at what the people consider to be a 'fair price' (Scott 1976: 75, Engel 1997, Thompson 1971).

Although Scott and Thompson regard industrialisation and the development of a market-driven nation-State as circumstances under which defence of the moral economy by such popular action becomes impossible, in the Soviet Union, the opposite occurred. The emerging State championed the moral economy of bread, and made it a core value of its own ideological program. One influential advocate of the involvement of the State in ensuring adequate supplies of bread was the Russian anarchist Kropotkin, who entitled his clearest exposition of his vision of anarchist society, *The Conquest of Bread*. Kropotkin argued that France's three popular movements – of 1793, 1848 and 1871 – failed because 'they discussed various political questions at great length, but forgot to discuss the question of bread' (1906/1995: 52). He insisted that 'bread must be found for the people of the revolution, and the question of bread must take precedence of all other questions ... in solving the question of bread we much accept the principle of equality' (1906/1995: 55). The Bolsheviks, in adopting the slogan 'Peace, Bread and Land' (Engel 1997: 721), allied themselves with the moral economy of the poor, as advocated by Kropotkin, embracing both equality and the importance of fulfilling the poor's basic needs. In so doing, they made the provision of 'bread', both particular and generic, integral to their program and practice.

Kotkin notes that 'bread came to symbolise the official urban supply network run not by individuals for private gain by the state as a service to the people' (1995: 238). Bread's two political aspects, as a moral symbol of basic rights, and of the state's (insufficient) provisions for bread distribution, were significant during the Revolution. The Petrograd crowds' calls for bread helped topple the tsarist government, given the chaos and panic that both contributed to and resulted from the lack of bread (Lih 1990: 8). The moral economy, on which revolutionary demands for bread were based, was an industrialised development of that of the peasantry; most bread rioters were new female workers, many of them soldiers' wives. 'Those who came from the village brought traditional expectations concerning the right to subsistence and the affordability of essential goods, as well as a more modern sense of entitlement derived from their connection to men at the front' (Engel 1997: 718).[16]

In response to famine, rationing was introduced in the late 1920s, and repeated during other periods of Soviet history. 'Rationing seem to have been widely appreciated ... Underlying rationing and purchase limitations ... was a popular expectation of social justice, an expectation that the regime encouraged and in its own way tried to meet' (Kotkin 1995: 268–69). The popularity of bread rationing, and the association of bread with equality, is illustrated by workers' discontent when rationing was abolished on 1 January 1935. There was considerable concern that the price of bread would increase, and indeed many saw the murder of Kirov, Leningrad Communist Party leader, in December 1934, as a protest against the

---

16   See Alexei Tolstoy's 1938 novel, *Bread*, for a fictional account of the role of bread during the Revolution.

end of rationing. 'They raised the prices for bread, so that's what you get,' declared one factory worker (Rimmel 1997: 483–84). Many felt that the rich would benefit while the poor would suffer. In short, the new policy was felt to represent unfairness and hierarchy (1997: 494), everything that 'bread' stood against. Given the regime's symbolic espousal of bread, 'for some people the end of rationing threatened the very legitimacy of the regime as "socialist"' (1997: 496).

Rationing of bread, its importance in the diet, and its position as symbol of equality, did not come to an end with the collapse of the Soviet Union. During the scarcities of 1990, people felt they would survive as long as there was bread. But when bread started to disappear – that is, the state could not provide it – Muscovites felt a turning point, of material and symbolic significance, had been reached (Ries 1997: 136–37). A decade later, bread rationing was introduced in the region of Krasnodar in which I was based. Two loaves were allowed per family, regardless of the size of the household. An article in the local paper explained the need for rationing. In Krasnodar (politically nationalist-Communist) flour is allocated to the bakeries in each region according to their population. This flour is used to make the 'cheap' bread, costing 2.30r.[17] Almost identical loaves are made, in the same bakeries, from 'commercial' flour, made from wheat purchased from private farmers, and sold for 4r. This latter was not rationed, and was always available.[18] Rather than merge the flours and the prices, and make sufficient bread, Kondrachenko, the region's Governor, maintained the low price of bread.

People did not blame the lack of flour on Kondrachenko. As one Meskhetian Turk noted, with muted approval, 'Kondrachenko doesn't like other nationalities, doesn't want other nationalities to live here, only Russians, Russians, Russians. Moscow doesn't like him either, they want him to go. But he has held the price of bread. He is strict'. Kondrachenko is generally disliked by Meskhetian Turks, and Armenians, in the region, for his policies towards particular minorities: refusing them citizenship, and encouraging propaganda against their presence in the region. Given this, the approval of his rationing of bread is even more striking, and demonstrates that bread remains a symbol of equality and of the expected role of the State.

During the rationing, villagers began reserving their place in the bread queue at 9 am, although bread was often delivered after 2.30 pm. Queues in Russia are virtual rather than physical: the new arrival asks who is last, and tells that person that she is next. She must then wait until another villager arrives to 'occupy the queue', but thereafter may go elsewhere and return later to take her place. As the time for the bread van's arrival nears, villagers gather, chatting, around the village shop. When the bread arrives they squash into the shop, watching the person in front closely, but allow pensioners and pregnant women to jump the queue.

When Ries asked, 'What do Russians do for spiritual peace?', she was told, 'We stand in lines! We stand in lines, share our worries and health problems, and become a collective there and then, inseparable' (Ries 1997: 133). While the villagers are far from inseparable, and invariably shout at one another for pushing

---

17 Approximately six pence.
18 Note that the continued provision, during rationing, of two differently priced kinds of bread occurred also in 1934. 'Power sees that the people have begun to live only on rations, and no one buys unrationed bread at the expensive price ...' (Davies 2000: 63).

in, the bread queue (which occurs even when bread is unrationed) is the one occasion on which a significant proportion of the residents do indeed collect. Election posters are displayed by the village shop, and the communal cow herding is discussed while waiting for bread. Soviet intelligence officers knew the significance of this social interaction, and used comments overheard in bread queues as the basis for reports on popular sentiment (Engel 1997, Rimmel 1997: 484).

The Meskhetian Turks and their neighbours interacted over bread when they first arrived in Krasnodar, and bread continues to serve as a site of both conflict and co-operation. One man declared that it is not the local Russians who are bad, because they helped out when they first arrived. When the children were sleeping on the bare floor, local Russians gave them cloth, a mattress, or some money for bread. Another man said they were helped by an Armenian wood-yard owner who 'gave us money for bread'. But others were not so welcoming, and their hostility was expressed through concerns over bread. One woman related that, 'When we were first here, Russians said to us to "You are eating our bread". We said, "We also work; if we sat at home doing nothing, then you could say we are eating your bread. But we work for it"'.

The tensions have lessened, and Meskhetian Turkish poverty is no longer such that they are reliant on neighbours for the most basic of foodstuffs. Yet, talking of his good relationship with his Armenian neighbour, one man said, 'we even share crumbs of bread', rubbing his fingers together to emphasise the point. Both men are relatively comfortable, certainly not reliant on one other's crumbs of bread, but they help each other, to mend a car, provide plastic sheeting for a wedding marquee, or indeed lend a loaf of bread when the shop is shut. But these comments are a reminder that bread continues to stand for equality and friendship amongst post-Soviet peoples, and that when a person speaks of 'bread', he refers to wide field of needs and desires.

CONCLUSION

Falk Moore notes that 'attributing moral significance to political ideas is one way to sacralise them and remove them from the category of the debatable' (1993: 1). I suggest that in this case, the opposite is true: the Bolsheviks took the existing peasant morality of bread and made it a core symbol of the socialist political programme. That bread did, and continues to, express morality in the relationship between Meskhetian Turks and the State depends in part on the continuing (post-) Soviet fear of famine. But the fact that there was no real threat of hunger in 2000,[19] yet rationing remained acceptable, demonstrates that there exists a more ideological component to the people-bread-State relationship. I suggest that bread's ongoing significance in this relationship depends upon its role in other spheres: in constituting relations within and between households, and in communion with ancestors and Allah. With or without the State, Meskhetian

---

19   Flour was still available at much the same price as before; indeed some Meskhetian Turks responded to the limits on bread purchases at the end of the summer by recommencing bread baking.

Turks build and maintain social networks which provide both physical and non-tangible security and sustenance, in which bread acts, on multiple levels, as a symbol of otherwise implicit morality.

BIBLIOGRAPHY

Campbell, J (1964) *Honour, Family and Patronage*, Oxford: Clarendon

Carsten, J (1989) 'Cooking money: gender and the symbolic transformation of means of exchange in a Malay fishing community', in Parry, J and Bloch, M (eds), *Money and the Morality of Exchange*, Cambridge: CUP

Carsten, J (1997) *The Heat of the Hearth: The Process of Kinship in a Malay Fishing Community*, Oxford: Clarendon

Davies, S (2000) '"Us against Them": social identity in Soviet Russia, 1934–1941', in Fitzpatrick, S (ed), *Stalinism: New Directions*, London: Routledge

Delaney, C (1991) *The Seed and the Soil: Gender and Cosmology in Turkish Village Society Berkeley*, CA: California UP

Engel, B (1997) 'Not by bread alone: subsistence riots in Russia during World War I' 69 *The Journal of Modern History* 696–721

Falk Moore, S (1993) 'Introduction', in Falk Moore, S (ed), *Moralizing States and the Ethnography of the Present*, Arlington: American Anthropological Association

Hirschon, R (1989) *Heirs of the Greek Catastrophe*, Oxford: Clarendon

Kotkin, S (1995) *Magnetic Mountain: Stalin as a Civilization*, Berkeley, CA: California UP

Kropotkin, PA (1906/1995), *The Conquest of Bread*, Cambridge: CUP

Lih, L (1990) *Bread and Authority in Russia 1914–1921*, Berkeley, CA: California UP

Mintz, S (1996) *Tasting Food, Tasting Freedom*, Boston: Beacon Press

Moskoff, William (1990) *The Bread of Affliction: The Food Supply in the USSR During World War II*, Cambridge: CUP

Pina-Cabral, J (1986) *Sons of Adam, Daughters of Eve: The Peasant Worldview of the Alto Minho*, Oxford: Clarendon

Ries, N (1997) *Russian Talk: Culture and Conversation during Perestroika*, Ithaca and London: Cornell UP

Rimmel, L (1997) 'Another kind of fear: the Kirov Murder and the end of bread rationing in Leningrad' 56(3) *Slavic Review* 481–99

Scott, J (1976) *The Moral Economy of the Peasant: Rebellion and Subsistence in Southeast Asia*, New Haven: Yale UP

Smith, R and Christian, D (1984) *Bread and Salt: A Social and Economic History of Food and Drink In Russia*, Cambridge: CUP

Thompson, EP (1971) 'The moral economy of the English crowd in the eighteenth century' 50 *Past and Present* 76–136

Tolstoy, A (1938) *Õëââ* [Bread], London: Gollancz

White, J (1994) *Money Makes Us Relatives: Women's Labour in Urban Turkey*, Austin: Texas UP

'TRUTH' AND CHANGE: MORAL DISCOURSE AMONG PROTESTANTS AND CATHOLICS IN THE NETHERLANDS

Tony Watling

INTRODUCTION

This chapter aims to analyse the way in which morality, in this case religious morality, rather than being a set of static norms, can be seen as a fluid concept, capable of adapting to new developments while still providing guidelines and existential support for individuals in their negotiation of an increasingly diverse and complex world. The term 'morality' derives from the Latin *moralis*, meaning 'custom'. It relates to the term 'moral', meaning pertaining to 'right' or 'wrong', 'good' or 'bad' conduct, and means conforming to 'moral principles' regulating such conduct (usually associated with 'religion', or belief in a 'God' who defines 'right' and 'wrong') (Hawkins 1988: 543).

As Howell (1997: 4, 9, 11) argues, morality should be recognised as complex and plural. There is a dynamic relationship between moral values and practice, ideals and realities, between the 'ought' and the 'is' (Bauman 1999, Bowker 1999, Overing 1985, Parkin 1985).[1] Morality is at once public and private, social and individual. The focus, therefore, should be on morali*ties*, or *moral discourse*, on the way in which morality affects and is affected by people's actions, resolving or causing conflict, constructing or deconstructing self-identity (see Howell 1997: 14). Analysing and understanding morality in this sense may allow an understanding of how individuals and groups can negotiate change, how they can retain their identities and traditions while accepting and assessing new developments, rather than simply rejecting them or being overwhelmed by them.[2] It may allow an understanding of the processes of stability and instability, empowerment and disempowerment.

---

1   This is particularly relevant to Dutch religion, which is highly ordered with clearly defined ideas. During my fieldwork I often felt that the information I was gathering was about what Dutch religion 'should be' rather then what 'is'. It sometimes seemed as if religion was 'planned' rather than 'lived'. However, in reality this planning *is* Dutch religion and involves a constant negotiation of ideals and practices where what 'should be' (the 'ought') is at the same time implemented as what 'is'.

2   In this respect 'morality' may be related to 'identity', a concept that is also recognised as dynamic and plural, providing a flexible framework through which people can interpret the world around them (see Bowker 1999, Giddens 1991, Lash and Friedman 1992, Watling 1999).

The idea of morality as an agent for engaging with change has important implications in the contemporary world. It has been argued that in the 'postmodern' 'globalised' world rapid change has fragmented the frameworks that previously supported or controlled individuals. This has freed them from social obligations, creating a diversity of authorities and identities and therefore moral codes (Featherstone 1990, Giddens 1991, Lash and Friedman 1992). These developments are seen to cause a decline in 'traditional' ways of understanding and believing. In particular religion, traditionally seen as the arbiter of morality, is thought to decline as individuals become less dependent on the authoritative legitimation of religious images and rituals by institutional churches and as the latter lose their control of areas of social life, such as education, gender, politics, law, to secular bodies and secular ideals (Beyer 1994, Bruce 1996, Woodhead and Heelas 2000). Recent change, therefore, seems to have threatened what has been understood as 'traditional morality' – the historically developed rules and practices that discipline individuals and populations to believe and act in similar ways – something that is usually associated with religion. Such 'truths' no longer seem relevant to the fragmented nature of society or the diversity of beliefs and actions, and are challenged by new social and technological developments (Bauman 1999, Giddens 1991).

However, such 'morality' may never have been so unitary. Dominant religions, such as Buddhism, Christianity, Hinduism or Islam, may have defined large populations but they have created very different moralities. Within themselves they have also been diverse. Furthermore, while there is some consensus that recent change has led to secularisation, 'religion' and 'morality' may still be valid ways of ordering personal and social beliefs and identities, and may include forms of 'secular morality'. Although changes may be occurring, individuals and groups may seek to order and control them, lessening their impact. In this respect 'traditional' religions and moral values survive, albeit perhaps with more implicit influence. They may be involved in a process of reform as much as decline, either towards 'tradition' (conservatively understood) and unity as in the case of fundamentalisms, or towards 'innovation' and diversity as in the 'liberal' religious traditions, or as expressed by the 'new' moralities found in New Religious Movements or secular bodies. This may be particularly significant, since recent changes, although possibly emancipating, may create instability and isolate individuals from moral resources (Bauman 1999, Beyer 1994, Giddens 1991, Griffin 1989a, 1989b, Grove-White 1993, Woodhead and Heelas 2000).

This chapter analyses the construction of such diverse moralities, moral rules, organisations and practices among a number of churches in the village of Aalten in the province of *Gelderland* in the east of the Netherlands. The aim is to understand how diverse religious groups (in this case Reformed Protestant and Catholic) negotiate their identities, their moral boundaries, in relation to each other and to a changing world. The discussion aims to explore in what ways they might change, rejecting, adapting or reinforcing tradition, and either cause or resolve conflict. Morality in this sense may be seen as a catalyst to action, allowing religious believers to interpret religious ideals and create moral rules and actions that encourage or resist change, creating emancipations or constraints. In the Netherlands religion has played an important part in the nation, being a fundamental organising principle for society, and something that may still colour Dutch mentality (Boissevain and Verrips 1989: 3, see Andeweg and Irwin 1993, van der Laarse 1989, Watling 2001b). Since the Reformation, which began at the same time as the Dutch Revolt and the formation of the Dutch nation (and influenced it) religion has been intertwined with economic, political and social developments. Religion could be said to have guided the development of the Dutch nation and national, local and individual identities. Religious morality, therefore, specifically Reformed morality, has had an important impact on Dutch identity; Catholicism has been a secondary influence. It may have enabled the Netherlands and the Dutch people to accept diversity and negotiate change (Watling 2001b). The rest of this chapter, therefore, uses the Netherlands, and specifically the village of Aalten, as an ethnographic example to explore 'morality(ies) in action'.

RELIGION IN THE NETHERLANDS: SCHISM AND ACCOMMODATION

The religious situation in the Netherlands has been intimately tied to the political and cultural process, particularly the creation of the Dutch nation after the Reformation and Dutch Revolt in the 16th and 17th centuries, and political and social emancipations in the nineteenth and twentieth centuries. These influences, expanding upon an already existing localist system of government, created a plural and discursive, religiously inflected, Dutch national identity, somewhat obviating class, ethnic or racial divisions (Andeweg and Irwin 1993, Shetter 1987, van der Laarse 1989, Watling 1999). Until the Reformation there was one church in the Netherlands, the Roman Catholic Church. Since then, religion has split into diverse churches, each claiming to define the 'truth'. These church schisms arose from the localised nature of the Reformation and the Dutch Revolt, which reinforced each other in their quest to establish autonomy from the Roman Catholic Church and from Spain. Indeed, in Calvinist thinking (dominant at the time) the Revolt and the aspiring nation existed for the sake of the Reformed church, it was seen as the 'sacred' struggle of the 'chosen people'. Other influences, such as other religious beliefs, the Enlightenment, the Scientific Revolution, and the State, forced a compromise with these ideals. However, the Reformation initiated important changes in belief, doctrine and society, which were influential, notably in that individuals could be as 'spiritual' as the clergy and that the local church was the most important religious unit, which highlighted diversity and responsibility.

In the 19th century a tension between innovation and tradition came to the fore, culminating in social emancipations (Wintle 1987). The Reformed churches were also reorganised in 1816 into the Dutch Reformed Church (*Nederlands Hervormde Kerk*), a State church run along hierarchical instead of the traditional Reformed Presbyterian lines. This led to schisms, with 'orthodox' groups splitting to reclaim Reformation ideals, forming new Re-Reformed (*Gereformeerde*) churches. In 1834 the Afscheiding, or Secession, occurred and in 1886 the Doleantie, or Protest, both of which may also have been in part social revolts (Wintle 1987). The latter initiated a philosophy of devolution or 'sovereignty in the individual social spheres', where different groups demanded to control their own affairs and influence the government. This was officially consolidated in the political system known as *verzuiling*, or pillarisation. It involved the creation of separate 'pillars' or sub-communities based on different ideological ideas, Protestant, Catholic and 'General', as well as smaller divisions, co-ordinated by the national government (Lijphart 1975). This allowed and accommodated diversity, and further schisms occurred in the 20th century and may still occur. Reformed belief is in movement, constantly searching for the 'truth' and seeking to create a morally perfect society. Its links to the political system may have widened this to encompass Dutch society as a whole, which may be seen as in constant moral discourse, attempting to create a 'truthful' existence.

The Catholic Church in the Netherlands has been in a disadvantaged position throughout most of Dutch history since the Reformation, since Reformed belief has dominated national development. Because of this two things have occurred. First, the church became insular, unified and staunchly 'Catholic'. However, the Reformed thinking that dominated national identity was also influential. The former allowed Catholics a solid base to seek emancipation in the *verzuiling* system; the latter may have influenced the major changes in the church from the 1960s, after Vatican II, when parishioners (and clergy) sought to create a new egalitarian church (Coleman 1978). Although this 'theological revolution' initially stalled, resulting in a lack of priests and rejection of the church by parishioners, the Dutch Catholic Church has since embraced change, at least 'unofficially', resulting in what could be termed a belated 'Catholic Reformation'. In this respect it is increasingly being organised along similar lines to the Reformed churches and, not coincidentally, entering into ecumenical discussion with them in an increasingly organised ecumenical movement.

The historical developments detailed above have shaped the way present day churches are structured, the way belief is expressed and the way Dutch society and nationality are experienced. The Reformation emphasised the individual and made the local church central, producing diversity of belief and in parallel disempowering the clergy and encouraging more responsibility for the laity (see McGrath 1994). The 19th century developments consolidated these changes and legitimised them through the intimate connections between religion and the political process. It is important therefore to examine the 'Reformation morality' thus produced, which provides the institutional background to the experience of belief and social action. The Reformation was essentially a moral conflict, delineating 'right' from 'wrong' and appropriate ways of behaving to reach the 'truth'. Morality became a personal quest rather than mere obedience to the Catholic Church. The early Reformed churches consolidated this by delineating moral rules through which to best experience this quest (Calvinism, especially, was important through its stress on discipline and order). Later church schisms refined this process by defining different 'moralities': different ways of channelling the 'truth' and ordering society within moral rules, roles and tasks. Individual experience and social order in this sense are morally appropriate, a way to approach 'truth'. Reformed believers aim to personally experience the 'truth' and act responsibly in society, thus creating a morally appropriate society where others can also experience the 'truth'. This is termed *roeping* or 'calling' (Watling 1999; see Belzen 1999, McGrath 1994, Weber 1991). Reformed churches, therefore, are essentially federations based around church councils (*kerkenraden*) of elected representatives, termed *ambtsdragers*, who officially take responsibility for the organisation of the church and belief. This is the *ambt* or 'office'. The *ambt* is essentially the social manifestation of the roeping. It represents the choice of devoting oneself to God and the church (and ultimately society). An *ambtsdrager* is a religious 'official' (morally) sanctioned by the church and by God. However, although *ambtsdragers* have most responsibility, the ambt could be said to be expected of all members. All experience the *roeping*, and all are seen as having roles and tasks suited to their abilities. This is thought to promote dynamism by allowing new ideas. Members interpret events according to their personal belief and through their personal responsibility, acting according to different abilities. The church organisation provides a democratic basis for the negotiation of these diverse actions and a controlled arena for engagement with new issues.[3]

Because of these Reformed (Calvinist) influences, religious groups in the Netherlands construct moralities allowing 'ordered' diversity and dynamism, thereby somewhat controlling developments. Members experience their individualities via moral guidelines; however they discourse with these, challenging as much as 'following' them. Through this they also discourse with wider society, creating a 'moral compass' to engage with change (Watling 1999). By encouraging such a moral discourse, Dutch churches provide existential resources for negotiating the world. In this sense they may both be constraining, in that they limit individual expression by providing obligations, and yet also empowering since these obligations encourage such expression.[4]

These developments have had important implications for the Dutch nation, for the development of Dutch identity and thus for Dutch Catholicism. They have been influential in the Dutch state and in local political councils, and may still affect the way Dutch society develops. What they and the political process may have developed is a 'flexible' identity, allowing diversity within dialogue (Shetter 1987, Taylor 1983, Watling 2001b). The Reformation and Dutch Revolt and economic, political, religious and social emancipations which culminated in *verzuiling*, may have formally consolidated Reformed morality in a bureaucratic structure and national identity, based around common dialogue. Andeweg and Irwin (1993: 231–33) point out that underlying diversity in the Netherlands is consensus. Conflicts are not about defining the nation but about how to run it. The nation therefore may revolve around the ideology of social partnership, a constant re-affirmation of difference and co-operation. In reality this may not always be so harmonious. It can also be oppressive, revolving around obligation as much as

---

3   This is not to say *ambtsdragers* lack power. Especially in 'orthodox' churches, there is an element of social control. *Ambtsdragers* observe members in their actions, discuss their lives and administer help or admonition. They are seen as respected and responsible individuals, best exemplifying the 'truth' of Reformation ideals the *ropeing* and the *ambt* which means they can attain prestige. In the past, and still today in 'orthodox' churches, they were seen to be 'morally higher' than normal members, needing to be more educated or experienced individuals, usually older males.

4   Some ('orthodox') churches may favour more constraint, while others ('liberal') more emancipation.

free choice, this oppressive situation being known as *zwaren* or 'heaviness' (Belzen 1999, Knippenberg 1992, Tennekes 1988, Weber 1991). It can also involve competition as different groups strive to express and promote their moral vision. Nevertheless, if anything links the nation it may be the calling, diversity, dynamism and order inherent in Reformed morality (Watling 2001b). In this sense, although there will be a variety of moral expressions (Protestant, Catholic, secular) negotiating change in different ways, these may be influenced by similar common moral principles (see Howell 1997: 4–11).

RELIGION IN AALTEN: A MORAL DISCOURSE NEGOTIATING THE 'TRUTH'

The history of religion in Aalten has followed religious developments in the Dutch nation as a whole, diversifying after the Reformation, although showing a Re-Reformed emphasis. At present the village has around 14 main church groups comprising around 16,000 members, in a population of around 18,000. Four can be considered the most influential, representing three areas of 'morality', 'orthodox' and 'liberal' Reformed Protestants (c 11,400 members) and 'Catholic' (c 4,000 members). These churches, influenced by the Reformed beliefs described above, themselves comprise 'orthodox' and 'liberal' elements, the former favouring 'tradition' the latter 'innovation', emphasising the need for diversity in an overarching organisation. They extend this to inter-church interaction, aiming to create a forum for religious discussion, a local 'moral discourse'. The village also has a strong ecumenical movement, therefore, existing as an organised arena for the churches to engage in religious dialogue and social activism. Religion is also in evidence in other areas of social life. The dominant political party is the Christian Democratic Alliance (*Christen Democratisch Appel*) and there is a growing 'orthodox' party, the Reformed Political Federation (*Reformatorische Politieke Federatie*). All but one of the 10 schools are denominational: three primary schools are Dutch Reformed, three Re-Reformed and two Roman Catholic; the one secondary school is ecumenical. There are also various Christian social groups relating to leisure, sport or work. It is the churches, however, which are central, competing to define the village's 'moral discourse'. They each aim to set a standard and lead the way by promoting their values and expressing it in action. In this way they hope to persuade the others and the wider public that they hold the 'truth' of belief.

'Orthodox' moralities: limiting and protecting the 'truth'

The schisms, or 'Re-Reformations', that have occurred since the Reformation itself have defined Reformed belief and practice into *rechtzinnige*, or 'orthodox', and *vrijzinnige*, or 'liberal', streams of thought. The former show a more strict application of Reformation ideals than the latter that accept new developments (Knippenberg 1992: 244–47). 'Orthodox' groups aim to search for the 'truth', defining it with reference to 'liberalism', and then protect it by creating small, isolated communities and effectively controlling their members' lives. They define appropriate ways of reaching the 'truth' through behaviour, with authoritative church personnel (albeit elected) administering rules and regulations to prevent the 'truth' becoming diluted or compromised.[5] These churches conform to somewhat 'fundamentalist' ideals and practices, looking inward to retain control, although they do compromise in certain areas such as dress, food or work (Beyer 1994, Bruce 1996, Woodhead and Heelas 2000).

In Aalten, 'orthodox' views mostly occur in the Christian Re-Reformed Church (*Christelijk Gereformeerde Kerk*), which traces its roots to the *Afscheiding*. This church restricts its 400 members' experiences, apart from work, to church occasions and 'disciplines' them to believe and behave the accepted 'Christian Re-Reformed' way (members are also bound more closely by kinship ties than 'liberal' churches). In this respect the church is more isolationist and less ecumenical. The church council (*kerkenraad*), made up of male *ambtsdragers* only, guides an explicitly 'moral community'. Its members are 'moral guardians', responsible for ensuring that other members are supported in their religion and their lives, and thus create a church morally in line with Reformation ideals. To do this they organise services, committees concerned with finance, leisure and missionary work and discussion groups based on age and sex that serve to 'discipline' members by providing controlled arenas in which they interact. However, this 'discipline' is not only formal, based around *ambstdrager* teaching and church rules, but also informal through peer pressure. It is both social and personal. By accepting organisational regulations and acting within them, members show their commitment to each other in public. They publicly demonstrate personal morality, showing their commitment to (and embodiment of) Christian Re-Reformed belief. Services, committees and workgroups are an expression of belief (the *ambt*). They are where members learn a particular 'Christian Re-Reformed' morality and where they experience and express their belief (the *roeping*).

This 'discipline' is why 'orthodox' churches are often seen to be especially *zwaar* or 'heavy'. Their belief can be an oppressive burden, weighing on members' consciences; they are dependent on it, it is what legitimises their lives (Belzen 1999, Knippenberg 1992, Miedema 1989, see also Tennekes 1988, Weber 1991). However, 'orthodox' morality may not only be oppressive. Members choose to be involved. It is an active commitment as much as a passive 'following'.[6] This is why members stay in a church that disallows certain behaviour and puts many of them in a secondary position. This can be particularly seen in two sections of membership who would seem to be most at odds with the church: women, who

---

5   This conflict over the 'truth' is why schisms occur (alongside personal and group differences) 'orthodox' groups split from 'liberalising' churches to reclaim the 'truth'. In fact, the 'orthodox' see the 'liberals' as schismatic because to them they embrace new ideas and thus reject the 'truth' (the terms are relative, therefore, encompassing a variety of interpretations: some 'ultra-orthodox' churches see 'orthodox' churches as 'liberal').

6   There are formal means to restrict and control members. They have to be baptised (although the church accepts any Christian baptism, including Catholic) and confirmed (only confirmed members can take communion or serve as *ambtsdragers*). Should anyone decline to be so active and committed *ambstdragers* would enquire why, try to find an acceptable solution, possibly show disapproval and ultimately administer sanctions (denying communion, rejecting from the church). The aim, however, is to encourage moral conscience so that members themselves choose to be active or leave.

are denied the chance be *ambtsdragers*, and young people, who are thought to most value 'liberal' or secular 'freedom'. Women, for example, are active members of the church. They are involved in all committees and workgroups and hold responsible and influential positions. They are taught the same catechism and take the same confirmation oaths as men. Many have important careers outside the church. However, they are denied church authority. Christian Re-Reformed interpretation of 1 Corinthians 14 and 1 Timothy states that women should not be in authority or undertake spiritual teaching duties, and prescribes a more implicit 'pastoral' role for them (UBS 1991: 217–18, 259–64). This poses a dilemma for them. They are encouraged to be emancipated, active and responsible individuals. Yet they have to defer to men. That they accept this is because they develop a 'Christian Re-Reformed' moral conscience that teaches them that they have different religious tasks to men. The church is seen as a community of likeminded individuals putting shared experience above individual desires.

Christian Re-Reformed women experience their femininity via the church (see Brasher 1998).[7] They and other members learn to become what is termed *bekeerd*: they learn to turn to God. The Christian Re-Reformed morality becomes a personal conscience (publicly demonstrated by their actions). They learn to experience their emotions through the church, engaging new developments via its 'discipline'. Such 'discipline', therefore, is a self-discipline, relying not only on the enforcement of doctrine but also on experience. As Brasher (1998) argues, individuals frame fundamentalism as much as vice versa, in other words they *embody* it. In the Netherlands this is termed *bevindeljkheid*, the hold of 'inner experience', as opposed to the hold of *orthodoxie* or religious doctrine (Belzen 1999: 239–48, Knippenberg 1992: 246–47, van der Laarse 1989: 442). Different churches have different levels of *bevindelijkheid*; the 'orthodox' have more of it than the 'liberals', and thus are termed *bevindelijke* churches. However, although difficult, taking a great deal of self-control, this allows members to feel fulfilled through giving their lives a purpose, and giving them a standard to cope with the world. Members are critical, indeed criticism is seen as a moral act since it demonstrates conscience and an ability to challenge 'liberalism' and secular society rather than merely following them. 'Orthodox' churches are not static. They value tradition but they also recognise the need to develop. Their aim, however, is to do so in a highly *controlled* way.

'Liberal' moralities: diversifying and expanding the 'truth'

In contrast to 'orthodox' churches that do not look far beyond their boundaries, 'liberal' churches are willing to explore different beliefs and wider issues. They revolve around the same Calvinist Reformation normative frameworks, but show greater tendencies to elaborate their moralities rather than clarify them. They do not attempt to control or promote a defined message. Rather, they embrace

---

7   Christian (Re-)Reformed women assess what the church offers in terms of community, education, family values, religious experience and standard of living, balance the options (in relation to 'liberal' or 'secular' values) and choose to commit to the church (although this is not simply a rational choice, through their experiences they also 'believe' the rules, it is a Christian Re-Reformed directed choice).

diversity. Their moral orientations are wider. They stress 'innovation' as much as 'tradition' and constantly seek new ways of experiencing their beliefs, embracing ecumenism and the secular world. This has led to secularisation and schism as their members have been freed from church commitments. The challenge for them, therefore, has been to retain diverse categories of members alongside coherent moralities, and prevent conflict while accepting change.

In Aalten 'liberal' moralities are represented by the Dutch Reformed Church (*Nederlands Hervormde Kerk*) and the Re-Reformed Church (*Gereformeerde Kerk*), the two largest and most influential Reformed churches in the Netherlands (in Aalten the former has around 5,000 members, the latter 6,000 members). The former is considered the semi-official church of the Netherlands, and contains diverse groups within its boundaries, from the extreme 'orthodox' to the extreme 'liberal'.[8] It does not promote one 'truth' or one morality, therefore. Rather, it co-ordinates many. This has traditionally differentiated it from other (schismatic) Re-Reformed churches, the largest of which are the Re-Reformed Churches (*Gereformeerde Kerken*), founded after the *Doleantie*, to which the latter belongs. Before the second world war these were considered 'orthodox'. However, since then they have 'liberalised' and correspondingly have had much contact with the Dutch Reformed Church. These churches have converged somewhat. They no longer need to create opposed moralities to define themselves (although much depends on locality).

Despite their changes, these 'liberal' churches still rely on somewhat 'traditional' organisational forms (that is, the *ambt*). Their beliefs are still experienced via church roles and in committees, services and workgroups, and both are structured around their church councils made up of *ambtsdragers*. However, the application of this organisation is less rigid than formerly. It is no longer used to 'discipline' members: rather, it is used as a resource enabling them to educate themselves. The churches are more 'academic' channels to gain knowledge, with *ambtsdragers*, the 'experts', guiding this (Giddens 1991). In this way they aim to address wider secular concerns while retaining their religious base. They do not merely construct a bounded morality, keeping opposing moralities and the secular world at bay, but expand morality, adapting to and encompassing diverse moralities and negotiating with the secular world. These churches emphasise that 'reformation' is no longer only an 'orthodox' option – returning to a morally 'pure' belief defining and defending the 'truth' via opposing 'outside' views – but that it can also involve engaging with such views, accepting diversity and doubt, previously 'impure' beliefs, and widening and adapting the 'truth'.

This reluctance to control or 'discipline' their populations has meant that these churches congregations are more diffuse than in 'orthodox' churches. This is termed *randkerkelijken*: a small core of 'active' members (*kernleden*) surrounded by

---

8   To retain membership the church has, throughout its history, had to officially recognise and institutionalise these differences as (from 'orthodox' to 'liberal'): *Gereformeerde Bond* ('Reformed Alliance'), valuing tradition; *Confessioneel* and *Ethisch*, centre groups, which have now mostly united in a 'middle-orthodox' category, comprising the majority of members; and *Vrijzinnige*, or 'liberal' groups, stressing freedom of expression.

a large rim of 'passive' ones (*randleden*) (Knippenberg 1992).[9] Consequently, the churches have had to seek *ambtsdragers* from a wider spectrum of members, including women and younger members. This has caused a change in beliefs and practices. Members are no longer dependent on church organisation, religious specialists or particular ways of believing. They are less controlled and more reflexive. Because of this, the role of *ambtsdragers* has changed, from being authoritarian 'leaders' to being 'colleagues'. This challenges the assumption that they are moral guardians, and further individualises morality. Instead of showing members the morally correct way of acting, they negotiate with them, adapting morals to their individual situations (something that may be less demanding but more confusing; they sacrifice moral clarity for moral learning). Of course, this 'liberal' thinking is not without its detractors. Because the churches are large and diverse (the Dutch Reformed Church has three pastors (one female), the Re-Reformed Church five (one female), all with slightly different beliefs), some members are 'orthodox' and prefer 'traditional' moralities and 'authoritarian' leaders. Thus morality is contested and expressed as discourse. The churches see this as stimulating debate, something that is needed to cope with diverse future possibilities. Members still experience the roeping to be active. There is still a constant search for moral perfection. However, this occurs outwardly rather than inwardly. The ambt has been widened, and is interpreted in a future-oriented rather than a tradition-bound way. This shows a willingness to compromise ideals and adapt beliefs, something that increasingly involves discoursing with the previously rejected Dutch Catholic Church.

Catholic moralities: 'official' and 'unofficial' 'truths'

The Dutch Catholic Church is in the process of change, re-defining authority, ritual and symbolism in a more democratic way. However, this is somewhat 'unofficial'. Dutch Catholicism is split between two traditions/positions. One the one hand, 'official' structures stipulate belief in transcendent images, hierarchical discipline, male domination and rejection of ecumenism. On the other hand, parishioners are developing new perspectives on moral conscience, on a par with and in dialogue with Reformed churches, rejecting transcendence, favouring egalitarian structures and embracing female emancipation. Aalten Catholic church demonstrates this well. It is developing a 'community of belief' where clergy and laity work together on equal terms. It is ordering Catholic beliefs in a new democratic way, initiating lay workgroups, enhancing individualism and entering ecumenical contact. However, much of this is 'unofficial', not sanctioned by the church authorities (or moral structures). This causes some tension and the

---

9   It is difficult to be precise concerning figures for this. Knippenberg (1992: 249) argues that 39% of Dutch Reformed and 73% of Re-Reformed members may be 'active' (he defines 'activity' as attending a service once a fortnight). In Aalten Dutch Reformed Church, around a fifth of members attend a service once a week, while in the Re-Reformed Church it may be around a third to a half. There are several services a week, possibly attended by different members, which may up the figures, as may the fact that with a change in emphasis from 'leadership' to 'dialogue' many members who do not attend services may be active in committees or workgroups. A loose estimate, therefore, would be that around a quarter to a third of Dutch Reformed and over half of Re-Reformed members may be considered 'active' in the sense I describe it.

number of 'active' parishioners within these arenas is, therefore, small at present. The church has even more numbers of *randkerkelijken* than the 'liberal' Reformed churches (Watling 2001c).[10]

The church has around 4,000 members and revolves around the parish council (*parochiebestuur*) and parish meeting (*parochievergadering*) made up of elected representatives. These groups decide parish policy, initiate new developments and stimulate activism. They delegate tasks and responsibilities to parishioners, who are encouraged to learn about religion for themselves in consultation with local clergy and local and national church organisations and use it in society. They are encouraged to experience a 'calling' and to apply it, as in the Reformed *roeping* and *ambt*. This is not an easy process, because by rejecting an 'official' belief and bounded morality based on dogma and habit, parishioners have to learn to create their own beliefs and encourage others to do the same. Criticism replaces obedience, something that risks loss of faith. This is why the local community is emphasised, enabling individuals to support each other. To expand and co-ordinate this development, therefore, the councils also supervise workgroups concerned with catechism, liturgy and pastoral work, which are seen as interlinked catalytic areas assisting parishioners to develop the moral responsibility needed to create a new, egalitarian and future-oriented Catholicism. The new ideas developing within them are envisaged as having two applications in the community: liturgical celebration and social activism. The former involves the services. These are still valued and still represent the 'official' show of clerical authority (preaching the gospels, leading the praying and confessions, blessing communion). The laity are more 'active' than formerly, however, reading lessons and physically 'taking' the communion rather than 'receiving' it on the tongue. This shows a change in ritual communication and material symbolism. The power of traditional images and their control by the clergy is no longer effective. A new symbolism is being celebrated in Aalten: one of 'community'. This is why social activism is regarded as important: it involves protecting the community, something that involves local, national and global concerns. Catholic boundaries are being widened and consequently the church is also becoming more inclined towards ecumenical dialogue.[11]

These changes also affect the images and roles of clergy and laity (particularly the position of women). Aalten parishioners reject the idea that someone 'higher' knows more of the 'truth' than they do, and want a redefinition of clerical authority. They want less hierarchy and more democracy. This has in fact been occurring in Aalten since the 1960s, especially in the decade or so when the community has been without a full-time priest. This has led to lay autonomy. In other parishes it has led to lay parishioners, working as qualified 'pastoral

---

10 Again it is difficult to be precise about figures. Knippenberg (1992: 249) argues that 37% of Dutch Catholics attend a service once a fortnight. In Aalten around a tenth of parishioners attend once a week, but adding activism in councils and workgroups I estimate that around 20–25% may be 'active'.

11 This is not to say ritual and symbolism are not valued. They may be. But parishioners want more control of them. They want to use them to legitimate their experiences rather than following the interpretation of the church hierarchy (see Dillon 1999). They value 'Catholic' 'tradition', the 'living faith', but not so much '*Roman* Catholic' 'tradition', the customary ways of organising faith (see McBrien 1994: 63).

workers' (titled *pastor* – a priest is titled *pastoor*) taking on the full priestly role. These workers study theology and pastoral work, often for as long as a priest, and include women.[12] 'Officially' they cannot perform sacraments, except in revised forms. However, inevitably many now do so. In some situations bishops have disciplined these workers, but generally the situation is accepted because the communities within which they work choose them and because without them the church would not function. They have a difficult task, juggling two roles, being 'politicians' as well as 'pastors'. In many cases the tension they create is eased by them working together with priests, who provide the 'official' seal to their 'unofficial' process.[13]

There is a struggle for re-definition of Catholicism occurring in Aalten, creating a moral dilemma of negotiating between 'official' doctrines and 'unofficial' actions, tradition and change. Because of this parishioners are somewhat alienated from the 'official' church. Their existential dilemmas cannot be assisted by its moral framework. This has led to decline. However, local level commitment is giving parishioners belief in their community in their personal and local moralities. These 'unofficial' principles and structures are creating, at present in dialogue with 'official' doctrines and structures, a new diverse and dialogic church. The results of this in the long-term may be varied. Reasserting tradition might cause schism, as might accepting radical change. A more likely result would be that the situation continues as it is, 'unofficially' diversifying and developing 'officially' promoting the Catholic 'image', something that may have always been the case with Catholicism anyway (Dillon 1999, McBrien 1994, Watling 2001c). However, recent 'unofficial' developments have led to ecumenical contact, suggesting that, in an ecumenical movement at least, the 'unofficial' Dutch Catholic morality may become consolidated 'officially' and gain in influence.

Moralities in competition and dialogue: the ecumenical movement

The decline of the *verzuiling* system, allied to secularisation, initiated ecumenical contact between Dutch churches as they came to recognise their (human) similarities more than their (church) differences. Since the second world war this has been increasingly organised in an official 'ecumenical movement'. This takes the form of local councils organising activities concerned with gender, liturgy, pastoral issues, social inequalities or third world issues, co-ordinated by a

---

12 The position of women is, perhaps, the area where new developments are most highlighted. Many women now take an active role in church affairs; in Aalten as many if not more women than men. Many take on 'official' roles as pastoral workers (at present only 'officially' allowed to work in care homes, prisons or hospitals). In a similar way to the Reformed churches, these women bring new ideas to the church. They are not concerned with authority or rules but with people. Their activism concerns practical, pastoral motives with social work as much as with church-based or spiritual ones (although they see the two intertwined) (see Watling 2002).

13 This change in the nature of Catholic authority is why celibacy is not so much of an issue in the Netherlands. It is challenged by new developments; parishioners prefer someone on their level, with similar experiences, to guide them. However, because most of the church workers these days are laity the issue does not arise. For the time being the clergy remain celibate ('officially', many may not be).

national committee, called the *Raad van Kerken* or Council of Churches (Watling 2001a). This is seen as the expression of a community of churches, a meeting place for mutual exchange rather than a 'superchurch'. Any 'ecumenical morality', therefore, is inherently plural, a multitude of actions and expressions. There is recognition of an ever-changing, diverse world and a recognition that moral views will need to be similarly diverse. A complexity of resources and solutions to combat the complexity of moral problems is seen to be required. However, this 'competition' between moralities is thought to allow for many possibilities (which is why despite 'liberal' morals being dominant, 'orthodox' morals are seen as valid and encouraged).[14] The important point is to express moralities 'in common', in dialogue. Individual believers and churches are encouraged to produce their own moral agendas (the *roeping*) but to work in unison, mutually supporting each other in their engagement with a secular society that is initiating challenging developments (the *ambt*).

Aalten *Raad van Kerken* involves the Dutch Reformed Church, the Re-Reformed Church and the Catholic Church (plus some smaller groups). It aims to be involved with contemporary issues, and to not just challenge them but define them. Its participants, therefore, are becoming morally obliged to be involved in the active creation of new forms of existence, be they economic, political, religious or social. Ecumenism is promoted as a way of life, something beyond religious boundaries (although it is based on Reformed morality). At present this involves a network of workgroups divided into 'educational', 'spiritual' and 'social' arenas, arising from and extending church arenas of catechism, liturgy and pastoral work. Education is seen as important because individuals are encouraged (and expected) to learn their own moral code. The 'Education Committee', therefore, organises discussions on a variety of religious or social topics, aiming to bring different churches together around a variety of often sensitive issues and situations, such as abortion, euthanasia, incest and environmentalism, in the hope that they can reach solutions jointly, controlling events rather than being controlled by them. Aalten churches feel it to be important to address new issues, as they pose new existential questions and moral dilemmas that traditional beliefs struggle to resolve. Spiritual issues are also discussed, therefore, challenging traditional liturgical forms and theological ideas. The *Convent van Pastores* or pastors discussion group includes pastors from all member churches (plus the Christian Re-Reformed pastor) who share experiences, research religious questions and advise the *Raad van Kerken*. This is seen as important, for as pastors continue to meet, find common ground and develop a new theology, so it is hoped other members will also. Similar lay groups occur, therefore. One, the 'Committee for Ecumenical Services', promotes ecumenism through more traditional arenas of prayer and sermon. It organises ecumenical services (five times a year, given in the Dutch Reformed, Re-Reformed and Catholic churches in rotation; a Catholic pastor in a Protestant church, Dutch Reformed in Re-Reformed and vice versa) and ecumenical communion. The latter

---

14 At present 'orthodox' groups refuse to be part of the process. They see it driven by 'liberalism' and secularisation, thereby compromising religious ideals and diluting the 'truth'. They, therefore, form their own 'Reformed' movement. They do take part in particular activities, however those with an evangelical bent where they can promote their moralities, which opens up the future possibility of them joining the overall process.

is considered a big step to take, even though some areas have already done so, because 'officially' it is forbidden, at least by the Catholics. The major stumbling block concerns transubstantiation. Many Protestants still think that Catholics believe in a literal change of bread and wine into body and blood. This to them is idolatry ('officially' Catholics do believe in this, even if 'unofficially' they do not). Protestants are also refused Catholic communion 'officially' (ie, it is not sanctioned by the Church). However, they take each others' communion 'unofficially' (at the discretion of local pastors), which is the stimulus, and the churches work this way. Protestants would like more 'official' agreement as for them 'rules' come from personal morality, and they struggle to understand that, for Catholics, 'practice' is morally correct for individuals while 'rules' are theological ideas interpreted locally by the clergy. However, at present they work within this hypocrisy as they realise ecumenism needs to be adaptable.

The need for adaptability shows that ecumenism (and any 'ecumenical morality') is practical. It involves acts rather than rules. Social activism, concerned with human needs or inequalities is, therefore, considered important. Social activism is envisaged as common to all churches; less likely to cause conflict by threatening different 'truths' but instead to put diverse beliefs to common use. Ecumenism, therefore, provides a neutral arena for different churches to enter dialogue and come to common ideas and actions. This is not to say it is altogether harmonious. It can cause tensions, as it challenges traditions and as different churches (or workgroups or individuals) 'compete' to see who can be most active and 'moral'. Nevertheless, although boundaries are challenged they are also legitimated, which means churches can confront change on their terms but also within a support network of mutual dialogue.

CONCLUSIONS

Recent change is seen as challenging 'traditional' forms of religion and morality, favouring independent individuality. Instead of merely 'following' 'authoritative', religious or moral rules and regulations, individuals are now seen as having the freedom to actively create their own, choosing to accept, adapt or reject traditional authoritative forms, thereby creating a diversity of views. However, as this case study shows, religion and morality may still survive and be valid ways of ordering personal and social life and engaging with the world. They may still give meaning to individuals lives and social practices, although perhaps now in a greater diversity and flexibility of forms. In this sense they may be agents for change and empowering as much as inhibitors to change and constraining. Much depends perhaps on context. Individuals may enter dialogue with 'orthodox' or 'liberal', 'bounded' or 'flexible' moralities and commit themselves to one or the other at particular times and in particular places.

In the Netherlands such individuality and religious choice may always have been the case, at least since the Reformation (Knippenberg 1992). Dutch 'religious (moral) consciousness' is a consequence of the centuries-long religious heterogeneity and the intimate links between religion, politics and culture (Watling 1999, see also Knippenberg 1992, Shetter 1987). What these influences may have produced is what Taylor (1983: 73) calls an 'elastic conservatism', a balance of 'orthodoxy' and 'liberalism', tradition and change. This is something Knippenberg (1992: 2, 246) argues as a struggle to crystallize Dutch consciousness between *preciezen*, or those 'defining' beliefs, and *rekkelijken*, or those 'stretching' beliefs (van der Laarse 1989: 26, Wintle 1987: 5). Dutch history, therefore, has, since the Reformation, been involved in a particularly dynamic moral discourse, a contested, plural domain negotiated by independent individuals. To this end the *roeping*, or 'calling', and the *ambt*, or 'office', may have been of importance because they may have allowed and encouraged (and at times forced) individuals to think about the world in moral terms, what van der Laarse (1989: 30, 377) calls a 'moral contract', something that encourages a dialectic between the personal and the social (see McGrath 1994: 131, Taylor 1983: 16).

The central driving force of the Dutch moral 'consciousness', affecting the present transformations in Dutch religion and the development of Dutch society (possibly even a Dutch 'nationalism'), may be a 'critical facility' or self-reflexivity (Watling 1999, see also Giddens 1991, Griffin 1989a, 1989b). The *roeping* and *ambt* may have influenced Dutch individuals, both Protestant and Catholic (or secular), directly via religious discourse or indirectly via the national identity, to empower themselves and critically engage with society, in varying 'orthodox' or 'liberal' (or secular) degrees, in dialectical interaction with church (or secular) moralities. This may allow them to integrate thought and action (the 'ought' and the 'is') when faced with religious (or secular) issues and developments, enabling them to control their religious (and to some extent their secular) destiny. In this way they are able to accept differences and negotiate change, rather than pursuing separatist views or feeling disempowered. The churches' role in this is to provide moral options rules, practices and communities from which individuals can choose to use to face the world, while attempting to morally influence events their way by promoting their 'moralities'. This Dutch (religious) morality may, therefore, involve 'competition' as much as harmony, a struggle for (moral) power. Each church, group or individual may compete to 'work' 'better' or more morally (according to basic Reformed principles). To achieve such moral superiority, however, may not be the outcome of economic, political or social domination, but of proving that one's ideas and actions can create a more moral (in Reformed terms) society. This concentration on moral discourse may also be why the Netherlands is keen to be at the centre of a European identity and why the Dutch may accept economic, social or technological change comparatively readily. Their particular form of moral literacy may enable them to incorporate such changes, influencing their development in a specifically (Dutch) moral way. Because of this, 'moral domination' may occur as different groups (for example Muslims, to name but one group of growing importance in the Netherlands) have to learn of and abide by what is essentially a Christian morality. Furthermore, the Dutch may impress their contractual, dialogic morality on other, less emancipated or less powerful countries who have moralities with different bases (for example, conflict, hierarchy, different religions; see Kapferer 1988).[15] Nevertheless what this

---

15 This is where a form of Dutch nationalism might be identified. The morality engendered by Dutch Reformed (Calvinist) Christianity may in this sense be similar to what Kapferer (1988) calls the 'ontology' at the base of nationalism, the underlying habitual conditions created via Dutch religious, political and social history where ideas and action, society and self, are created (see Watling 2001b).

shows is that particular individuals, religions or societies at particular times and in particular contexts may develop implicit and explicit moral strategies to negotiate change. In this sense, therefore, 'morality' may still be an organising principle and existential anchor for individuals and societies.

BIBLIOGRAPHY

Andeweg, R and Irwin, G (1993) *Dutch Government and Politics*, Basingstoke: Macmillan

Bauman, Z (1999) *Postmodern Ethics*, Oxford: Blackwell

Belzen, JA (1999) 'Religion as embodiment: cultural/psychological concepts and methods in the study of conversion among "Bevindelijken"' 28(2) *Journal for the Scientific Study of Religion* 236–53

Beyer, P₁(1994) *Religion and Globalization*, London: Sage

Boissevain, J, and Verrips, J (eds) (1989) *Dutch Dilemmas: Anthropologists Look at the Netherlands*, Assen: Van Gorcum

Bowker, J (1999) 'Introduction: raising the issues', in Holm, J, and Bowker, J (eds), *Making Moral Decisions*, London: Pinter

Brasher, BE (1998) *Godly Women: Fundamentalism and Female Power*, New Jersey: Rutgers UP

Bruce, S (1996) *Religion in the Modern World: From Cathedrals to Cults*, Oxford: OUP

Coleman, JA (1978) *The Evolution of Dutch Catholicism, 1958–1974*, Berkeley, CA: California UP

Dillon, M (1999) *Catholic Identity: Balancing Reason, Emotion, and Power*, Cambridge: CUP

Featherstone, M (ed) (1990) *Global Culture: Nationalism, Globalization and Modernity*, London: Sage

Giddens, A (1991) *Modernity and Self Identity*, Cambridge: Polity

Griffin, DR (1989a) *God and Religion in the Postmodern World*, New York: State University of New York Press

Griffin, DR (ed) (1989b) *Varieties of Postmodern Theology, New York*: State University of New York Press

Grove-White, R (1993) 'Environmentalism: a new moral discourse for technological society?', in Milton, K (ed), *Environmentalism: The View from Anthropology*, London and New York: Routledge, pp 18–30

Hawkins, JM (ed) (1988) *Oxford Reference Dictionary*, London: Guild Publishing

Howell, S (1997) 'Introduction', in Howell, S (ed), *The Ethnography of Moralities*, London and New York: Routledge, pp 1–24

Kapferer, B (1988) *Legends of People, Myths of State: Violence, Intolerance and Political Culture in Sri Lanka and Australia*, Washington and London: Smithsonian Institution Press

Knippenberg, H (1992) *De Religieuze Kaart van Nederland: Omvang en geografische spreiding van de godsdienstige gezindten vanaf de Reformatie tot heden*, Assen: Van Gorcum

Laarse, R, van der (1989) *Bevoogding en Bevinding: Heren en Kerkelijk in een Hollandse Provinciestad, Woerden 1780–1930*, StichtsHollandse Bijdragen 21, s'Gravenhage: Stichting Hollandse Historische Reeks

Lash, S, and Friedman, J (1992) *Modernity and Identity*, Oxford: Blackwell

Lijphart, A (1975) *The Politics of Accommodation: Pluralism and Democracy in the Netherlands*, Berkeley, CA: California UP

McBrien, R (1994) *Catholicism*, London: Geoffrey Chapman

McGrath, AE (1994) *Reformation Thought: An Introduction*, Oxford: Blackwell

Miedema, N (1989) 'Orthodox protestants and enforced marriage', in Boissevain, J and Verrips, J (eds), *Dutch Dilemmas: Anthropologists Look at the Netherlands*, Assen: Van Gorcum, pp 5–23

Overing, J (1985) 'Introduction', in Overing, J (ed), *Reason and Morality*, London and New York: Tavistock Publications

Parkin, D (1985) 'Reason, emotion, and the embodiment of power', in Overing, J (ed), *Reason and Morality*, London and New York: Tavistock Publications, pp 135–51

Shetter, WZ (1987) *The Netherlands in Perspective*, Leiden: Martinus Nijhoff

Taylor, L (1983) *Dutchmen on the Bay: The Ethnohistory of a Contractual Community*, Philadelphia: Pennsylvania UP

Tennekes, H (1988) 'Religion and power: modernization processes in Dutch Protestantism', in Quarles van Ufford, P and Schoeffeleers, M (eds), *Religion and Development: Towards an Integrated Approach*, Amsterdam: Free University Press, pp 31–52

UBS (United Bible Societies) (1991) *Good News Bible: Today's English Version*, Glasgow: HarperCollins

Watling, T (1999) 'Negotiating religious pluralism: the dialectical development of religious identities in the Netherlands', unpublished PhD thesis, University of London

Watling, T (2001a) 'A new Reformation for a "secularised" world? Retaining "tradition" while accommodating "change": the dialectics of the ecumenical movement in the Netherlands' 16(1) *Journal of Contemporary Religion* 85–104

Watling, T (2001b) 'The continuing Reformation? Religious processes and national identity in the Netherlands' 25(1) *Dutch Crossing: A Journal of Low Countries Studies* 1–25

Watling, T (2001c) '"Official" doctrine and "unofficial" practices: the negotiation of Catholicism in a Netherlands community' 40(4) *Journal for the Scientific Study of Religion* 573–90

Watling, T (2002) '"Leadership" or "dialogue"? Women, authority, and religious change in a Netherlands community' 63(4) *Sociology of Religion* 515–38

Weber, M (1991) *The Protestant Ethic and the Spirit of Capitalism*, London: HarperCollins

Wintle, MJ (1987) *Pillars of Piety: Religion in the Netherlands in the Nineteenth Century, 1813–1901*, Hull: Hull UP

Woodhead, L and Heelas, P (eds) (2000) *Religion in Modern Times: An Interpretive Anthology*, London: Blackwell

MORALITIES IN CONFLICT: AMBIGUITIES OF IDENTITY AND SOCIAL CONTROL FOR FILIPINA DOMESTIC HELPERS IN MALAYSIA

Michelle Lee Guy

INTRODUCTION[1]

Increased cross-border movements of people, business and industrial organisations have transcended geographical and cultural boundaries. On the one hand, the dissemination of information, people, goods and materials is accentuated; on the other, a more fluid and mobile population of transmigrants is established. While mainstream studies of migration have largely focused on migration flows, international production, law, history and the division of labour,[2] the ambiguities of identity and moral values faced by migrants in relation to their culture, community and personal aspirations have less often been analysed.

The conflict of moral values between migrant community and personal self-interest, as well as the negotiations of social control imposed by the host community, affect the process of identity construction for migrants. This chapter explores the relationship between identity and morality through an ethnographic analysis of Filipina migrants' experiences as domestic workers in Malaysia. As migrants and workers, Filipinas are inevitably subject to the social values, moral judgments and expectations based on their gender, whether in their home or host societies. The interaction and negotiation of power are especially intense for Filipina domestic helpers and their (female) employers, due to the intimacy of their regular interactions in the employer's house. Outside the house, Filipinas have to deal with close surveillance by local authorities, as well as by the Filipino migrant community, which expects normative (Filipino) behaviour and the maintenance of collective morale. In addition, migrants are caught in the dilemma of the need to fulfil moral obligations to their families, and to satisfy their own individual aspirations. The development of migrants' self-identity is filtered through social expectations, values and surveillance in the host and home countries. Although Filipinas are vulnerable both as migrants and women, they

---

1   This chapter is a part of my PhD research. I would like to thank Dr Nanneke Redclift (UCL), Professor John Gledhill and Professor Shamsul Amri (UKM) who have given me precious advice and support. All names referred to in the chapter have been changed to preserve anonymity.

2   See, for example, Skeldon 1992, Sassen-Koob 1983, Nayagam 1992, and Wang 1997.

have their own ways of demonstrating resistance to unreasonable treatment. This chapter examines these conflicts of self and collective morality, in the context of the disciplinary mechanisms exerted by employers and among the migrant community itself.

CONCEPTS OF SELFLESSNESS AND RELATEDNESS

Due to a rich and diverse cultural mix resulting from a relatively long period of colonisation, a variety of social values and practices can be identified in the Philippines.[3] However, prevalent and dominant values centre around notions of selflessness and relatedness. It is not unusual to find that there is a tension between self-assertion (individualism) and the collective values shown by individual Filipinos. This could be exemplified by their much appreciated skill of building smooth interpersonal relations, meant to preserve harmonious and reciprocal relations with each other or within a collective group/community; while at the same time, personal interests can be negotiated. An exploration of the ambiguous demonstration of self-identity and obligations to the collectivity is therefore necessary.

Shaping the moral domain are the key concepts of *utang na loob*, *pakikisama*, *hiya* and *amor propio*. *Utang na loob*, a concept and practice with a long history, is still proudly observed in Filipino society (Andres 1984, Cannell 1999: 11). The term means 'debt of the inner self' or a 'feeling of indebtedness which is incurred when one receives a favor, service or good, and a deep sense of obligation to reciprocate when the appropriate moment comes' (Andres, 1984: 25, see also Gochenour 1990). This pattern of reciprocity requires that every indebted person should return a token of favour to the creditor, involving a moral obligation for a lifetime (Trager 1988: 77–78). For example, children are expected to be eternally grateful and generous to their parents or older siblings who have looked after them. If a person gets a job from a friend, a lifetime of kindness is owed to the friend as well as the readiness to return a favour whenever necessary. The expectation to return the 'favour' or kindness is a common moral obligation for many Filipinos. To their families, sacrifice and the suppression of personal aspirations are needed to fulfil such an obligation. This value of moral indebtedness is commonly observed, and if neglected an individual is marked as immoral, irresponsible or *walang utang na loob*.

Moral obligation and indebtedness also go hand-in-hand with pakikisama (belongingness or to get along with) and *hiya* (shame). *Pakikisama* denotes an essential sense of belonging to a community or a group. It stresses the solidarity and *utang na loob* existing amongst members – who could be friends or peers, gangsters or relatives – and therefore strengthens collectivity or relationship. *Pakikisama* reinforces family, kinship and in-group ties; members can always get help from each other in terms of financial assistance, services, employment, emotional support and other sorts of favours. This is particularly evident in the popular Filipino practice of god-parenthood or *compadrazco*. Godparents are

3   The Philippines were colonised for more than 350 years, first by Spain and later the United States. It obtained independence in 1946.

accepted as the second parents for the godchild. They are expected to provide support and kindness to the child, and its parents should the need arise, and the child is supposedly indebted to the godparents as long as it lives. The relatedness in this system illuminates a closely-knit social network or safety net.

Betrayal, wickedness or bad behaviour in relation to family, relatives, community or a creditor causes *hiya* or shame. It leads to humiliation and resentment, causing the individual to be regarded as *walang hiya* or without shame. Hence, *hiya* is a social sanction that can regulate behaviour, a measure of right and wrong, social approval and disapproval. It is, I would argue, a moral tool used, consciously or unconsciously by Filipino migrants to 'monitor' their own behaviour, while at the same time, it strengthens the ties among them wherever they are, reminding them about the purpose of their migration, their families and country.

To avoid *hiya*, *amor-propio* (self-respect, self-esteem) is essential. Migrants strive to sustain amor proprio by adhering to cultural and religious practices, and maintaining smooth interpersonal relations and family pride. Thus, respect and priority given to family and kinsmen always comes first, frequently at the individual's expense, often leading to the sacrifice of individual needs or welfare. Nevertheless, an *utang na loob* to an opposing group or a family enemy is considered *walang hiya*, and *walang amor-propio*.

Filipinos are constantly aware of their behaviour and their social environment; they consciously avoid hiya and conflicts with others in every way, and maintain their own *amor propio*. Thus, 'smooth interpersonal relations' (SIR) are essential in daily life. On occasion, in sensitive situations that may bring embarrassment, conflict and tension, an intermediary may also be needed. An intermediary or go-between acts as the middleman to avoid face-to-face encounters, and would tactfully 'smooth' a harsh situation. However, graft and bribery are often the accompanying factors required to achieve personal interests. In this case, the receiver is obliged to fulfil the 'task', while the provider owes him a long-term favour, that is, *utang na loob*. Thus, this further reinforces and perpetuates the sense of obligation in social interaction and reciprocity (Steinberg 1990: 4–6).

This web of moral obligation, relatedness and self-interest is an intrinsic part of migrants' presentation of identity. Because they come from the same country and have a common economic ambition abroad, they share a collective identity. However, achieving ambition is a personal goal, backed by different individual's experiences. The negotiation of self and collective is thus indispensable to sustain smooth interpersonal relationships.

Migrants therefore develop and maintain diverse identities both in their home and host societies. As Rouse (1995) asserts, 'it is necessary to go beyond the assumption that identities are invariably "localized" and recognize that many (im)migrants have in fact developed multi-local and transnational affiliation', and that transmigrants 'have acquired multiple identities, combining old and new in a broadened repertoire of possible associations', as well as in 'the multi-local settings that now frame their lives' (Rouse 1995: 354). The Filipina migrants in my research illuminate such complexity and flexibility of identities and these are often unveiled in their interactions with local residents, employers, fellow immigrants and local authorities. The effects of transnationalism (see also Rouse

1995 and Schiller, Basch and Blanc-Szanton 1992) and collectivism are also revealed when they confront unequal treatment, demand immigrants' and workers' rights, or look out for each other.

REPRESENTATIONS OF PERSON AND COMMUNITY

My research suggested that the word 'we' would be used rhetorically to represent oneself and/or the community, or the whole nation. The word 'I' was usually articulated only when a conversation is carried out in a more interpersonal setting, such as one to one or in a small group. This is not without reason, as migrants are cautious in presenting individual opinions in the presence of fellow Filipinos, particularly to those who are older and/or possess influential social status in the community.

In the presence of other fellow Filipinos, migrants often said, 'we are used to helping our families whether we are married or single', 'it is normal for Filipinos to take care of their families' and 'religion is very important for us'. However, in our one-to-one interviews, they tended to say, 'I want to help my family, even though I have to sacrifice'; 'I plan to set up a business after I finish my contract here'; 'I want to go to the United States, but it's impossible to do now because I haven't got enough money. My children's education is more important'; 'I'd like to go to school, I'd like to study ... but I know I can't continue. So I work together with my sister to earn some money to help my parents'; 'if it's possible, I'd like to stay in Malaysia'.

In another example, referring to the case of Narina, a victim of repeated rapes by her employer, most members of the migrant community appeared to be sympathetic and concerned about her unfortunate experiences. When the case was brought up during my meetings with the Filipina community, they unanimously expressed support for Narina and a fund was collected to help her and her mother, who was also working for the same employer. In our private conversations, however, they showed different reactions. I was told, 'I don't think she was actually raped'; 'she just accused him of raping her because her plan failed. I think she wanted to have a relationship with her boss, so that she could live a better life like her sister did in the Philippines'; 'she is lying. She told me on the phone that she had sex with her boss seven times, but she told the police that she was raped four times. How could she have remembered all the dates?'; 'I don't think she was raped, because I talked to the neighbour and she told me, and told the police, that she saw Narina and her boss were kissing and hugging lovingly on the veranda'. These expressions of personal views contrast with the collective identity, formed and expressed in the presence of other community members to conform to *pakikisama*, avoid *hiya* and to protect *amor propia* both as an individual and on behalf of the nation.

The manipulation of metaphors accentuates the ambiguity of identity. When a Filipina uses the term 'we', it could mean 'I' (as an individual) or 'the Filipinos' as a nation (as a collective identity); this further justifies the relatedness and the sense of being recognised as a member of the community (*pakikisama*), henceforth the obligation to protect the community. Nevertheless, such protection and perpetuation of a collective image may enhance the boundary between Filipina workers, and their employers and host society as will be discussed later.

INDIVIDUALISM AND COLLECTIVITY

As Lukes argues:

> it was in the United States that 'individualism' primarily came to celebrate capitalism and liberal democracy. It became a symbolic catchword of immense ideological significance, expressing all that has at various times been implied in the philosophy of natural rights, the belief in free enterprise. (1973: 26)

These values underpin the illusion of the 'American Dream', which has drawn people around the world to the United States. It provides the background for the formation of cross-cultural identities closely linked to the effect of colonisation, which has in turn enhanced the growth of 'the "new diasporas" created by the colonial experience and the ensuing post-colonial migrations' (Cohen 1997: 131). In the Philippines, the legacy of American colonialism resulted in the celebration of democracy and liberalism and accelerated the formation of individualism. Post-colonial migration encouraged the spread of Filipino diasporas all over the world. Based on the imagination of and admiration for the west and the values of liberalism and prosperity, Filipino migrants often envisage 'greener pastures' overseas, in their effort to find ways and means to emigrate for work, escape from hardship at home, and elevate the social and economic status of their families.

Despite the emphasis on close-knit family and kin ties, as shown in the concepts of *pakikisama* and *utang na loob*, there appears to be a strong sense of individuality woven in the collective image of the migrant community in Malaysia. Affected by American culture, the ideology of freedom, democracy, free enterprise, and individual liberalism and the extended impact of capitalism on self satisfaction, recognition and consumption; many Filipino migrants strive courageously for economic achievements, ambition and freedom across national borders. For those who stay in the country, the imagination of the 'American dream' and Western 'superiority' also plays an important part in their lives and are articulated in various ways.[4] Filipina migrants in Malaysia reveal the complexity of identity asserted by Cohen:

> selfhood, the representation of one's own community and other communities, as well as the differences between the two are ... negotiated in strange, hitherto unexplored and fluid 'frontlines' and 'borderposts' of identities.

He argues that this is a result of the 'overlapping edges, the ambiguities, the displacements of difference, and the mixing of cultures, religions, languages and ethnicities' (Cohen 1997: 129).

Thus, in the case of transmigrants, the contradictions (within oneself, and between one's community and the host societies) and the ambiguity of identities are reciprocal effects of transmigration process.

---

4   Such as through consumption (eg, fast food, beverages, clothing and speech), media (television, magazines, printed advertisements) and sports (basketball, American football and rugby).

In relation to personal identity, the representation of self not only prevails in personal behaviour and the use of metaphor. It is also prevalent in the Filipino migrant community, and traceable in their interactions, communication and expressions of feelings toward each other, and to others outside the community. The representation of self and interactions in the community is an interdependent and reciprocal practice that, according to McTaggart, is structured in such a way that 'the individual is an end, the society is only a means' (cited in Lukes 1973: 50). In other words, besides acting as the representative of the migrant group, the Filipino migrant community in the guise of its formal organisations (which include the Filipino Ministry, church, and community social and religious activities) are also utilised as the means for personal achievement. In this sense, the individuals' ultimate ends are to work and earn wages to fulfil their own and their households' immediate needs. While these needs are individually based and not a collective objective or practice, the migrant community and formal organisations can also be used or exploited to provide support and grounds for achieving personal objectives. Collective images are therefore, mobilised by individual transmigrants to portray uniformity and transnationalism. This phenomenon echoes the research by Basch *et al* (1994) on Filipino organisations in the United States. These organisations mobilise Filipino migrants in the US to contribute financial and political support for political campaigns in the Philippines.

Collectivity within the migrant community in Malaysia, is reflected in organised activities, such as the celebration of Philippine Independence Day, outdoor and/or religious activities, conferences between the community, Malaysian authorities, and employers, or meetings with local NGOs' representatives. This collectivity is also evident when migrants confront non-Filipinos, or when there is a national or community message to be articulated as a collective interest such as issues pertaining to the minimum wage or rest days.

Selected examples exemplify the complex representations of self and collectivity. The issue of the regulation of the migrant's day off provides an important case in point. During the period of my fieldwork for this project, arrangements were made for the parties involved to meet and discuss the issue. It was agreed that the migrants would discuss collective interests before the meeting and the questions or suggestions also represent individuals' interests. However, during the meeting, any questions asked or any suggestions made would comprise a collective voice. In retrospect, in all the focus group meetings I held with the migrants, each participant tended to speak for herself or to put her own point of view, even if this involved raising her voice. However, when I raised a subject pertaining to 'the Philippines' or 'Philippine society', most of them would be quiet, listening to the eldest participant, who spoke for the group.

Another issue is that of dealing with conflict. When a conflict of interest occurs between an individual and the migrant community or other formal organisations, discussions are held or the individual refers to other resources, such as kin or other social networks. Nevertheless, formal organisations are likely to be blamed when individual's interests are not upheld. This was clear in Narina's case. She felt that she was not given enough support or concern from the Philippine Embassy in Kuala Lumpur and the Filipino Ministry. A meeting was held between

Narina, her mother, and the advisor and other members of the Filipino Ministry. In the meeting, Narina wanted the advisor to apologise and resign for her alleged incompetence to lead the Ministry, and to stop spreading gossip about the allegation of rape. She also accused the Ministry and the Philippine Embassy of treating her and her mother unjustly, citing bad accommodation, lack of money and problems with her visa extension.

Despite the migrants' expectation, relevant organisations such as the Philippine Embassy and the Filipino Ministry in Kuala Lumpur cannot do everything for them. Their dependence on these organisations appears to put pressure on bureaucratic relations and rapport with local authorities. Nevertheless, migrants are bound together by these formal organisations that provide not only a place to seek comfort, but more importantly, to form a collective group which serves as a safety net; or as mediators for collective bargaining with the Malaysian and the Philippine governments. Additionally, these formal organisations are established and operated on the basis of two factors – nationality and Christianity. In Malaysia, Filipinos are only allowed to form official associations and activities based on their religion. This is no doubt a strategy of the host country to regulate their activities. However, it has strengthened religion (Christianity) as a symbolic institution for Filipino solidarity.

The tension between individualism as opposed to collectivity is significant. Collectivity, in the case of the Filipino migrant community in Kuala Lumpur, is used as a protective measure and a portrayal of national image. This can also accentuate barriers between the community and the host society, and minimise assimilation. In addition, it crystallises boundaries and differences based on ethnicity, cultural practices and personal values between employers and employees in the intimate setting of the home. Furthermore, when surveillance is widespread and freedom is circumscribed, individualism is accentuated and community may also provide a vehicle for the pursuit of personal goals.

SOCIAL CONTROL AND DISCIPLINE

This section discusses the disciplinary mechanisms used by employers in relation to their helpers. Bounded by a work contract and relevant immigration rules, and flooded by news or allegation of migrant deviance, employers feel that it is their responsibility to keep domestic helpers out of trouble. Control and careful monitoring are therefore deemed necessary. However, social control and discipline are also in evidence among the migrant community itself and gossip is not only used as a way of communication and interaction, but also to enforce conformity and adherence to cultural values.

The stratification of social status and power between the helper and the employer is clear. Differences of culture, social status, ethnicity, nationality and religion create the context for hierarchical relationships between employers and helpers. They give rise to the imposition of power and control by the employer, which in turn strengthens the distance between the two. The practice of power is exemplified by the rules and regulations set by the employer, and the employer's practice of placing a relative in the house to keep an eye on the helper at all times. Barriers (between employers and employees) are further enhanced by giving the helper a small bedroom at the back of the house, denominating the space and time for her every activity, by insisting that she addresses the employer 'Sir', or 'Ma'am', or by setting detailed work and time schedules for the helper and monitoring her activities outside as well as inside the house.

Domestic helpers usually work very long hours. Many are required to get up before six in the morning and do not retire before nine. Some have to extend their work hours into the night, especially if there are infants, elderly or sick people in the household. For example, Lynn often had to attend to her employer's baby when she cried at night, while Jenny had to offer her services whenever a social function is held at a relative's house.

Some employers also used to phone home at least once a day from their workplace. They would either speak to the children, to a live-in relative or to the helper, to find out if everything was all right and to make sure that the helper was doing what she was told. Control was also extended to the image and identity of the Filipinas in the public sphere: managing the time (and frequently the space) for helpers to work, rest or interact with others, and their dress and appearances when they leave the house. They were seldom allowed to wear 'pretty' clothes, adornments or make-up; they are allowed to go to the church but must be back at a certain time. Some employers even take their helpers to church on Sundays and pick them up, to make sure that they do not go astray.

This kind of control has also been documented in other locations. Filipina domestic workers in Hong Kong face similar treatment and the practice is extended to personal or physical appearance, such as making sure that the helper's hair is cut short before her first arrival in the employer's house (Constable 1997a, 1997b). Furthermore, the helper's personal belongings are regularly scrutinised. Chin sees such practices by middle class employers in Malaysia as resulting from their superior status as the 'household supervisor-manager' (Chin 1998: 130). But disciplinary practices can also be seen as more far-reaching, extending to the State's exercise of control through its implementation of stringent, yet often inconclusive, immigration rulings and strict selection of migrants (Lee Guy, 2003).

Social control and the exercise of power by local society or employers are closely connected to public concern about Filipinas' images pertaining to their migrant status and occupation. Relevant news, public xenophobic opinions, a number of cases of apparent misbehaviour (such as running away, crime, involvement in the sex trade and infidelity), and international communication furnish the source for the circulation of information and gossip. Because little is generally known about their culture and there are various unfavourable reports about their home country (such as political instability, widespread poverty, etc), most members of the host society choose to only see or interact with Filipina migrants in a public and impersonal capacity. For the migrants, gatherings on their day off frequently involve carrying out in public what are generally considered by the local population to be private or indoor activities, such as nail polishing, hairdressing and comforting, and they speak in languages that most locals do not understand. This is seen as a threat or moral challenge to existing patterns of local norms and authority. Unfortunately, all these heighten public concern and suspicion toward the migrants.

The concern over the allegedly immoral, provocative and promiscuous behaviour of migrants in public, particularly during free time, also accentuates public suspicion about their sexuality. This is perhaps due to the belief that the helper's sexual desire and freedom, strictly restrained when they work in the house for 28 days a month, would consequentially be given full rein on their day off. Unfortunately, gossip and the exchange of news and information about migrants 'misbehaviour' amongst the host society is inevitable. Therefore, many of the employers whom I talked to said that they felt it necessary to control to constrain the helpers' mobility and sexual expression, and thus naturally, impose their own moral values on them.

On the other hand, Filipina migrants are fully aware of the 'reputation' associated with their nationality and occupation and take initiatives to sustain self-discipline and to monitor each other's behaviour as a response. Intra-community gossip is also one of the mechanisms used to curtail deviant acts in order to manage the favourable collective image which is particularly important for them in terms of job security.

As a form of communication and interaction, gossip is an exchange of information about the character or actions of others. The accuracy of such information is, however taken for granted; and often, the truth or root of the information is not pivotal. In other words, there is something to talk about although the listener(s) or the informer(s) may not have access to the reality of whatever they are gossiping about. It usually involves some form of impression, information and/or reputation management on the part of the speaker and can, on occasions, be a source of empowerment for the person who talks about or makes moral judgments on others. It also has social and psychological functions that tie individuals together, provides information, and enforces normative behaviour.[5]

Gossip has frequently been defined in social anthropology as a forceful mechanism through which cultural normativity is reinforced, thus marking the boundaries of a moral community (Gluckman 1963). As an act of information transaction, it therefore becomes an indirect impetus to propel individuals to conform to socially sanctioned patterns of normative behaviour (Abraham 1970). It is presumed that individuals, in a particular social setting (or an encounter where the gossip takes place), share an awareness of the moral codes and patterns of acceptable/unacceptable manners. On the one hand, the setting reflects a particular social structure where the performance of gossip is embedded, be it in a community, group, institution or between two persons. On the other hand, it also demonstrates the social relations in an encounter (between the performer and receiver), the purpose and expectation of that encounter, whether this is explicit or not.

For example, Rima has been going out with a fellow Filipino for a while and they had spent a lot of time together away from the migrant community. Her absence had, however, caused suspicion among the community. They started to

---

5   See Handelman (1973), and Abraham (1970) for details on purposes, and anthropological perspectives on gossip.

gossip about her intention of keeping the boyfriend out of the community; saying that she was selfish and only interested in his money. After a while, the gossip began to affect their relationship, so Rima disclosed the relationship and explained to others that she wanted to be certain and confident about it, before she could introduce the boyfriend to everyone.

Self-consciousness and discipline is important to enable each individual to be accepted by fellow migrants. This is extended to migrants' reputation as 'good' helpers, and it also carries national pride. Migrants are particularly sensitive about gossip pertaining to their intentions in relation to migration and job selection. They resent the news that circulates in the host society that Filipina migrants are poor, promiscuous, stupid and their work as domestic helpers is low status. They believe that as long as they do their job well, they deserve respect and reasonable pay. To avoid being labelled by fellow migrants and members of the host society, many migrants such as Gin and her friends prefer to take part in activities in the church, or spend most of their day off in the community. They asserted that they could save some money and from being accused of being lazy, 'man-hunters' or as sex workers.

Criticisms and teasing are also used among migrants as a way of ensuring the maintenance of discipline and normative image, particularly in terms of clothing and self-presentation. Interviews and observations during the research period suggested that there was a common code of dress and image connected with being a domestic helper, and a notion that if one is not dressed accordingly (too revealing, excessive make-up and accessories), it would cause trouble. This might include public objection, attempts at molestation by the employer or by men in general, or comments that she does not behave like a domestic helper should. Filipinas who wore revealing clothing were often teased by others in the community, either by asking if they were going to a party, or saying that they were selling their body or trying to attract men. Although often done humorously, the message is straightforward.

Constable's (1997a) research revealed that Filipinas in Hong Kong also exert control and discipline over each other through the reiteration of stories, jokes and fellow migrants' experiences, and by writing and publishing articles, poems or letters in local community magazines. The magazines described by Constable appear to be similar to the newsletter *Sandigan* published in Kuala Lumpur. *Sandigan* mostly publishes official news related to immigration and labour rules, overseas Filipino workers, and reports of the Philippine Embassy in Kuala Lumpur, but also contains a small contribution of letters, poems and articles from Filipino workers in Malaysia, mostly to express feelings and experiences. These writings not only show Filipinas' own motivation towards self-disciplinary practices, they also illustrate the tendency of migrant workers to accept and internalise their subservient positions.

Gossip and the articulation of personal stories or grievances between a female employer and her helper also occur within the house. In such situations, it is understood that the female employer is perhaps seeking support, sympathy and relatedness from the helper. The helper may see this as a gesture of confiding in a friend or a family member; but she may also see it, on the contrary, as an emotional burden which she does not need to add to her own endurances. For example, Mimi's employer often talked about her restricted physical mobility and helplessness since she had a bad fall, when formerly she had assisted her husband in his business and managed the household on her own. However, her excessive demands and ill temper caused irritation, exhaustion and apathy on Mimi's part.

In other instances, gossip about foreign helpers takes place between employers. They exchange stories and strategies, or accumulate news and information from other employers or newspapers about foreign helpers' misfortune and misbehaviour. These are then transferred to the helper in order to justify that she has been very lucky and well treated. However, the helper's discontent, sufferings and lack of support may not be the employer's concern.

SUBTLE RESISTANCE

It is not unusual to find that migrants have to deal with discrimination and disrespect on a daily basis and there are limited channels for them to voice their anxieties and complaints. This is particularly true for domestic helpers who are restricted in the house and by their employers. In most cases, even the most subtle resistance is likely to generate a very tense, hostile or mechanical relationship between the employer and the helper. Due to surveillance by local authorities and insufficient support from the Philippine Embassy, widespread public protest is almost impossible for migrants in Malaysia. However, even though they are not as articulate and aggressive as their counterparts in Hong Kong who utilise public protest and demonstrations (Constable 1997a), Filipinas in Malaysia have shown subtle forms of resistance and reacted to unfair treatments and subordination in their own way. For example, Elena was often requested to do extra work for her female employer (such as going to the bank, doing photocopies or helping out in the Chinese temple). Instead of saying no, Elena told her male employer and his adult children that she could not cope with so much work. In this way she used the male employer as a conduit to his wife. To show silent protest, Elena would sometimes take a long time to complete her tasks outside the house, and would go to the shops on her own to make telephone calls to her friends in Kuala Lumpur.

In another instance, Mona had to work in the house and a laundry shop owned by her employer. She did not like the long hours she had to put in for the limited salary she receives. So, she would slow down at work when her employer was absent or she withheld customers' requests and delayed deliveries. On the other hand, Ilona negotiated her terms and conditions of work with her employer as a reaction to her employer's request for her to work in another house on a regular basis. As a result, she gained half a day off on Saturdays in addition to her weekly day off on Sundays; and she was allowed to go out in the evening during the week.

Raids in churches or other public spaces by government authorities also generated discontent among migrants. The authorities' disrespect for their religion and disapproval of their public gathering on Sundays have not diminished migrants' faith, and their persistence in maintaining social networks and meeting in public. Filipinas continue to attend Sunday masses and gather at and around the church. Various services and goods (including beauty services, adornments, stamps, clothing, food) are sold either by locals or migrants, at the vicinity of the Cathedral. This is made possible because the migrants pay money to local council officers who are in charge of the area. Furthermore, an advance notice or tip-off will be given to vendors or hawkers before official raids. They assert that after six days of obedience and abiding to rules in the house, they have the right to socialise and enjoy their day off. They sometimes wear make-up, accessories and clothing that are normally not allowed in the house; or see their boyfriends, cook Filipino food in their friend's houses, and listen or dance to the kind of music they like. Many Filipinas enjoy doing manicures, having their hair done or going shopping, or having fun with friends and relatives at their gathering place in the vicinity of St John's Cathedral. Apart from paying low rates (compared to local services) and helping other migrants, it is a direct way of reminiscing about home.

Some of the complexities surrounding protest are also illustrated in the case of Narina which we have already discussed. She reported the alleged rapes to which her employer had subjected her to the police and the press made extended coverage on the case. This would appear to be a positive assertion of her personal rights and resistance to abuse and discrimination. However, Narina's action produced two repercussions. First, apart from losing her job, she also had face the loss of *hiya* and *amor propia* in relation to the Filipino community itself. Secondly, Narina and her mother were avoided by fellow migrants and, as we have seen, there was negative gossip about her allegation. Her ex-employer made a statement to the Malaysian Foreign Affair Ministry, in which he claimed that the sexual initiative came from Narina and he did not have sex without her consent.[6] Despite the sexual vulnerability of migrant workers and the gender/power dynamics of the case, which might have led to pressure for further legal exploration of the facts, the gossip about the case amongst Filipino migrants was a subtle protest against Narina and her mother who had brought moral opprobrium and a somewhat negative public attention to the migrant community.

GENDER, SUBORDINATION AND AGENCY

Filipina transmigration and the relationships between (female) employers and domestic helpers illustrate the significance of transactions between women in domestic service and their social networks. The processes of transmigration and domestic service suggest that, despite the subordination of migrants in the host society and domestic sphere, women are moral agents.

Previous studies of transmigration and the discourses of the public and private spheres emphasised the subordination experienced by women. I would also suggest, however, that despite the inequality inherent in their structural position, a certain marginalisation of men is also implicated in Filipina transmigration for domestic service. Although decisions for transmigration are made as part of their household survival strategies, Filipinas are eager to establish networks with their female kin on whom they particularly rely. For example, in

6   The statement was faxed from the Ambassador's country of origin when he was retrieved by his employer. It was published in local newspapers.

getting financial assistance for overseas placements, childcare, and to handle remittances, Filipinas usually go to the foreign employment agencies by themselves or accompanied by a girlfriend or a female family member. They would often borrow money from their aunts, and as noted, the majority of married women left their children in the care of their mothers or female relatives.

In domestic service, there are also several indications of co-operation between women, rather than between men and women in the household. Sharing of household chores and childcare, communication and resolution of differences are usually done by female employers and Filipina helpers. Domestic service is inherently women's 'business'. This was clearly indicated by some of the male employers I spoke with, who often told me to 'talk to my wife, she handles this. It's women's business'. Interactions between female employers and employees are mainly household-based; however, even when the female employer was away from the house, there were still limited interactions between the male employer and the helper. Female employers would communicate with the helper and give instructions through telephone calls. For instance, Gin's female employer called from Canada on a holiday to tell Gin to do certain chores for the male employer who stayed behind.

In terms of gender relations, the Filipino's notion of the private and public spheres is related to household and kin relationships, and the political and economic relations outside the household. Without hesitation, Filipinas in my research applied the term 'useless' to describe men who were unable to provide for their families. Men were seen as peripheral not only in the process of Filipina transmigration, but also in the continuity of their households. Men were also seen as inefficient in maintaining a household without women's help and support. This resulted in the practice of Filipina migrants leaving their children with female kin. Although male partners were inevitably included in the web of romantic love and women's notion of relatedness, they are not embedded in Filipinas' ideology of sacrifice. Children, natal family members and kin were often at the core of this ideology.

Beyond this marginalisation of men, the subordination of women, particularly of transmigrants, prevails. Within the Malaysian households I studied, collective income and financial collaboration between the husband and wife illustrates an underlying co-operation between them. The complementary manner of gender relations may signify the accommodation of differences. However, it does not diminish the subordination of women in the household, which can now be diverted to Filipina domestic helpers who are relatively vulnerable and of a lower status. This is highly relevant to the power relations and juxtapositions of employers and employees as mentioned earlier. The intersection of the public (waged work and transmigration) and the private (the household) in domestic service created a more complex stratification of power and the subjugation of women by women, as well as co-operation among women in the household (female employers and helpers relations).

THE PARADOX OF FREEDOM AND DEPENDENCE

Transmigration for work has given the opportunity for Filipinas to generate income for the survival of themselves and their families; it also provides the pathway to freedom and independence. The appreciation of freedom and independence amongst the Filipinas is not difficult to trace from their verbal and physical presentations, as well as their behaviour. Although Filipinos in general have a flair for beauty, which is shown in their regular beauty pageant competitions and elaborated celebrations of all kinds (such as birthdays, anniversaries, baptisms, weddings), financial constraints limit the frequency of these forms of expression, particularly in the poor areas where most of the Filipinas came from. In Kuala Lumpur, Filipina migrants often dress up on their day off. Conversations, more often than not, revolve around appearance, accessories, and the presentation of new purchases. This is one of the reasons for the flourishing direct sales business among the migrants.

Being away from home means being free from parental domination and local social constraints. The ability to earn an income themselves means the Filipinas have control of their own salaries. Even though there are always reminders from home to send remittances, they reserve the decision on the amount and regularity of remittances. Being far away from home, and from parental and home community surveillance, the Filipinas are relatively autonomous in their movements and social engagements outside the household or workplace. It is hardly a surprise that engagement in sex work, conjugal relationships, and adultery whilst abroad are kept secret from their families back home. Migrants themselves seldom discuss these subjects within their community, or with outsiders. I encountered this secretiveness on several occasions. For instance, when I tried to talk to one of the local employment agents outside St John's cathedral, his Filipino wife who was standing beside him turned and walked away and he was reluctant to disclose her occupation. When Mona started to develop a relationship with her Filipino boyfriend in Kuala Lumpur, they were very cautious not to show any signs of mutual interest when they were in the migrant community. Later, when I had seen them walking or dining together, she revealed the relationship.

Freedom and independence are therefore, not without constraints. In fact, they are often susceptible to stigmatisation and subjective moral judgments, due to social expectations. For instance, Flora was a polite and pleasant girl. She however had a habit of borrowing money from her friends in and outside the Filipino Ministry. Apparently, she spent a lot of money on food for herself and her friends, and purchased goods on her day off, but she failed to pay her loans back. Nonetheless The news spread and the Filipino community boycotted her and her unacceptable behaviour was reported to the church vicar. Eventually, Flora went home after her work contract terminated without paying all her loans.

In another instance, the effect of the prevalent ideology of femininity on migrants was apparent in the dispute between Jenny and her Filipina friends in the neighbourhood where she worked. Jenny revealed that her close friends refused to talk to her. Stories circulated in the community about Jenny 'stealing' her girlfriend's 'lover', who is also a Filipina. Jenny was furious because she thought that being a lesbian was despicable. She said: 'They are crazy, why can't they see. They are all women and it is very big sin to God!' She further asserted that a woman's life is incomplete without having a family – husband and children – like her mother: 'if you are not married, you can't pay back your mother; you have to have children, like your mother.' The intent of *utang na loob* is apparent. Jenny further added that although she was not sure when she would get married, she would definitely stop working as a helper and stay home to take care of her children, like her mother did.

Jenny's experience shows a clash of moral practices in relation to sexuality. Religiously, Jenny thinks that it is unacceptable to develop passionate feelings for members of the same sex, but she wants to be friendly to her fellow migrants. Even though homosexuality is not uncommon in the Philippines,[7] the majority of the Filipinas who participated in my research claimed to dislike the idea of being personally involved. Therefore, apart from personal values and discipline, the general perception of morally acceptable behaviour poses challenges to individual moral identity.

CONCLUSION: MORALITY, SUBJECTIVE OR OBJECTIVE?

The international division of labour is highly gendered. Male and female migrants are channelled towards specific occupations. In the context we have discussed domestic service appears as a transaction between women in which men are largely peripheral. Filipinas' participation in transmigration, particularly for domestic service, demonstrates a contradiction: they experience increased freedom and agency, but at the same time have to endure subordination, surveillance and moral judgment.

This chapter has suggested that apart from work pressures and the negotiation of control and discipline, Filipina migrants, as their stories show, also face the dilemma of the competing demands of moral obligation and personal aspiration in the process of maintaining existing identities and dealing with new ones. As autonomous individuals they have personal preferences, education, experiences, beliefs and desires. They make judgments and decisions based on these subjective individual qualities. However, as an individual, he or she must live within the context of the collective norms and expectations that are frequently imposed upon the individual (by both the migrants and local communities). Their choices and actions are bound to be constrained and affected by these social attributes. Particularly in the vulnerable situation in which migrants find themselves, it is impossible for an individual to live outside any kind of community, or to assert personal will and needs without manipulating or being coercive of others. This paradox or conflict between the personal and communal indicates two points: (a) that there appears to be a set of authoritative and independent principal values or sanctions in each community which may be in tension; and (b) that in the migrant context personal emotions and preferences are particularly likely to be circumscribed by conflicting collective values and social constraints which must constantly be negotiated by the individual.

7   See Johnson (1997).

Although the final decision to migrate was made by each individual, it was usually made on the basis of the cost and benefits for their households. The ideology of moral obligation propels Filipinas to take up the responsibilities of household maintenance and reproduction. They endure various hardships while working abroad, and consistently conforming to the obligation of *utang na loob*, sustaining *pakikisama* both in their home and host societies, and protecting *amor propio*.

Because of this recognised 'sacrifice', migrants are seen by their families and government as heroines. In the host country, they will be accepted by the migrant community if they observe objective/communal moral values. They have to suppress subjective or personal desires not only to fulfil cultural obligations, they have to submit to the host society's (including the employers') moral expectations. Although Filipinas could negotiate between the subjective and the objective (through subtle resistance, and the imagination/hope of earning 'enough' money and to move on), they have limited resources due to the variety of constraints that their narratives have revealed.

The practice of gossip as a form of communication and control seems intriguingly effective among Filipino migrants. Although migrants are vulnerable to dirscrimination, they face it with courage and discipline. To sustain this, members of the migrant community have to assist each other, but at the same time, exert control and constraints among themselves. Therefore, transmigration illuminates the paradox of freedom and dependence. In the same context, migrants are caught in the dilemma of whether to hold on to personal aspirations or abide to collective values. This gives rise to a certain fluidity of identity, mobilised in different situations. In turn, the ability to negotiate their difficult circumstances reveals the flexibility of their language, culture and survival strategies.

BIBLIOGRAPHY

Abraham, RD (1970) 'A performance-centred approach to gossip' 5(5) *Man* 290–301

Andres, TQD (1984) *Understanding Filipino Values*, Quezon City: New Day Publishers

Basch, L, Schiller, NG and Blanc, CS (1994) *Nations Unbound: Transnational Projects, Postcolonial Predicaments and Deterritorialized Nation-States*, Switzerland: Gordon & Breach

Cannell, F (1999) *Power and Intimacy in the Christian Philippines*, Cambridge: CUP

Chin, CBN (1998) *In Service and Servitude: Foreign Female Domestic Workers and the Malaysian 'Modernity' Project*, New York: Columbia UP

Cohen, R (1997) *Global Diaspora: An Introduction*, London: UCL Press

Constable, N (1997a) *Maid to Order in Hong Kong: Stories of Filipina Workers*, Ithaca: Cornell UP

Constable, N (1997b) 'Sexuality and discipline among Filipina domestic workers in Hong Kong' 24(3) *American Ethnologist* 539–58

Gluckman, M (1963) 'Gossip and scandal' 4 *Current Anthropology* 307–16

Gochenour, T (1990) *Considering Filipino*, Yarmouth, USA: Intercultural Press

Handelman, D (1973) 'Gossip in encounters: the transmission of information in a bounded social setting' 2(8) *Man* 210–27

Johnson, M (1997) *Beauty and Power: Transgendering and Cultural Transformation in the Southern Philippines*, Oxford: Berg

Lee Guy, M (2000) *Female Transmigration in Southeast Asia: Filipina Domestic Helpers in Malaysia*, unpublished PhD thesis, University College London

Lee Guy, M (2003) 'Globalisation dilemmas: immigrants in Malaysia', in Welsh, B (ed), *Reflections: The Mahathir Years*, Washington, DC: Southeast Asia Studies, Johns Hopkins University/SAIS

Lukes, S (1973) *Individualism*, Oxford: Blackwell

Nayagam, J (1992) 'Migrant labor absorption in Malaysia' 1(3–4) *Asian and Pacific Migration Journal* 477–94

Rouse, R (1995) 'Questions of identity: personhood and collectivity in transnational migration to the United States' 15(4) *Critique of Anthropology* 351–80

Sassen-Koob, S (1983) 'Labor migration and the new international division of labor', in Nash, J and Fernandez-Kelly, MP (eds), *Women, Men and the International Division of Labor*, New York: State University of New York Press

Schiller, NG, Basch, L and Blanc-Szanton, C (1992) 'Towards a transnational perspective on migration: race, class, ethnicity, and nationalism reconsidered' *Annals of the New York Academy of Sciences*, pp 1–259

Skeldon, R (1992) 'International migration within and from the east and southeast Asian region: a review essay' 1(1) *Asian and Pacific Migration Journal* 19–63

Steinberg, DJ (1990) *The Philippines: A Singular and a Plural Place*, Boulder: Westview

Stivens, M (1998) 'Sex, gender and the making of the Malay middle classes', in Sen, K and Stivens, M (eds), *Gender and Power in Affluent Asia*, London and New York: Routledge

Trager, L (1988) *The City Connection: Migration and Family Interdependence in the Philippines*, Ann Arbor: Michigan UP

Wang, G (ed) (1997) *Global History and Migrations*, Boulder: Westview

PART 3

MORAL RHETORIC:
MEANINGS OF CONFLICT AND
VIOLENCE

CHAPTER 9

THE MIGRATORY MEANING OF TERROR: MORAL CONVERSATIONS FROM 'OTHER' AMERICAS

Nanneke Redcliff

Moral concepts have always been used to pursue political agendas. However, since the events of September 11 2001, the pervasive language of terror and freedom has come to dominate the global public sphere to an unprecedented degree. This generalising rhetoric conceals a myriad of complexities and is in turn likely to generate responses whose significance is only beginning to be understood. This chapter makes a preliminary attempt to look beneath this monolithic discourse. As Halliday (2002: 213) warns, the two conventional responses to great historical events, to say that nothing has changed or to say that everything has changed, are both misleading and preclude accurate analysis. Rather than assuming change, I take 9/11 as a critical moment or historical 'conjuncture' (Sahlins 1981), in which a new event radically inter-relates and re-combines existing beliefs and assumptions. Drawing on fieldwork in Mexico immediately after the attack on the Twin Towers, I examine the varied nature of the morally inflected conversations that developed in one specific place in reaction to news of the attacks. I explore the way in which critical events (Das 1995) and new historical conjunctures can generate a power of 'disclosure'. They lay bare incipient tensions and commitments, revealing a hitherto imperfectly grasped state of affairs, and generating a process of evaluation that is itself a social exchange. Taking an ethnographic example outside the immediate and misleading nexus of 'West' or 'Islam' helps to reveal the various ways in which people understood and responded to the moment of impact, made meaningful within the framework of their own beliefs, values and concerns.[1]

The concept of disclosure captures a moment when what is already incipiently in existence, but as yet unstated, becomes explicit, a point at which the unsayable is enacted, or apparently familiar territory re-codified. If Ground Zero can be thought of as an instance or site of such a process of re-signification, witnessed globally, how was it seen and interpreted in the myriad contexts of its spectators?

---

1 This paper is part of a broader project on the politics of cultural imagination in Yucatan, Mexico (2000–05). I would like to acknowledge the support of the British Academy and University College London for part of this research. I would also like to extend particular thanks to the many people who generously spent time talking to me during and after the period discussed here. All names used are fictitious, unless people gave permission or specifically asked for their names to be used; any errors of interpretation are entirely mine. The difficulties of writing about an emergent process that is still unfolding in the present are clear. Yet, perhaps, as Upendra Baxi notes: 'The grave narrative risks that one runs in writing about September 11 and its aftermath, pale into insignificance when set against the background of ever proliferating justificatory strategies and stratagems, on all sides, for the practices of politics of mass cruelty' (Baxi 2001).

Such a critical event, and its diverse audiences, may also lead us to question our conceptual models: of consciousness and culture, of war and power. These models must try to respond to the developing reality of the post-post-Cold War social formation, at both the widest and the narrowest human level. They also need to be scrupulous in avoiding apocalyptic language, or an over-reliance on the rhetoric of the 'new', since continuities, or at least the perception of continuities, may be as important as any real moments of change.

Following the logic of this inquiry further suggests a need for analyses of social interpretation and identification, which do not simply 'relate' the local and the global, the macro and the micro, the nation and the community, but considers their 'simultaneity' in cultural practice and in individual ontology. A definition of simultaneity might therefore encompass the ways in which a critical conjuncture is instantiated in a variety of settings. It might also be used to conceptualise a train of events that unfolds in diverse ways in different contexts. Such a concept also tries to move beyond the synthetic simplicities of the term 'global', and its dichotomy, while reflecting the immediacy, transmitability and translatability of contemporary images, ideas and moral formulations, as well as their unpredictable appropriation by a varied world of viewers.

The discussion that follows examines some aspects of this process of simultaneous disclosure. Its point of departure is that critical events have power beyond their own immediate point of impact, a ripple effect that is often unforeseeable. It is a dynamic that reveals some of the fault lines of representation and some of the implications of the moral language of freedom and terror. There is much classic social science to build on in developing a more clearly disaggregated analysis, and a significant literature on the sources of resistance and rebellion to draw upon, most of which has been strangely absent from current commentary. The rich anthropology of remembering and forgetting is of great significance here.

President Bush's much quoted phrase, 'a plane flying in a clear blue sky will never look the same again', is resonant of the transubstantiation of objects in the context of human meanings. But it can also be seen as a very American reading of that particular 20th century symbol, a particularly local and culturally rooted image of the aeroplane as an icon, and of its incarnation as a 'dense transfer point' for ideas of both progress and power (Foucault 1976/1984). Foucault used this phrase in relation to the body's particular propensity to condense meanings, relations and values. However, it might also usefully be applied to the symbolic powers of technological objects, an interpretation that also reveals some of the complexities of history and representation; for surely the plane has always also been an instrument of destruction? Many elderly Europeans might still recall the sound of a plane's engines in the dark as a harbinger of fear. Were we to try to construct a geography of those nations that might endorse an innocent reading of the plane as simply a machine for overcoming the limitations of time, what would such a map look like today?

The US, however, having waved its B52s off on so many missions of death elsewhere, beyond its own domestic horizons, has managed to preserve a boundary of apparent artlessness and distance. The language of 'stealth bombers', 'collateral damage' or 'friendly fire' preserves a euphemistic abstraction. The provenance and implications of such terms are shrouded in techno-speak, mystified into the morally nobler domain of protection and foresight planning. Thus, 'Dubya's' plaintive comment perhaps reflects a peculiarly American loss, not only of security but also of orientation, of worldview even. His statement captures the shift from innocent myopia to the grainy world of infrared night-sight, where the price of power is to be ever-vigilant. A shift that, according to Charles Krauthammer, marked the end of America's 'decade-long holiday from history' (quoted in *Economist* 2002: 23). There may also be imperceptible but crucial changes in the 'subsoil' of society, such as an altered balance between security and civil liberties, the justification of previously intolerable actions in the name of a supposedly higher moral purpose, or a re-evaluation of the moral legitimacy of particular persons or groups, so that 'to be more safe [people must] become willing to run the risk of being less free' (2002: 25).

The difficulties of constituting the US as a field in its own right suggest, first, that some recent analyses can usefully be taken as social texts and representations which themselves reveal tacit values and aspects of misrecognition. Bourdieu's use of the term *meconnaisance* (1977) draws on the Marxist concept of false consciousness but might be said to have some subtle difference from it. While the Marxist concept is fully inscribed in a hierarchical relation of power, in Bourdieu's sense, although dominance is fundamental, all human actors can be said to live within forms of *meconnaisance* at different points and in different ways. It becomes the more generalised condition of partial knowledge. Thus the first two sections of this chapter discuss the 'idea' of America by commenting on two programmatic statements that preceded and followed the destruction of the Twin Towers, examining their discursive orientation, and suggesting that there is a particular need at this juncture to reflect on their underlying assumptions of standpoint and voice, ie, where? By whom? On behalf of whom?

Secondly, it also suggests that the level of abstraction at which some recent interventions have operated could be complemented with a more anthropologically grounded examination of the plurality of responses. 'The meaning of America for others' then becomes a specific terrain of inquiry. The third section therefore considers 'meanings of terrorism and meanings of America' from a specific social and cultural context, that of Mexico, the US's symbiotic neighbour, the gateway to the 'other' Americas. The final section of the chapter examines the implications of this juxtaposition and the particular challenges it raises for anthropological analyses.

CONSTITUTING AMERICA AS OBJECT

Not the least of the many ironies of the post-9/11 period is the fact that an attack, which in the most simplistic reading might seem to result from the exclusion, penetration and impoverishment of the 'Third World' or the 'south', is having its most serious impact on that world itself. That this reading is itself partial only serves to underline the fact that spatial labels become even more inadequate and misleading than they have always been as the underlying socio-historical configuration of the events becomes clearer. A certain 'post-September 11 global melancholy' (Halliday 2002) seems to stem from the generation of a new kind of conceptual uncertainty. Confronted with the imponderables of an obscure anti-terrorist campaign that has unforeseeable goals; compelled to endorse a military intervention whose rationale is sometimes opaque and antecedents obscure; forced to bear witness to major conflicts, which somehow evade the instituted framework and meaning of 'war', yet involve many of it consequences, both politicians and analysts inevitably have recourse to the security of old models and a search to reinstate the status quo. Yet there is also growing awareness of an unsettling vacuum, the sense that beneath the return to *plus ça change* a more intractable seismic shift has taken place, akin perhaps in its occult transformative power to the splitting of the atom or the invention of the contraceptive pill. The complex alignments of non-Western elites and their patterns of recruitment and identification, for example, the common cause forged between disaffected Saudi billionaire intellectuals and dispossessed youths from inner-city Bradford, may defy conventional sociological analysis, but should probably not surprise us. However, the diverse ramifications of this conflict, like widespread nuclear fall-out, are more perplexing and more revealing. They have begun to lay bare chains of dependency, networks of trade, finance, information, control and alignment, and conflicting moral evaluations which transcend simple references to 'nation', 'culture' and even 'globalisation'.

In an important discussion piece written shortly after the attacks, Edward Said pointed out that the internal diversities of the categories 'West' and 'Rest' are far more telling than such 'labels, generalizations and cultural assertions', and far more relevant in understanding the processes which had been unfolding (Said 2001). Samuel Huntington's post-Cold War thesis claimed to identify the 'cultural' basis of emerging conflict between the 'Islamic' and the 'Christian' worlds (Huntington 1993, 1997). His theory and its reception provides one of the most troubling examples of the way in which forms of analysis take on discursive power in their own right, nourishing self-confirmatory positions. His argument has been dangerously easy to assimilate into general public consciousness, because it gave intellectual weight to popular processes of moral 'othering' that were already entrenched and because it seemed simultaneously to prefigure and to justify both the crisis and the response to it. As Said noted, reifications, such as those espoused by Huntingdon, create false couplings, between West, moral order and good versus Islam, moral degeneracy and terrorism, thus blurring the many important connections that also exist 'between apparently warring civilizations' (2001: 3).

Strangely, however, Said's intervention, like Bush's comment, also seems curiously trapped by its own perspective. While it exemplified the subtle cultural positioning of one of the founders of post-colonial and hybrid transnational scholarship, someone who always decried attempts, like those of Huntingdon, to 'survey the entire world from a perch outside all ordinary attachments and hidden loyalties' (2001), it seems nonetheless uncharacteristically uni-dimensional, reflecting a curiously American lens. Said noted that Huntington's language of gigantism and apocalypse has been taken up by the European and American press to fan the flames of a self-righteous polarisation that has gathered pace since the events of September 2001. There are two points to make about this.

First, it is right to note that such reductionism is neither accurate nor clarifying. However, in Britain as well as in other parts of the world, although this might have been a prevalent tone in much media and popular analysis in the immediate aftermath, there has also been a more nuanced, more pluralist, more ambiguous and doubting discussion to be heard. To read the British 'view' from the British press, which somewhat schizophrenically has tended to espouse the 'war on terror' while expressing some nervousness about the rhetoric, would be simplistic. The 'view' from 'British' communities would be altogether more multifaceted. Furthermore, being against the US ('if you're not with us you're against us') does not necessarily mean being 'for' the other side (Jack 2002). Central and South American nations, for example, have long suffered from the aggressive interventions of the US, but this does not necessarily make them pro-Taliban or even pro-Islam. NGOs in El Salvador sent an official protest to George Bush on 22 November 2001 in which they rejected both terrorist actions and military reprisals in equal measure, stating that, 'criminal acts should be punished by justice and not by vengeance'. It is noteworthy that they made explicit their view that the roots of the events have to do with US foreign policy, of which they themselves have frequently been the victims in the past, without espousing any simple polarities. Nor did Said mention the anti-bombing lobby throughout the world, which had gathered momentum at the time he writes and which in some places has been pro-Islam in the Huntingtonian sense, but which in many others, both in the so-called 'West' and the Rest, has been pro-international justice, pro-dialogue, pro-diplomacy. In response, 'terrorist' forms of 'counter-terrorism', an all too familiar historical phenomenon in the south, are likely to increase as a consequence of these cross currents. The murder of the student Carlos Blanco Lequizamo by the police during an anti-globalisation/anti-bombing demonstration in Colombia (*Por Esto*, Merida, Mexico, 22 November 2001) is a case in point. The word 'terrorist' has always stood for particular interests. Thus the Zapatistas of Chiapas are labelled freedom fighters or bandits according to the political persuasion of the speaker, while President Putin proclaimed his support for the American position, using it as an argument for support against the Chechens. The invocation of the term, in sweepingly generalised form, as an instrument of international policy, has revealed these linguistic strategies in a new way (Silberstein 2002). It also had other complex transnational-local effects.

At the same time, however, decrying these generalising labels, or seeing them merely as Huntington's invention as Said tended to do, may also be too simplistic. Regrettable as they are, they were also already in use in previous conflicts, as mobilising weapons, monolithic shields with which to pursue other agendas. Said tends to respond to them merely in their incarnation as limited analytic categories, invoked by a sloppy thinker. However, they are not just dead and inappropriate labels, but have acquired significant moral force, however spurious. They need to be understood and unravelled as an aspect of practical politics, cultural production and identity formation. In real life conversations, people conjugate many contradictions unawares.

Secondly, the use of examples in Said's 2001 article is also revealing, giving most space to a discussion of the diversities of Islam. While undoubtedly for an American (or European) audience this needs as much explanation and emphasis as possible, he pursues this reading rather than making any attempt to explore beneath the skin of the US. Commenting on articles published by the newspaper *Dawn* in Pakistan, he offers an insightful reinforcement of the salience and variety of anti-rightist, anti-fundamentalist Muslim opinion. This serves the important purpose of illustrating the multiplicity of Islamic positions. Alluding to Conrad, he deftly underlines the fragile construction of northern European certainties and his invocation of history serves to remind us of the extent to which Islam is indeed part of our own heritage, 'on the inside' as he puts it. These points are very valuable. However, they run the risk of attacking one stereotype (that Islam equals fundamentalism) while confirming another (that the 'problem' is Islam), leaving intact the assumption of America as subject, 'the Muslim world' as object.

The view *from* 'west Asia' might ask other questions. How has this amnesia (Baxi 2001) about the shared roots of knowledge and religion come into being? How are different versions of this history being used today as forms of political representation (Harshberg and Moore 2002)?:

> Much is made of the colonial past and of globalisation in the causes of 11 September. But here it is pertinent and right to listen to what the self proclaimed perpetrators themselves have said. They do not seem to care for global inequality as such or about what has happened in the cold war in Africa, Latin America or East Asia. They hate their own *munafiq* or 'hypocrite' rulers, but they also hate the Shi'ite Muslims who live in their midst in the Arab world – Iran, Pakistan and Afghanistan – and have, on the evidence, a sinister and deeply felt hatred of women. For the leadership of al-Qa'ida the conflict goes back, so they say, 80 years: this means it is dated to events, not exactly specified, in the Middle East of the 1920s. This is most likely a reference to the consequences of the fall of the Ottoman empire, including, as a possible list of starting events, the imposition of British and French mandates in parts of the Arab world in 1920, the abolition of the califate of Turkey in 1924, the rise of Jewish immigration to Palestine. It may include, perhaps not least, the establishment of Saudi Arabia in 1926. More immediately, the leaders of al-Qa'ida have dated the starting of their activity to the Kuwait war of 1990–91 and the stationing of US forces in Saudi territory. That this latter point is a sophistry, implying that the whole of Arabian peninsula, rather than just Mecca and Medina and their environs, is sacred territory does not detract from its ideological appeal. It also ignores the rather significant fact that there are Americans, that is, American Muslims, in Mecca. Whatever the antecedents may be, and one may suspect that history is more pretext than cause, antecedents there are. (Halliday 2002: 214)

Halliday's macro-political interpretation already pushes well beyond the polarities of civilizational clash and glimpses at the nature of the historical consciousness that so urgently needs to be understood. This is a task that is generally easier to do on the past rather than in the present, but it is surely vital to accord the interactions of structure and agency as much significance in the contemporary as in the historical world. Not all Islam is 'fundamentalist', as Said is also anxious to stress, but in addition not all Islamists are fundamentalists, and not all Islamists or fundamentalists necessarily subscribe to this particular reading of history.

'EMPIRE' AND FREEDOM: THE INSIDE AND THE OUTSIDE

A second text that is instructive here and which I suggest we might examine as a social representation and as an expression of the politics of knowledge, is the recent best-seller *Empire* by Michael Hardt and Antonio Negri. The surprising sales figures of this work indicate extensive popular consumption and a readership which must be prepared to invest money in search of enlightenment, even if many people claimed to find it 'unreadable' and even if they failed to find the answer therein. The proliferating and contradictory commentary on the book from both sides of the Atlantic, often violently pro or anti, also gives it a social relevance that goes well beyond its intrinsic qualities of thought or argument (Balakrishnan 2000). The particular claim of this piece of writing is that it sets out to provide a radically new theoretical perspective on the New World Order. Its (self-aggrandising) project is to set out a diagnosis of late extreme capitalism to match that of Marx for an earlier era.

Reduced to outline, Hardt and Negri's point is that an older imperialism, in which a dominant sovereign power was counterposed against its subjects, through a spatial hierarchy of metropolis and colony, is giving way to a new kind of amoeba-like field of force. The authors call this entity (or process) 'Empire', or sometimes 'the coming Empire'. This network-like power lacks a clear centre (2000: 200, 384), but is powerfully diffuse. It is not based on the old kinds of military and political might, but has enormous multilateral conscriptive energy. This new trancendence is expressed through its control of 'biopower', a term purloined from Foucault, to convey the way in which the multitude under its sway comes to incorporate its own domination. Thus it is not just 'governed' but comes (by choice? by coercion?), through participation in transnational markets, informatics and media, to internalise the goals and meanings of Empire in its very being and life projects, even as it is exploited by them. 'Government and politics come to be completely integrated into the system of transnational command' (Hardt and Negri 2000: 307). The familiar dualistic oppositions characteristic of imperialism: sovereign and territory, administrator and administrated, colonists and colonised, superior and lesser race, have been replaced (or are being replaced, the status of the concept is not always clear), by this radically different amorphously potent network surpassing the scope of the nation State. This spreads out imperceptibly like a web, with ever encompassing reach and its own spatial and temporal logic. Hardt and Negri imagine it contradictorily as both acephelous or de-territorialised, but also as a pyramid at whose 'pinnacle' sits the US (2000: 247–48).

There is not enough space here to delve further into the inconsistencies of this somewhat over-written tome, nor to examine their invocation of 'the multitude' which is said to be both within and against Empire. However, two issues are worth debate. The first is the idea of the development of a very specific moral rhetoric of 'freedom' from the externalisation of the original project of the American Constitution that developed from historical conditions of frontier society. Hardt and Negri turn this into an epic with distinctive features and suggest that these unique historical circumstances distinguish it significantly from the tired old European version of democracy. They write, 'liberty is made sovereign and sovereignty is defined as radically democratic within an open and continuous process of expansion' (2000: 168). The continuing symbolic power of the frontier in American thought, as a self-concept and source of self-belief, is of thus of pervasive relevance. However, their reading is careless history. Possibly it owes more to cinema than to documentation. What is important and revealing, though, is the throwaway thought, which they pass over all too quickly, that the idea of liberty 'hides ingenuously a brutal form of subordination. North American terrain can be imagined as empty only by wilfully ignoring the existence of the Native Americans' (2000: 169). This idea alone deserves much fuller elaboration, for it could be argued that it is not so much the epic of democracy, as the ingenuous erasure that characterises pronouncements about freedom in the past as well as in the present. Its latest incarnation, 'Enduring Freedom', cynically appropriates a universalising moral rhetoric for particularist ends. That the original erasure might persist as a political *leitmotiv* is one of the most telling points the book never intended to make.

The second issue that is relevant to our discussion is the authors' use of the ideas of 'inside' and 'outside'. They seem to intend by this a contrast with imperial regimes. In such previous regimes a distinction could be made between the colonial power (euphemised perhaps as the 'mother country'), which had its 'inside', its own culture, society, people, state and values, external to which were its occupied territories, controlled, ordered and defined 'from within' the hegemonic power itself. However, 'In the passage from modern to post-modern, and from imperialism to Empire', Hardt and Negri tell us, 'there is progressively less distinction between inside and outside' (2000: 186–87).

This is an extremely provocative thought, but probably not in the sense that the authors intend it to be. As Peter Fitzpatrick insightfully points out (Fitzpatrick 2001 and nd) this book purports to be a critique of America and has certainly been taken by some reviewers to be a marxisant, radical and deconstructionist epic, producing cries of outrage from the US right. However, in their exegesis of 'inside' and 'outside' Hardt and Negri appear to be endorsing a very conventional and uncritical thesis of 'Americanization', which like its twin 'globalisation' cries out for more serious and specific analysis (for example, see Miller 1997). In other words, they seem to believe that we are all American now. To repeat: the view from 'west Asia', from Mexico or elsewhere, would not deny the spread of the market, nor the 'beauty and power' of things American (Johnson 1999). But it would point to the significant contradictions and tensions involved in this process, creative of new kinds of differentiation and self-definition. It would highlight the agency of individuals and societies in appropriating, rejecting and making anew their relationships with the market of goods and ideas. *Empire* has been seen as especially timely, since it was written before the events of 9/11, yet appears to provide a place of refuge for some of those seeking answers to the imponderables of that moment.

However, the thesis that the 'outside' has come to an end is largely challenged by those events themselves. There are clearly people who desire to re-mark the distinctions between inside and outside, to challenge the amoeba on its own ground. Surely the very force of the act was symbolically to penetrate and distanciate, to bring the outside in? Like Said, Hardt and Negri seem to remain trapped within a predominantly American optic and moral vision, reinstating the myth, unwittingly celebrating the legend instead of unmasking it. Even their title is redolent of Hollywood, and their prose is certainly galactic in its weightiness. In this they at least perhaps confirm their own thesis.

But it is a thesis that leaves the important questions unanswered. If, as they suggest, Islam is the repressed consciousness inside the Euro-American mind, what is the West in the ontology of 'others'? What is 'America' (or 'West' or 'North') for a Chinese rice farmer, or a Thai businessman, for instance? What is America as forged in the life-experience of the 17-year old sweatshop worker in Cuidad Juarez on the Mexican American border? Or the Hispanic waiter in a California bar, perhaps one of the 28 million (or 10% of the US population) whose language of the home is Spanish, making America the fourth largest 'Spanish speaking' country in the world. In contemporary eastern Yucatan, southern Quintana Roo, or the highlands of Guatemala there are Maya populations who may have spent time as migrants in the US, or who have family members there, who work as easily with the temporal distinctions of the Long Count as with those of Gregorian Calendar, who combine distinctive systems of numeration without necessarily giving it much thought. The inside and the outside are entering into new conjunctions. The very processes of internalisation that Hardt and Negri propose may also lead to new kinds of critique and differentiation and to inter-relationship that are much more complex than those they espouse. In comparison, Said's commentary recognises these layered realities to a considerably greater extent, but he, too, has concentrated his attention on the view *from* America, rather than the view *of* America. The hegemony of the view from America is insightfully dissected in Peter Fitzpatrick's deconstruction of the nation of 'enduring freedom' and its concomitant legal apparatus. This, he argues encodes a responsibility *for* the other, not responsibility to the other (Fitzpatrick 2001). This is only the prologue to what we need to understand.

The factors that lead to a crystallisation of resentment against a dominant power often have their roots in a multi-faceted history. The Mayan rebellion of 1847 in Yucatan (usually referred to as the 'Caste War') is a case in point. The Canadian historian Marie Lapointe, in her analysis of this uprising, which was one of the most important indigenous revolts against 'white' dominance in the Americas, effectively demonstrates the limitations of the 'clash of cultures' argument. In her discussion of the factors that led only some sectors of the nineteenth century Maya population of Yucatan to move beyond 'everyday forms of resistance' and to take up arms against the *criollos*, she unravels the mosaic of positions that were derived from the underlying ethnic relation. These included: micro-regional racial/cultural demography, critical mass, a level of autonomy and resources, fratricidal conflicts between the whites themselves, and the experience of both cultural and economic restrictions that significantly threatened the reproduction of a 'way of life and belief'. These are all familiar ingredients, but they are ones that mobilised particular people and not others. They shifted certain groups in particular regions of the Peninsula from alienated and complicit debt peons, to people whose 'field of social consciousness' had catalysed. Her point is that to understand the wellsprings of this conflict it is necessary to understand as much about the society of '*los blancos*' as that of the Indians, and the intricacies of hybridity, internalisation and cultural memory are central to the analysis.

Transposed to the current context this implies that understanding the complexity of views *of* America in the social imaginary of others may be important. The following section makes a preliminary contribution to such a discussion with some reflections on the process of disclosure that was set in motion by the events of September 11 in one particular place, Mexico, whose relations to the US is one of the most special in the world. The process of disclosure as experienced and interpreted from eastern Yucatan revealed things that had always been present, but posed them with a new clarity, differentiating people from one another in the process. The discussion suggests that four things were re-articulated from different standpoints by this moment: the 'value' of Americans and the integrity of the US as a nation; perceptions of the disjunction of moral orders; ideas about the future and strategies through which to confront it; and lastly the power of access to information itself to create distinctions.

THE DAYS OF THE DEAD?[2]

On the day the two planes crashed into the Twin Towers, 28,000 Americans were on the coast of the Yucatan Peninsular, mostly in the vacation megalopolis of Cancun. With many holiday packages coming to an end that day and flights suddenly at a standstill, paradise beach quickly turned into departure lounge hell as the back-log of passengers began to build up. Transformed in an instant from powerful visitors to pitiful refugees, with no chance of returning to their comfortable hotel rooms, they were shocked and cast loose, their golf clubs, snorkels, surfboards and luggage in piles around them. Plans in disarray, commitments back home abandoned, anxious about the situation they were watching unfold on Mexican television and in the newspapers, they could only camp out and wait in the small Cancun terminal building.

As the days unfolded in disbelief and confusion, and cancelled flights piled upon cancelled flights, many of the homeless Americans ran out of money. Even '*gringos*' have their holiday budgets after all, and not all could draw on funds from home. Gradually the fragility of the tourist relationship began to leak out from behind the accommodating screen of the 'system'. Some local hoteliers, invoking 'traditional' Mexican hospitality, took pity and offered crisis accommodation. For others in the local market, however, while a rich American is tolerable, a necessary piece of the daily jigsaw of survival, a poor American is little better than a dog, at least when out of his home context. There is always a lively discussion in the regional newspapers about the 'quality' and '*poder adquisitivo*' (purchasing power) of particular tourist cohorts at different times of year or in specific places. The shipwrecked travellers of September 11 suddenly found themselves at the bottom

2   Material from this section is derived from a series of structured and semi-structured interviews, formal and informal discussions with a wide spectrum of different individuals, workers, farmers, professionals, shopekeepers, entrepreneurs, tourists, etc, conducted between September and December 2001 in eastern Yucatan and central and southern Quintana Roo, Mexico. I would like to thank all those who so generously participated. Personal names have been changed to preserve anonymity.

of the ladder in this hierarchy of worth. Mexico has for so long lived in the shadow and under the thumb of the dominating 'north' that it seemed hard for some residents of Cancun to conceal a measure of satisfaction in seeing the tables turned. *'Ahora* ... now, now they might see what it felt like' was the almost inexpressible thought.

Not entirely tacit, however. When operators of the airport's food concessions refused even to give the stranded passengers water, the local paper, *Por Esto*, reported that this was an 'inhuman' act which would be viewed very seriously by the local municipality (*Por Esto*, 11 November 2001). The religious imagery of water and brotherhood was invoked to express the thought that this most fundamental gesture of compassion should be extended, even to your enemy. Such a short step from valued guests to despised aliens! And such a thin line between the intimate discourse of tragedy and sympathy and the detached analysis of the 'military-industrial complex', a term that seems to have dropped out of the European intellectual vocabulary, but has never quite left the Mexican stage. The attempt to convey the sense that these were terrible acts, but that everyone – apart from the victim nation itself – could clearly identify the logic of their genesis, left many of those I interviewed struggling for the best way to express the conflictual morality of their spontaneous responses.

As the bombing in Afghanistan expanded, the complexity of these representations persisted and deepened. In villages and towns in the Yucatec interior, the manifestations of an unsteady global economy had already been having an impact, as it so often has in the past. The attack on the Twin Towers seemed to be yet another natural disaster to add to the recent list. These included the *marea roja* (a marine micro-organism which infected the northern coast of Yucatan and destroyed both tourism and the fishing industry in 2001), the poor octopus catch, layoffs in the *maquiladoras* (assembly plants), and the epidemic of dengue fever in the summer months were, like the predictable failure of the new PAN (Partido de Accion Nacional) government to be any better than the old, mostly beyond human control.

Many people returned to their communities and *barrios* because jobs on the coast dried up, as the tourist industry went into decline, a fact of great concern to families and to local municipalities. Not only is there the large scale circular migration of workers, particularly young men but also women, from the interior of Yucatan and Quintana Roo, to the coast, but all the secondary services that feed the tourist industry are also a vital part of local livelihood. Food provision, consumer goods, the artisan sector were all affected. In communities such as Piste, near the monument of Chichen Itza, which has witnessed an extraordinary expansion in the last 10 years, the burgeoning artisan trade virtually collapsed for a time. Choices made with one evaluation of the future in mind preclude other options, which may then no longer be there as a fall-back position.

The continuance of the subsistence base of *milpa* agriculture in the countryside is partially complemented, but also undermined, by new markets and new sources of employment. The different alternatives for the older and the younger generation which tourism has created during the last 15 years are hard to reverse now. If, in some families or communities, children have begun to be raised with the expectation that they will be able to make more money away from the land, they now lack he skills or the inclination to go back. So much hangs on this perception of the future, which particularly in the 'Maya World' revolves around selling the cultural past to outsiders.

Thus, the tourists of September 11 were reduced to vagrants, but a few months later any tourist was once again a good tourist. The arrival of the first cruise ship from Florida in the Port of Progresso on 15 November of the same year gave rise to acrimonious disputes about who should be the beneficiaries – locals or tour operators. The cruisers were greeted with an almost hysterical reception. Every manifestation of local pride, from food, *jarana* dances and *trova* groups (trios playing regional Yucatec music), to newly cleaned streets, was marshalled to attract them. The intensity of the debate surrounding who should benefit from this 'cargo', and how the tourists should best be 'managed' for the benefit of the population continues with a fervour that soon regained its force. Each week reports circulate of the numbers of cruise ships expected, or predicted for the next week, the next year.

The disclosure of the fragility of the '*industria sin chimeneas*' (industry without chimneys), as tourism is called, as if to evoke a false image of purity and beneficence, is a terrible awakening. A young man, studying for a career in tourist hospitality, compared it to the boom and bust of previous extractive economies in the region, the era of the 'greed gold' of henequen (Sisal) production, or of *chicle* (the resin used in chewing gum), both destroyed by shifts in the world market. Tourism had been implicitly seen in contrast as a new era of never-ending demand. Yet, now it could perhaps never again be quite the answer it had seemed to be. Although dreams will still be spun and investors will still be wooed, a number of people noted that the reality of the rest of the world had come suddenly nearer and that more than one strategy is needed. While children still read comics, watch *tele* and fly kites on waste ground near the town, their parents developed new worries and began looking for different solutions. Those who had jobs in the public sector, who might before have been regarded (and have regarded themselves) as less adventurous and less 'of the moment' than those who worked in tourism, for a time acquired a new confidence.

For example, Tomas, a worker in the state electricity company, congratulated himself on diversifying around this secure job, which entitles him to various benefits, rather than having given it up to get more time for his other projects, a shop, house building, a plan for a café. Resistance to globalisation began to take on new meaning, not as the mass protests of politically conscious internationalised activists, but in the small ways of retrenching, recouping and finding a 'safe' state job or some immediate, neighbourhood-based form of livelihood. The more secure could afford a more sanguine comment. From the viewpoint of an hotelier from a well-connected regional family, people's desires are unquenchable and their memories short. There have been other terrible conflicts, yet the market place of pleasure ultimately restores order, fears are forgotten and normal life is resumed. 'The war will end, better the devil we know, tourists will come back.'

The Day of the Dead, always an important Mexican festival, and followed by the Mayan celebration of *Hanal Pixan* (the feeding of souls) which takes place eight days later, was, in the context of 2001, discussed by a number of people as a particularly significant moment. Perhaps, they suggested, extra piety could be a way of restoring sanity to a crazed world? So many unknown strangers dead, so much distant death, it surely strengthened the need to join with the known family members who must be fed and welcomed into the living world. 'Madness breeds madness, it has been met by madness, but faith and God remain', as one shopkeeper commented. The creation and tending of shrines and altars restored moral order and served as a witness to a sense of the enduring nature of metaphysical and collective values which could support disassociation from either side in the conflict.

In the towns of the Yucatan Peninsular, an everyday discourse of tolerance is quite prominent, notwithstanding due cynicism about particular acts of intolerance at the party political level. The ideals of the Mexican Revolution, freedom, equality, justice, distorted as they have been by the history of the corrupt Mexican state, often discussed with sceptical sarcasm and now generally celebrated every 20 November, largely through images of sport and culture, still provide a conventional way of speaking about things, a sort of moral talisman, a narrative framework to ease the wheels of quotidian communication. In a strongly pious community, made up of many different kinds of believers, such tropes are also a learned framework of common dialogue. Deeper into a conversation, however, for example with Jose Enrique as he mends a bicycle in his repair shop, with Manolo as he grills a chicken on the street corner, other ideas come to the fore. Jose Enrique is a non-Maya speaker who nevertheless regards himself as Maya, in common with approximately 50% of the local population. We were chatting about the contemporary state of the world and the impact of the events of September as he changed the wheel. Despite the ambivalence towards the US and the sense that there was some understanding of the sources of hatred underlying the attack, which was so uneasily conjugated with sympathy in the immediate aftermath, as time went on and the American response began to crystallise, other views came to the surface. 'Well, terrorism had to be defeated, they had to do it some way or other,' said Jose Enrique. 'After all we know what the Arabs are like [rubbing his thumb and forefinger together and speaking as if instructing], we businessmen know they drive a very hard bargain ...' 'But,' I say, 'there isn't a very big Arab population in Yucatan, surely? Hasn't the Lebanese community in Merida been a well integrated part of the city for years?' 'Well, numbers don't really matter,' he counters, 'the point is they're all the same, they won't give an inch ...' As ever, tolerance in the particular is a different matter from general principles. It is in the interstices of communities that social and political attitudes are forged. Even for the Maya population of Yucatan, historically ennobled yet socially impoverished and excluded, there is no *necessary* common ground around social justice to be forged against 'white' power, even by those denigrated by it.

The American proclamation of 'freedom' evoked an anger that became quite widespread. In this sense something that was always known about 'Tio Sam' has come out of the closet in a heightened political form. A major long-term casualty of the bombings has been civil liberties in the US itself, as well as the UK, resulting in greater control on immigrants and increased policing of the undocumented workers. This is having a significant impact on Mexican migrants, and the hypocrisy of the rhetoric of freedom in the context of the denigration and absence of rights for many Mexican workers has made a new impact. The contrast had the effect of re-politicising the debate and led to new meetings at the diplomatic level and new initiatives to put greater pressure on the other side. Yucatan is not a large exporter of migrant labour, in comparison with states such as Michoacan, for example. But even those who have no migrants, or hopeful migrants, in their families are more likely to question the contrast between rhetoric and reality. 'The "Place of Hopes" has its dark side, we can see it now' a *seminarista* (ordinand) from the theological training school told me. His mother agreed, one might think again about plans that had been made for the future. He had once thought of going '*p'al Norte*' but since September had decided that the search for a better life lay with Christ, rather than in 'a society which talks so much of freedom but which is built on racism'.

From the phlegmatic response of those with some security, or those who draw moral lessons from the events, to the cynical take of youth. In a neighbourhood cyber café someone had downloaded a site called 'Yo Mamma Osama' – 'the events are tragic but a sense of humour helps us to get by'. On New Years Eve, 2001, *noche viejo*, when effigies of the 'bad' old year, often the current Mexican president, are placed outside houses or on street corners and later symbolically burnt, Osama bin Laden and George Bush were to be seen side by side, even hand in hand. 'The consumer is the processor, the turner of things into social and cultural values' (Strathern 1992: xiii).

On the corner of the street there is a more philosophical view: Manolo, setting up his food stall for the day, says that it is unthinkable, illogical even, to go to war over religion. Since each faith is simply a particular, human, way of reflecting on God, merely a set of ideas and images to help us grapple with mysteries we cannot easily encompass, each religious form is just the means we use to reach the same end. He suggests that another kind of politics lies behind the claims of *jihad* or crusade. His insight transcends his circumstances. He has a young son to support but has just been laid off from the local t-shirt factory. Fewer tourists inevitably mean fewer t-shirts. One day of death, one version of the meaning of terror, heralds a thousand others.

CONCLUSION

This, then, is perhaps where local meanings and moral orientations make a contribution to diagnostic discussion. These notes are merely an introduction to an exploration of the multiple interpretations of the discourse of terror and freedom, through which some of the over-unifying categories of recent debate might be grounded.

It is too early to predict the long-term transformations that may result from the events of September 11. A passable version of the *status quo ante* has in some senses been reconstituted in the US and in the rich world. US consumers, moved by a resurgence of patriotism and nationalism, bought more American products, in the months following September, to the eventual benefit of their own economy and balance of trade, but to the great detriment of the NAFTA countries, particularly

Mexico. The level of trust they expressed in their president soared for a time, prompting Mexican comment that the attacks had been instigated 'from within'. More importantly, the greatly diminished sphere of civil liberties that is being put in place is affecting immigrant populations above all. The lay-offs and decreased remittances that result are bound to have a major effect on any 'recovery' of the poor world, a further effect of which could be new forms of *conscientization* whose consequences are unforeseen. America's 'icons', including the aeroplane, are also, via globalisation, other peoples' icons, too. However, the nature of the 'ownership' of these representations is very different. For the majority, the change is likely to involve much more than the meaning of wings against a clear blue sky.

BIBLIOGRAPHY

Balakrishnan, G (ed) (2000) *Debating Empire*, London: Verso

Baxi, U (2001) 'Operation "Enduring Freedom": towards a new international law and order' 2 *Warwick Electronic Journal on Law, Social Justice and Global Development* (LGD), http://elj.warwick.ac.uk/global/issue/2001-2/baxi.html

Bourdieu, P (1977) *Outline of a Theory of Practice*, Cambridge: CUP

Das, V (1995) *Critical Events: An Anthropological Perspective on Contemporary India*, Oxford: OUP

Economist (2002) 'What September 11th really wrought', 12 January, pp 23–25

Fitzpatrick, P (2001) 'The Law of Enduring Freedom' 2(1) *Warwick Electronic Journal on Law, Social Justice and Global Development (LGD)*, http://elj.warwick.ac.uk/global/issue/2001-2/baxi.html

Fitzpatrick, P (nd) 'Laws of Empire', unpublished ms

Foucault, M (1976/1984) *The History of Sexuality: An Introduction*, Harmondsworth: Penguin

Halliday, F (2002) *Two Hours That Shook the World: September 11, 2001: Causes and Consequences*, London: Saqui Books

Hardt, M and Negri, A (2000) *Empire*, Cambridge, MA: Harvard UP

Harshberg, G and Moore, K (2002) *Critical Views of September 11 from Around the World*, New York: WW Norton

Huntington, S (1993) 'A clash of civilizations?' 72(3) *Foreign Affairs*, Summer, 22–49

Huntington, S (1997) *The Clash of Civilizations and the Re-making of World Order*, London: Simon & Schuster

Jack, I (ed) (2002) 'Introduction' 77 *Granta* (What We Think of America) 1–2

Johnson, M (1999) *Beauty and Power: Transgendering in the Southern Philippines*, Oxford: Berg

Lapointe, M (1983) *Los Mayas Rebeldes de Yucatan, Michoacan*, Mexico: El Colegio de Michoacan

Miller, D (1997) *Capitalism: An Ethnographic Approach*, Oxford: Berg

Redfield, R (1941) *The Folk Culture of Yucatan*, Chicago: Chicago UP

Sahlins, M (1981) *Historical Metaphors and Mythical Realities*, Ann Arbor: Michigan UP

Said, E (2001) 'The clash of ignorance' in *Z Net*, www.zmag.org/saidclash/htm

Silberstein, S (2002) *War of Words: Language, Politics and 9/11*, London: Routledge

Strathern, M (1992) 'Foreword: the mirror of technology', in Silverstone, R and Hirsch, E (eds), *Consuming Technologies: Media and Information in Domestic Spaces*, London: Routledge

TRAUMA, GUILT AND *ASSUJETTISSEMENT*: DISCOURSES OF MORALITY AND RACE IN CARIB HISTORICAL CONSCIOUSNESS

Paul Twinn

During an early visit to St Vincent I discussed my proposed thesis with a local woman living in the Central Windward district of the island. She knew that I was interested in Vincentian history and that I was planning to come back to research my thesis. I began to explain that I was specifically interested in the Caribs and that I planned to stay with them in Sandy Bay. I was rapidly stopped short however by her reaction; her jaw dropped and her eyes widened:

> Why do you want to go up there, with them people? Them Caribs are crazy! They get drunk all the time. When some aviation fuel got washed up there one time the government had to go on the radio to tell them not to drink it. But they did anyway! They'll drink anything, they're just crazy people!

I tried to explain that it was part of my research and that I was interested to learn more about them, but my response merely evoked a slow shaking of the head in resignation and the weary words of someone who knew better:

> Well, I know you are an educated man Mr Twinn but you don't know what you are doing. Them people aren't like us …

Until that conversation I had no real conception of the social distance that existed between the Caribs and some members at least of the wider Vincentian community. What made this conversation startling was that it was with a teacher, who had had a better than average education and who, I presumed at the time, was open to new ideas and would have been actively challenging the old prejudices of the past. But throughout my stay in St Vincent the views expressed by that informant were reiterated by many, though not all, of those non-Caribs I questioned. On several occasions informants, anxious to dissuade me from going to stay with them, described the proclivity of the Caribs to get drunk and/or fight. Given my position as a white Englishman from the University of London, my determination to do so tended to evoke a mixture of puzzlement and mild amusement. Occasionally the response would be a knowing nudge and wink, 'Dere's plenty ah ganja up there and dose Carib gals are plenty hot white man. You gonna have some good time'. This was a typical young male response and, though the clear inference was still that Sandy Bay was a wild place, the emphasis had shifted away from the wild as dangerous to a wildness based on excitement. These two connotations of wildness and the ambivalence that they evoked were reiterated in conversations with different people throughout my fieldwork. To some, who might be described as aspiring to respectability, the Caribs were the negation of all the virtues that they held dear, the Caribs were quick to anger, violent, hedonistic and feckless. They lived for today and, so long as they had the price of a quarter of rum in their pockets, cared little for the future. But for other Vincentians, those aspiring to *reputation*, these traits were an object for emulation. What immediately caught my attention, however, was the similarity between the statements of present day Vincentians and early reports by the missionaries of the seventeenth century regarding the Caribs. Three possibilities immediately presented themselves: first that the Caribs had maintained behavioural characteristics over 300 years despite the changes in their circumstances; secondly, that the discourse of the native Caribbean had been thoroughly internalised by the Vincentian population and it was this that had persisted; the third that occurred to me was that the situation might be a combination of both these factors.

The incident mentioned by my informant certainly seemed to bear out the depiction of the Caribs as wild men, but it was only later in my fieldwork that I began to realise the full significance of the paradigmatic event that had been related to me. This significance, however, was itself far from uniform and I rapidly learned that its effectivity as a symbol of *being Carib* had evoked responses from within the Carib community that sought to undermine that effectivity. The incident itself had been headline news in St Vincent at the time and had even been reported in the British national press, a rare event for Vincentian news even in today's media driven society, let alone the 1960s.

On Wednesday 19 November 1969, the 90 tonne schooner *Ruth 114* bound for Martinique from Trinidad ran into heavy weather and, having suffered damage to the sails and rudder, sprang a leak. Unable to stem the flow of water, the crew abandoned ship and made for the beach at Colonaire on the Windward coast of St Vincent at approximately 0300 hours on Thursday morning. After some nine hours the crew arrived in Colonaire and informed the local police. Despite a search by two ships from Kingstown the vessel was not sighted and finally, having drifted north for several hours, finally ran aground at Big Level, a beach immediately adjacent to the east of the village of Sandy Bay. A small group of men from the village managed to board the boat and began a salvage operation to remove the cargo and any items of value. This consisted of a small quantity of rum in wooden casks as well as the main cargo of 100 drums of methanol and 150 drums of aviation fuel. On finding the rum the men opened the casks and began to drink it. They then turned their attention to the other drums and sampled that too. One informant told how, having witnessed what was happening, he warned the men about drinking the fuel but was told that he was just a boy and didn't understand drink. This was 'Jack Iron' they claimed, a strong rum made in the Grenadines. The schooner was by then beginning to break up and the drums were floated and dragged ashore. By this time a large group of people had assembled and quickly began to distribute the liquid amongst themselves. News of the wreck had spread rapidly and it was believed to be a piece of good fortune for the inhabitants of the area. As news of the unexpected windfall spread people began to arrive not only from Sandy Bay but the nearby village of Owia. That weekend the community could have a party thanks to the boon they had received.

Within 24 hours the situation changed as the lethal concoction's devastating effects became apparent. People began collapsing from poisoning. Some of the recipients of the drums were lucky. One man informed me how he had seen a friend with an old truck loaded with drums of methanol and that he had been given one. Fortunately he had decided to put it aside for Christmas and so avoided poisoning. Many others were not so lucky. A frantic operation began with those unaffected trying to administer sugar and water to the sufferers. This prompt action may have saved many lives but the toll was still heavy. Nineteen people died, two were blinded and up to 600 people suffered poisoning through drinking the aviation fuel. Amongst the dead were two children, one of 11 and one of 12. The bodies of the victims of the tragedy were laid out in the small square outside the post office in Sandy Bay, whilst the survivors were taken to hospitals in Kingstown, Georgetown and Chateaubelair. The situation had been made worse by the absence of both telephones and electricity in the north of the island. Getting the sick to hospital, once the alarm had been raised, was made more difficult by the tortuous nature of the coastal road to Georgetown some eight miles away. Fortunately the Rabacca Dry River was not in flood and vehicles were able to cross the shallow ford in relative safety, but the isolation of the Caribs, beyond the Dry River as they were, was made starkly apparent.

Amongst the local inhabitants there was a sense of shock and a feeling of bewilderment at the events that had unfolded, feelings that were heightened by the euphoria that had preceded them. One man recounted to me the sight that met his eyes when he went to the post office. 'I remember going down to the square and seeing all those bodies lined up. They were just left on the ground with a sheet over them. People I knew. I had warned them not to drink it but they wouldn't listen.' Even after 30 years he was visibly shaken as he talked of the events he had witnessed. But amongst the wider Vincentian population, despite the genuine grief felt at the tragedy, the incident served to reinforce old prejudices regarding the Caribs. During the weekend after the wreck of the *Ruth 114*, the government had broadcast warnings of the dangers of drinking the liquid on the boat. These warnings had been ignored. Henceforth, the Caribs were subject to the accusation that they could not tell the difference between rum and aviation fuel. The objectification of the Caribs as wild men and the isolation of the community were complete.

On many occasions when discussing these events Carib informants expressed their belief that this was indeed the lowest point in their history. For years they had been neglected, regarded by the wider community as an incongruous oddity within the nation. They now felt the full force of their position as firmly anchored at the bottom of the social pile. But though the nadir of their social standing in St Vincent, the tragedy served to create a positive reaction in some young Caribs. The desperation of the situation provided the catalyst for a recognition that changes in their circumstances could only come from within their own community. As one man put it, 'After that I knew we could not depend on anybody else to help us. We had to do it ourselves'. Having been classified as wild men, categorised as stupid and ignorant and considered as beyond the pale of respectable society in St Vincent, a growing self-consciousness of their position emerged within the community. It was this self-consciousness that made possible a re-evaluation of their position within Vincentian society by the Caribs themselves. This is not to say though, that this self-consciousness developed on its own throughout the Carib population. It would be more accurate to say that the trauma had the effect of clearing or creating a space within which specific Caribs could constitute themselves as what Gramsci termed *organic intellectuals* (Forgacs 1988). That is to say, they constituted themselves as the dialectical opposite of their discursive characterisation. They could do this because the events of November 1969 provided such a stark objectification of what it was to be Carib that some at least were able deny it. The pre-existing models of normative behaviour summed up in the notion of 'respectability' provided an alternative to the wild man image of 'reputation' that dominated discourses of Caribness.

Gramsci elaborated the concept of the organic intellectual within the wider context of the role of education and the division of labour in class formation. Traditional intellectuals, such as academics, teachers, the media, artists and the clergy, were categorised in terms of the social division of labour that assigned to them the function of discursively elaborating the material interests of the dominant group in the society with which they were usually associated. But he was equally concerned with the struggle faced by subaltern groups, principally the proletariat, for whom the problem was how to 'challenge the existing order and become hegemonic in its turn, without becoming dependent on intellectuals from another class' (Forgacs 1988: 304). Therefore, in order to effectively challenge for hegemonic control of society, it was necessary for classes such as the proletariat to develop their own organic intellectuals, that is to say, to develop intellectuals who derived from within the subaltern group itself and who maintained practices that effectively constituted and maintained their relationship with that class. This was necessary since, according to Gramsci, intellectuals did not in themselves constitute a class but were linked to specific social classes, the paradigmatic example of this being the ecclesiastics who were 'organically bound to the landed aristocracy' (Gramsci 1988: 302). It was possible for an emergent class to win over, temporarily at least, some of the intellectuals of the dominant group, but, for Gramsci, it was only by the formation of its own organic intellectuals that an emergent group could challenge for hegemonic control. The constitution of such organic intellectuals was thus a major event in group formation, since one of its major functions would be to discursively articulate social identification within the category from which group membership could coalesce. It was precisely this process of constitution that the traumatic events of 1969 precipitated.

In this it contrasts with previous traumatic events, which had occasionally brought the Caribs to the attention of the colonial administration. Of these the most calamitous was the violent eruption of La Soufrière in 1902, which resulted in widespread loss of life and damage to property. This had induced the Caribs of Morne Ronde on the leeward coast of St Vincent to petition the King for relief. But, whilst the claim for land was endorsed by John Francois, who claimed the status of Carib Chief, and five headmen, the petition itself was signed by P Foster Huggins who is described as being 'Chief and Referee by election'. However, he is described in a colonial internal memo as 'a white man, some 60 years of age owning some small landed property at Calliaqua and at Rutland Vale'. In a further letter to Joseph Chamberlain at the Colonial Office, the Governor of St Vincent writes:

> I think it has probably escaped your attention that the so-called 'Chief and Referee' is Mr P Foster Huggins, recently pensioned from the public service … The Caribs as a distinct race no longer exist in any large number, they have intermarried with the descendants of the African slave Negroes and there are very few pure Caribs left. The people of Morne Ronde have received every consideration and have no substantial grievance …

Whilst the language of the Governor typifies the attitude to the Caribs that had prevailed in St Vincent since the beginning of the 19th century, the appearance of an ex-government officer acting on their behalf clearly caused some consternation to the colonial authorities. But despite the calamity that had befallen them, the Caribs had not developed spokesmen of their own but had had to act through the mediation of Huggins. That they were prepared to go to the lengths of making him an 'honorary chief' so that he might speak for them indicates both the desperation of their plight and the complete lack of self-confidence that prevailed. Whilst it can be argued that Huggins was acting as no more than an honest broker, it is equally clear that his was the only intervention regarding the Caribs that occurred and in the years that followed the disaster they disappeared once more from the colonial records. He was for the Morne Ronde Caribs, a traditional intellectual, in the Gramscian sense in that he was able to discursively articulate their grievances whilst they remained mute, and it was in this role that he mediated not with the colonial administration but directly with the King to whom the petition was addressed. The tone of the Caribs' plea was strangely reminiscent of that reported by Peter Carstens (Carstens 1991) for the Okanogan Indians who similarly held their relationship to Britain to be direct to the monarchy rather than through the normal channels of the administration. Shephard reports this attitude as far back as the beginning of the 19th century and the amnesty that brought to a conclusion the Carib Wars (Shephard 1832). Unlike the later disaster, subsequent to the wreck of the *Ruth 114*, the eruption of 1902 did not result in the emergence of organic intellectuals within Carib society. Indeed, the misfortune that befell the Caribs was shared by many others in the north of the island and although it was they who suffered most directly in terms of loss of life, the events were viewed as an act of God, a natural disaster that was part of the perils of living on a volcanic island. This is in marked contrast to the events of 1969 when the Caribs themselves were seen as the authors of their own misfortune. This was not a natural disaster but one that emanated from the proclivities of the Caribs themselves and served as proof of those proclivities. This disaster was not about living in a perilous location, but about the perils associated with being Carib; it confirmed, in the eyes of Vincentian civil society, the depiction of the Caribs that had been current in the literature from the time of Columbus. It is this aspect of the events that allowed their incorporation into the practices by which Carib individuals were constituted as Carib subjects. But it was the specificity of this constitution, its definitive rigour that created the possibility of denial. In order to elaborate how this constitution was possible, it is necessary first to consider how the incident of *Ruth 114* contributed to the objectification of the Carib as wild men, and only then can the complexity of its role in the constitution of Carib subjects be explicated.

Two key elements emerged from the incident regarding the objectification of the Caribs: the first was a confirmation of their alleged excessive proclivity to drink alcohol; the second reinforced the belief that they were unable to make rational judgements and were concerned only with the here and now, with scant regard for the implications of their actions. Combined, the two elements coalesced into a depiction of the Carib immersed in a mindless hedonism that precluded their inclusion in the wider society, with its aspirations at the time for modernity and independence. This objectification of the Caribs, internalised, as we have already shown in previous chapters, through the discursive practices of colonialism, could be reformulated by non-Carib Vincentians in terms of the event. Henceforth, it became possible for the incident of the *Ruth 114* to be used as a form of interpellation of Caribs by the non-Carib population. The way in which this occurred was described thus:

> After that people below the river [Rabacca] would see us and shout 'Jack Iron' – we were the stupid Caribs who couldn't tell the difference between rum and aviation fuel. That's what they thought of us – the tragedy of all those lost lives meant nothing, it was just a joke at our expense. We were just a joke and our lives meant nothing. Sometimes, even today, when you are just walking along the street, minding your own business someone will shout out 'Jack Iron'. Even today, after all these years they won't let us forget it. But it was much worse years ago. Then our people would really deny being Carib, they were ashamed. (Carib resident of Sandy Bay)

> Oh it's just a bit of fun, sometimes when the boys see one of them Caribs they'll shout out 'Jack Iron' just to tease them. (Non-Carib bar-owner)

These exchanges, for a response is clearly required and expected for it to be successful, were the most obvious means by which Caribs could be interpellated as subjects within a discourse which had a genealogy stretching back to the time of Columbus.

The term 'interpellation', as it is used here, refers to the work of the French Marxist philosopher Louis Althusser (Althusser 1971). In his article 'Ideology and ideological State apparatuses', Althusser posed the question as to the constitution of subjects in terms of the functional requisites of the reproduction of the means and conditions of production in capitalism. Althusser was specifically concerned with the reproduction of labour-power, embodied as it was in concrete individuals. In order to function as labour within capitalism, these concrete individuals were required to be 'competent, ie suitable to be set to work in the complex system of the process of production'. Moreover, the processes by which this competence was acquired lay, according to Althusser, outside the normal domain of production. But competence for Althusser was not just a question of technical know-how but was the attitude that should be observed by every agent in the division of labour, according to the job he is 'destined' for; rules of morality, civic and professional conscience, which actually means rules of respect for the socio-technical division of labour and ultimately the rules of the order established by class domination (Althusser 1971: 127).

This inculcation of knowledge thus served not only to reproduce the technical know-how necessary for capitalism but also the 'subjection to the ruling ideology or the mastery of its "practice"'. That is to say, the inculcation of knowledge served to reproduce class relations insofar as rulers needed to know how to rule and subjects needed to know how to respond to orders. The institutions of society that served to perform this function were termed by Althusser 'the Ideological State Apparatus' in order to distinguish them from the State Apparatus proper or, as he sometimes termed it, the Repressive State Apparatus. Whereas the latter manifests itself as a monolithic totality, the former presents itself as a plurality of separate social institutions such as schools and universities, trade unions, the media, literature and the arts and, perhaps most contentiously, the family.

Althusser's first thesis was that the role of ideology was to give a 'representation of the imaginary relationship of individuals to their real conditions of existence'. He does not claim that reality is illusory, but that the subject's imagined relationship to it is. This leads him to a second thesis: that ideology itself has a material existence, since:

> Every subject endowed with a consciousness and believing in the ideas that his consciousness inspires in him and freely accepts, must act according to his ideas, must therefore inscribe his own ideas as a free subject in the actions of his material practice. If he does not do so, 'that is wicked' ...

As a consequence of this Althusser claims that 'there is no practice except by and in ideology' and that 'there is no ideology except by the subject and for the subject'. This, of course is not to say a great deal, merely that human action is meaningful and that that meaning derives from individuals as subjects. But Althusser makes a further claim which is his central thesis, and it is at this point that interpellation emerges as the key concept, thus, although ideology is always by and for subjects and is thereby constituted, it does so only insofar as ideology itself constitutes concrete individuals as subjects. For Althusser therefore:

> In the interaction of this double constitution exists the functioning of all ideology, ideology being nothing but its functioning in the material forms of existence of that functioning. (Althusser 1971: 160)

That is to say, ideology is nothing more than the process by which concrete individuals become concrete subjects, and the means by which this is achieved Althusser terms interpellation or hailing. It is achieved, though, not through conscious ideology, that is, not by believing as a credo, dogma or matter of fact, but in practice through the acceptance of the hail. It occurs when the concrete individual responds to the hail through the recognition that he or she is being addressed. This is a crucial point, since for interpellation to be effective the concrete individual must already be a concrete subject, must already have internalised the depiction of him/herself as the subject of the hailing. As early as 1979, Paul Hirst argued that Althusser's concept of interpellation presupposed the existence of individual subjects prior to their constitution as subjects. 'This something which is not a subject must already have the faculties necessary to support the recognition that will constitute it as a subject' (Hirst 1979: 65, cited in Hall and Du Gay 1996). Even if, as in the example that Althusser gives of the policeman calling out 'Hey, you there', it is still required that the individual recognise that 'you' could refer to him or her and that he or she is 'there'. Thus to shout 'Jack Iron' in the street is an invitation for the hailed individual to recognise that he is not only a Carib but also that he identifies the hail as being for him as a Carib, ie, as an already constituted Carib subject. What is recognised is the *obvious* fact that Jack Iron denotes what it is to be a Carib, a fool who cannot tell the difference between rum and aviation fuel, and therefore to respond is not merely an act of recognition but also one of subjectification/subjection (Foucault's *assujettissement*) to the ideological discourse in which Caribs appear as wild men.

Interpellation is thus the process by which discursive formations (Foucault 1972) come to be internalised by individuals and, in the process, constitute those individuals as subjects of a *particular* discourse. During my fieldwork I only ever witnessed such an occurrence three times, and in all cases the Carib in question did not appear to respond but ignored the jibe. Unfortunately, on each occasion the context precluded me from ascertaining for certain whether the Carib in question had actually heard the 'hail' and deliberately chose to ignore it and, if so, what the reasoning was behind the response or rather lack of it. However, one Carib male, a member of what I have termed the *organic intellectuals* of Carib society related to me how he had been subject to such a 'hailing' in a work context and had been able to reverse the situation:

> When I first went to college in 1982 there were five of us from up here. That had never happened before; there had only ever been one person at a time. Even then there would be comments. One guy said, 'Four of you, we better get some Jack Iron in, we don't want you going to the airport to get a drink!' I said to him, 'Look, we don't need that kind of talk, we've come here to be professional and train that's what we want – just that! I didn't expect that kind of nonsense here. We're supposed to be professional people. We should act professionally.' We were under a lot of pressure. People expected us to fail. Two of the girls nearly buckled and thought of coming back. But I tried to hold us all together. I told them we would all stick together and pull through. We all passed but only three of us came back.

In this instance the Carib had taken the position of modernity, rationality and liberalism and claimed that the attempted act of interpellation itself designated the hailer as 'unprofessional', that is to say, in a modern context, 'uncivilised'. Nonetheless, the clear implication of this episode is that the Carib informant had accepted that Jack Iron referred to Caribs, had responded to the hailing function of the aside, but as an organic intellectual his response had been the dialectical opposite of the expected. There had been no quick denial as in 'I'm not like that!', but rather a denial of the hailer's competence to perform the function of interpellator.

One point that should be noted here is that in all three instances that I witnessed the Carib who was hailed was an adult male. Although the small number of examples precludes the making of generalisations, the impression that I received was that these exchanges were primarily a male activity. Certainly the exchanges with young Carib women would usually be far more sexual in nature and an initial 'hailing' of 'Jack Iron' would not have been an appropriate method of opening a conversation, though I suspect that such a trope could be utilised were a non-Carib male publicly snubbed by a Carib female. In all the attempts by non-Carib men to hail Carib women that I encountered in Georgetown, the interpellation attempted to constitute them as the subject of sexual desire. I have designated these attempts to initiate a response as interpellation only insofar as there was a specific reference to being Carib. Such activity was typical of young males 'liming' and was not in other ways different from their approaches to non-Carib females. A simple hail such as 'Hey, you there, Carib girl' was complex insofar as it was loaded with the ambivalence that surrounded attitudes to Carib women. It expressed both physical attractiveness and subaltern status. As such it could be used to hail fair skinned non-Carib females and combined both flattery and denigration.

One of the principle criticisms of Althusser's formulation of interpellation was that it produced a static system (see Butler 1997, Dolar 1993). Subjects were constituted through interpellation and since they were always/already so constituted any rejection of the hail became impossible. The functionalist concern with the reproduction of a system of power effectively produced a circularity from which Althusser could not escape. Yet Althusser did include something of a proviso that he did not elaborate when he stated regarding religious ideology:

> If it interpellates them in such a way that the subject responds: *'Yes, it really is me!'* if it obtains from them the *recognition* that they do really occupy the place that it designates for them as theirs in the world, a fixed residence … we should note that all this procedure to set up religious subjects is dominated by a strange phenomenon: the fact that there can only be a multitude of possible religious subjects on the absolute condition that there is a Unique, Absolute, *Other Subject*, ie God. (Althusser 1971: 166)

Here Althusser is concerned with the constituting Subject that is presupposed by religious ideology, but the inclusion of the term *recognition* allows the possibility of its opposite. To use Althusser's own example, we might imagine an individual who responds to the hail with 'Hold on, that's not me, I'm not like that!'. The more specific the hail, the more interpellation attempts to constitute the individual as a subject in totality ('That is what you are and that is all that you are!') then the greater the possibility that the hail can be denied. It is this liminal failure of interpellation that is expressed so clearly by the emergence of organic intellectuals within the category of people designated as Caribs by the interpellation 'Jack Iron'. But this failure itself highlights a further problem with the Althusserian formulation of the constitution of the subject. On the one hand, Althusser attempts to explain the reproduction of subjects as occupiers of particular positions which are an effect of particular discursive formations, for example the division of labour in capitalism, whilst, through his adoption of concepts derived from Lacan, he also sought to develop a general explanation of the constitution of the individual as subject. It was this aspect of hailing which led Judith Butler to ask, regarding Althusser's paradigmatic scene with the police officer who hails an individual and invokes a response, a turn:

> How might we think of this 'turn' as prior to subject formation, a prior complicity with the law without which no subject emerges? The turn toward the law is thus a turn against oneself, a turning back on oneself that constitutes the movement of conscience. (Butler 1997: 107)

An openness to the hail of the Law is therefore, according to Butler, a prerequisite of interpellation. In this sense Althusser's scenario appears to be derived from an *a priori* condition of guilt. But this in itself reiterates the conflation of interpellation as a discursive practise and as it occurs in terms of the Lacanian mirror stage that Althusser adopts as the blueprint for the constitution of the individual as subject, and it is essentially the paradox that derives from this confusion that Hurst had previously described.

After the events concerning the *Ruth 114*, Caribs became open to the hail of 'Jack Iron' but this does not necessarily entail a predisposition of guilt as an abstract concept, as Butler perhaps suggests, but rather with the internalisation of specific tropes associated with Caribness. These tropes, although part of what might be termed a hegemonic discourse, were nevertheless contextually constrained. As much as the events contributed to the depiction of the Caribs as wild men, and hence beyond normal Vincentian society, in doing so it positioned them within the conceptual opposition of respectability and reputation, and hence created the possibility for their reintegration within society by a process of self-constitution. Thus, while the incident provided a reaffirmation of the Caribs historical depiction, it provided the Caribs themselves with a more complex system of subjectification, a complexity borne of the various and contradictory strategies that were open to them in terms of their own identification. It was precisely because at the level of concrete individuals they never existed simply as Caribs, subject to a totalising discourse of *assujettissement* as in the case of Foucault's prisoner, but were always subject to heterogeneous discourses of identification emanating from discrete social institutions, that the possibility of the liminal failure of interpellation was always immanent. In one of those peculiar paradoxes with which history is littered, the very moment at which every calumny aimed at the Caribs of St Vincent appeared to be vindicated proved to be axis upon which new forms of *assujettissement* could turn.

BIBLIOGRAPHY

Abramson, R (1983) *The Man-of-Words in the West Indies: Performance and the Emergence of Creole Culture*, Baltimore: Johns Hopkins UP

Althusser, L (1971) *Lenin and Philosophy and Other Essays*, London: New Left Books

Butler, J (1997) *The Psychic Life of Power*, Stanford, CA: Stanford UP

Carstens, P (1991) *The Queen's People*, Toronto: Toronto UP

Dolar, M (1993) 'Beyond interpellation' 6(2) *Qui Parle*, Spring/Summer, 73–96

Forgacs, D (ed) (1988) *A Gramsci Reader*, London: Lawrence and Wishart

Foucault, M (1972) *The Archaeology of Knowledge*, London: Tavistock

Gramsci, A (1988) *A Gramsci Reader: Selected Writings 1916-35*, Forgacs, D (ed), London: Lawrence & Wishart

Hall, S and Du Gay, P (1996) *Questions of Identity*, London: Sage

Rubinstein, H (1987) *Coping with Poverty*, Boulder: Westview

Shephard, C (1832) *An Historical Account of St Vincent*, London: Frank Cass & Co

CHAPTER 11

WAR, SPACE AND THE LEGITIMACY OF VIOLENCE IN ERITREA

Michael Mahrt

This chapter concerns the spatio-political configuration of war and how it affects the moral configuration of violence and political control in the Highlands of Eritrea.[1] The Highlands border Ethiopia's northernmost province, Tigray, along the river Mereb. This region has been characterised by war for decades, although these were wars of different kinds and magnitudes. In this chapter I will focus on the two wars that define modern-day Eritrea: the liberation war against Ethiopian occupation (1961–91), which resulted in the creation of an independent State, and the more recent border war between the two countries (1998–2000). My analysis will highlight the impact of these two wars on the spatio-political configurations of violence and political control in the Highlands. I will argue that the liberation war, which was mainly a guerrilla war, was to a large extent compatible with existing conceptions of the political configuration of space and moral concepts in the Highlands. The recent border war, by contrast, posed a radical challenge to those conceptions.

The inhabitants of the highlands are mainly Tigrinya-speaking, Orthodox Christian, sedentary agriculturalists. The area is characterised by large plateaux and occasional rugged mountainous areas. It is interspersed with small seasonal rivers and intensively cultivated. Rocky areas, hillsides and ravines make a substantial amount of land unsuitable for plough-based agriculture. These areas, generally known as *Berekha*, are used mainly to collect firewood, honey and other natural products, for grazing animals, and of course to travel through to reach other villages. But the Berekha is also considered to be a wild place, home to hyenas, leopards, snakes, and evil spirits, and a hiding place for people outside the law. These people are traditionally known as *Shifta*, and I will return to them again later.

The term Berekha is rather vague, whereas its opposite, *Adi*, is very clearly demarcated. The Adi is the village with its cultivated lands, measured out in very precise parcels. The Berekha, on the other hand, is not defined so precisely, not even negatively as beginning where the Adi ends. In short, Berekha is a place with no permanent human habitation. Most villages have origin stories which recount how someone came to that specific place and chased away the evil spirits, and the lions that lived there, in order to make it habitable for people. In other words, human agency has the potential to change the Berekha into Adi. However, spirits

---

1   The paper is based on fieldwork in the central highlands of Eritrea, carried out between September 1999 and July 2001.

and animals are always a threat, and human agency is hence constantly needed to keep them at bay.

Village and household are the main features of organisation for the Tigrinya of the central Eritrean highlands. The household is to a very large degree an independent economic unit. Land is owned collectively by the village, but it is the households who uphold and exercise rights to use the land which is distributed evenly among them. Rights to land are dependent on rights to live in a particular village. This right can be obtained only if one can demonstrate that one's forefather, no more than four generations back in a straight line, actually lived and worked the land in a particular village. It is important to note here that the emphasis is placed on working the land, rather than on being born in a particular place.

In his study of Tigrayan peasants, Bauer notes the strong emphasis on the economic and political independence of the households (Bauer 1985). The importance of this independence in many respects overrides that of kinship. There is a saying that brothers should not build their houses next to each other. According to men, it would result in fighting amongst the women, since they will try to use kinship obligations as a way of getting help for the work in the household. Women explain that the brothers would fight, because each would expect the other to help with ploughing and other heavy workloads in the fields.

Decisions regarding village matters are taken by the traditional council, made up of all heads of households in the village. They meet at the central meeting point, the *Baito*, to discuss significant issues. Decisions are often taken by consensus, or an assessment of majority opinion (see Tronvoll 1997 and Bauer 1985 for more detailed descriptions). Today, more and more decisions are made by the administration, which imposes its decisions on the villagers. In terms of conflict resolution and other legal matters, the village is the main unit. Each village has a lay judge, or rather a mediator, known as the *Danya*. While he is usually elected by vote among all heads of households, in some areas he is, or was, appointed by the administration, in particular during the British Military Administration (1941–52) and currently, in the post-liberation period. The Danya is the man (always a man) to whom any dispute is brought. He deals with cases regarding quarrels over land, marital disputes, violence involving villagers, etc. His authority rests solely with the acceptance of all parties, and is limited to his own village or more precisely, disputes involving people from his own village. When conflicts and disputes occur between people from different villages, the plaintiff brings his case before the Danya of the accused's village. The rules guiding the Danya are laid down in the *Sereat Adgeme Milga*, the traditional law of the area formerly known as *Serae*. Other areas have their own similar versions.

As is evident from this brief description, a person is a legal subject within jurisdictions defined by his residence in a particular village. Furthermore, we have seen that villages have a flat power structure, organised horizontally with households as politically and economically individual units. We shall now look at anomalies to this – namely the Shifta.

SHIFTA

The Shifta were bandits, quite common in the Highlands until not so long ago. They were almost always men. Many of them had run away from the villages of their birth due to some serious unresolved conflict, or to evade the taxes of the administration of the day. The Shifta lived in the Berekha, sleeping in trees and riverbeds. They were often gathered in organised bands and robbed people travelling in the Berekha or in the villages after dark. They rarely killed people, except when they met with resistance. The Shifta were naturally feared, but not completely and unequivocally condemned. In fact, to become one was also regarded as a noble way of escaping the fate one faced after losing one's temper in a situation familiar to everyone, fighting over land. Furthermore, the Shifta targeted rich people, and never hit them so hard as to debilitate them economically. They were, in other words, an integrated part of the economy,

People who joined the Shifta often returned to their villages when their relatives had organised a settlement in the particular conflict in which they had been involved. This could be a matter of months, or years, depending on the seriousness of the crime, and the economic standing of the Shifta's family. In the case of murder of a white person (during the Italian and British periods) there was no such thing as return, except to face certain death. Most of those who attained fame as Shifta did so precisely because their crimes were spectacular, and because they had been Shifta long enough to become known by name, rather than being simply another anonymous outlaw. These leaders were famous, and are still remembered today in songs and sayings. For example, Debessai Drar was said to be immune to bullets, and other leaders were also praised for their bravery and courage in fighting with the authorities.

Occasionally a Shifta was hunted down, but almost always by the colonial authorities, and only if his crime was considered to be under official jurisdiction. As mentioned before, the local Danya had no police force to hunt down a Shifta. Apart from the administration, the only people who would be expected to capture a Shifta were the relatives of the victim of his initial crime. But the perpetrator often simply disappeared from the area, and since the farmers were rarely able to stay away from their land long enough to catch him, he was safe. The Shifta changed area almost daily, to avoid angering people enough to pursue them. I asked one informant to explain to me what a Shifta was:

> Shifta means *Amatsi* [a criminal]. Shifta means someone who is not with the government and who is also not with the people. They live in the Berekha and rob people and commit crimes against them. If they get a person who has gold or a goat then they will rob him and force him to bring them more. 'Negus Netsla, Gebri Netsla' ['We hate the king, we hate the tax']. This is what the Shifta say. They don't pay tax, they live outside the law and they live their life in the Berekha and spend their time stealing.

There are two themes in this quotation that I would like to emphasise. One is the fact that the Shifta is seen as being against the government, and against the people. We shall come back to that, when we look at the liberation movements and administration. The second is that they are seen as living their lives in the Berekha, outside the villages, and, in the same breath, that they are outside the law.

SPATIAL FEATURES OF VIOLENCE AND POLITICAL CONTROL

We should now be able to sketch out the spatial and moral features of political control, violence, and the institutions used to deal with violence. Violence, as it occurs between villagers, can be dealt with on the basis of their residence in a village and of institutional mechanisms that are based on horizontal relations between villagers. The basic principles guiding this are the basic principles of social organisation – those of the distribution of land.

Any male individual has a right to land in the place where, based on pedigree, he has a right to live. Upon taking up that right, he legally belongs to that village, and hence is under the jurisdiction of the local Danya. Should he commit a crime, or be accused of one, against someone from a different village – no matter where the crime takes place – he has to answer to the Danya of the victim's village. He will have to do so if he wants to continue to live in his village and work the land he has been allotted. I argue that this is jurisdiction based on a specific organisation *in* the land, rather than an organisation *of* the land.

The Shifta choose to opt out of the social organisation that revolves around agricultural work and the distribution of land. To do so they need to employ certain specific spatial strategies, such as not living in a village, and indeed not living in a permanent place. This naturally means that their economic strategies change too – they become robbers. They choose to live outside the law, both in a metaphorical sense and a literal sense. This does not mean that they are safe and free to do what they like, but that they are outside that particular jurisdiction with its particular institutions and functions, because they are outside the type of organisation that defines this jurisdiction. The Shifta perform a certain function in the land, and they use land in a completely different way than villagers. The violence that the Shifta employ is understood in these terms. It is understood as an economic strategy – a deplorable, but understandable economic strategy. Thus the Shifta's violence is placed within a moral framework, based on the conception of space as heterogeneous, as encompassing different forms of organisation, and different forms of moral value and human agency.

I have until now concentrated on intra- and inter-village jurisdiction and institutions. There were and are other institutions and functions. I shall now turn to the issue of administration, colonial and otherwise.

ADMINISTRATION AND THE MILITARY

Administration has been performed by military organisations for as long as anyone can remember in the Highlands. Up until the Italian colonisation, taxes were collected by various feudal lords who employed soldiers. When the Italians conquered the area at the end of the 19th century, they mainly took over the tax-collecting function in the beginning. Later on, they became more active regarding land reforms, military services, and building up modern urban centres with opportunities for wage-labour. This was particularly true during the build-up to the invasion of Ethiopia in 1936. This invasion eventually led to the downfall of the Italian administration, which was taken over by the British after they defeated the Italians in 1941. The British presence was also a military presence, as was the

Ethiopian administration that took over in 1952 as a result of a UN decision to federate Eritrea with Ethiopia. The Ethiopian emperor Haile Selassie kept a large military presence in Eritrea due to widespread resistance to the new administrators. This resistance grew into armed liberation movements around the time Ethiopia annexed Eritrea (1962). When the emperor was overthrown in 1974, a regime, known as the *Dergue*,[2] took power. From 1978 onwards, the Dergue stepped up the military presence in Eritrea even further, with the help of the Soviet Union.

The people of the villages see administrators as militarily organised 'others'. They are organised in vertical hierarchies, unlike the horizontal structure of the village. Moreover, they are highly mobile, and importantly they are always outsiders to the villagers. Administration in this sense comes from the outside and above, and is linked to military presence, both in the sense of the presence of armed people, and in the sense of the way they are organised. All sayings I recorded on the matter of administration emphasised its particular quality, rather than its legitimacy, as in this praise of the Italians as opposed to the Ethiopians: 'The King from Shoa[3] is *hasawi*.[4] But I have seen the King from Rome. He was just and true in his reign. He fed us and reigned as well as if it was his own life.' In general people are quite indifferent to who is actually carrying out the administration, they are much more interested in how it is done. The legitimacy of a government therefore stems from what it does and how it does it, rather than who is in it.

The problem of the Shifta was seen as a problem for the administration. They had the policing capacity due to their control of military strength, and they were also supposed to impose sanctions and punishments on those who left their villages to become Shifta. This did not automatically override the jurisdiction of the village. Indeed I have recorded several cases where a Shifta was caught and sentenced by the administration, only to return to his village after serving a prison sentence, to face other punishment, such as compensation for killing or causing bodily harm.

It has to be said that the administration was often not very successful in their hunt for the Shifta. This is very much due to the notorious inaccessibility of large parts of this very mountainous and virtually roadless area. However, the lack of co-operation from villagers also played a role. This is noted time and again in documents preserved from the Italian and British administrations, and was confirmed by my informants. They explained that there were two reasons for this lack of co-operation. First of all, it was known to be dangerous to provide information for the administration, since the Shifta might retaliate. Secondly, the problem was seen to be between the administration and the Shifta – it was thought to have little to do with the villagers, except that they were annoyed at being robbed. But as mentioned above, the Shifta rarely debilitated an individual household; they would simply take a little here and there, so they were tolerable to a local economy. Furthermore, their status was ambiguous, since they were not

---

2   Dergue means 'committee' in Amharic, the language of the Amhara people who dominated Ethiopian politics until 1991.
3   Shoa is the homeland of the Amhara people.
4   'Liar'.

unequivocally condemned. They were in fact often seen as heroes of resistance to the dreaded tax system and the constraints of village life. As such the Shifta were perceived as being mainly against the administration of the day, and certainly the administration's problem to deal with. It was not until the Shifta themselves chose to return to their villages that they would come under the local jurisdiction, at which point they obviously ceased to be Shifta, and became regular villagers once more.

To reiterate the points made so far, the Highlands are characterised by an enduring cohabitation of different kinds of people, defined by how they are organised in relation to their function in space. We have seen that a particular socio-political organisation in space is central to understanding the moral response to crime and violence and how they are perceived and dealt with. One form of jurisdiction is based on the social organisation revolving around the distribution of land to people. This system functions as a gravitational force that binds individuals to certain villages, and this is what supports the judicial system to deal with crime and violence at this level.

There is another layer of jurisdiction that is not derived from the form of social organisation revolving around the distribution of land. This is the jurisdiction that belongs to the administration, which, as I have stressed, has always been militarily organised, no matter who was in charge. A military organisation is by definition contrary to the organisation of the village. It is hierarchical, and it does not bind its members to the land in the same way as the people of the village. To the villagers, the administration has always come from outside, and has distributed its people in the land. These people of the administration were always strangers to the land. Though they might be resented for various reasons, it was rarely, if ever, their foreignness. It is simply in the very principle of organisation that they must be others, even if an individual serving that function might have been born in the area.

In the light of the above, land in the Highlands can be described as heterogeneous. The land supports different forms of organisations, notably the village, the administration, and the Shifta. It is within these forms of organisation that crime, violence, and political control are understood. This becomes even clearer when we take a look at the villagers' attitude towards the liberation movements that began to appear in the 1960s.

LIBERATION MOVEMENTS AND THE LIBERATION WAR

The first group to begin operations in the Highlands was the Eritrean Liberation Front, popularly known as *Jebha*. In the beginning this was little more than a number of clandestine groups operating in the area. They would perform attacks on government troops and buildings, but never villages. When they did enter villages, they would often ask to be served food, but rarely, if ever, did they steal. Nevertheless, the villagers today often refer to them as Shifta, or they admit that at that time they saw them as Shifta. This is not as strange as it may seem. They lived the same life as the Shifta. They were living in the Berekha, and were always on the move. Besides, their members were often people who had fled for exactly the same reasons as any Shifta, in that they were in opposition to the administration. They might have fled and then in the Berekha encountered the Jebha, who then tried to persuade them to join their movement. As mentioned before, it was quite common for the Shifta to gather together in bands. But most of all the Jebha resembled the Shifta in their opposition to the administration. The Jebha's political ideologies might have differed from that of the Shifta, but that was a moot point to most villagers. So the liberation movement was not an entirely new factor in the heterogeneous conception of the groups of people operating in the land. It was a variation of a theme that was well known to the villagers.

In the official historiography of Eritrea, this was seen as a liberation war, officially beginning on 1 September 1961. To the villagers, it was hardly any different from what had gone before. The administration had always been militarily organised. There had always been groups of people in the Berekha who had escaped the political control of the administration for one reason or another, and there had always been the odd risk of clashes between these opposing but similarly organised groups of people.

When such clashes took place, villagers in that particular area would flee to the Berekha, or to villages where they had friends or relatives they could stay with for a day or two. In other words, they used spatial strategies to avoid getting caught up in the violence. These strategies were possible for two reasons. First of all, the villagers were not targeted by any of the fighting groups. Secondly, it was possible for them to leave for a short time, because they always knew that they could return, no matter who had won and was in control of the area. These clashes occurred from time to time in any village, as indeed they had between groups of Shifta and the administration of the day, for as long as people can remember.

With the advent of a new liberation group, the *Shaebia*, things changed somewhat. They had grown increasingly powerful up through the 1980s and controlled more and more areas with the help of the *Weyane*, their Tigrayan comrades in arms. For an extended period of time they controlled the area where I did fieldwork, though not as far as the nearby market and administrative town of Mendefera. They established a kind of administration in the area, and hence took over the function of the Dergue. Later, their luck turned, and the Dergue forced them out of the area. However, they remained operative as guerrilla groups, and the Dergue grew more and more frustrated. They began targeting villagers, suspecting them of collaboration with the liberation movements. This grew steadily worse as villagers were beaten up by the Dergue, and in one tragic incident in the rainy season of 1989, several people were killed. The Dergue had had a group of soldiers stationed in a village. Late one evening, after dark, another group of Dergue soldiers approached the village. The group inside the village mistook the approaching group for a Shaebia group, and began firing at them. The group approaching under fire automatically assumed that the village had been taken over by the Shaebia and began firing back. The battle lasted all night, and many soldiers were killed, before the dawn revealed the mistake. In anger over the loss of their soldiers, the Dergue went on a rampage through the villages in the nearby area and killed seven or eight people. To many villagers this incident was a turning point, and henceforth the administration was discredited. At the same

time, the Shaebia managed to cut some of the Dergue's supply lines, and many
soldiers and administrators were left for long periods without supplies, adding to
their random stealing from villagers. As a consequence of these events, the people
in the villages began referring to the Dergue soldiers as Genie, which they
described as a kind of Shifta approved by the government.

It was around this time that the idea of the Shaebia taking over the control of
administration became a viable option in the eyes of the villagers. This was the
stated aim of the Shaebia, which villagers knew very well. In their eyes, the
Shaebia was a variation of the Shifta who were always opposed to the political
control of the administration of the day. The Shaebia were a kind of better-
organised Shifta group that wanted to take over a certain political function in the
land. When the Dergue overstepped their legitimate functions, and performed
illegal violence, the only counterforce to that were the liberation groups. They
were militarily organised, as administration had always been in the area, and they
had such aspirations.

The violence of the struggle between the Shaebi and the Dergue was seen as
unfortunate for the area and the people living in it, because it was a disturbance of
everyday life. It was only when the violence was directed against the villagers that
moral judgment was passed on it.

The end of the liberation war brought stability to the region for a while. This
was much welcomed by the villagers, since, at least at the beginning, it meant that
they could go on with their lives more safely. They were again able to travel here
and there without much risk, and for many it meant that they could be reunited
with family and friends. The administration was now left to the Shaebia, which
was still organised in a military fashion, and still seen, from the perspective of the
village, as radically different from village life. As such, they were far better than
the preceding administration, since they did not overstep their legal limits in
terms of violence. Yet they were not inherently different. This obviously contrasts
sharply with the view that the Shaebia held of themselves, namely as being a more
legitimate administration because they were from the same geo-political area. The
villagers do not share this view. To them administration comes from outside, is
militarily organised, and deals with a particular set of functions in the land. As I
have argued above, land in the village view is heterogeneous. It is occupied by
various agencies performing different functions. Thus it is function and
organisation which define political agency and give it legitimacy. Against this
might be argued that villagers do indeed get their legitimate right to a plot of land
from tracing their relations in the land. However, it is important that it is not
enough to be born in a particular village, or to have a patrilineal forefather in that
village. One must prove that that particular forefather worked the land in that
particular village. He has to have been a *gebar* (one who pays taxes and one who
works the land) and performed the function in the land related to that status.
However, the flip-side of this point is that the right to use land is all that is
legitimised by tracing an ancestor who actually performed that function.

From the perspective of the villagers, the right to govern is not related to the
right to work the land. The right to govern is achieved by force and, for as long as
anyone can remember, has belonged to outsiders who are militarily organised.
This 'layer of right' in the land is thus of a different kind and structure, and

derives its legitimacy from a different logic than that governing everyday economic and social activities.

THE BORDER WAR

After liberation, people were free to move across the border with Ethiopia for purposes of trading and visiting relatives and friends. The Weyane and the Shaebia had been close allies during the liberation war, and now they formed governments in Ethiopia and Eritrea respectively, so ostensibly relations were quite amicable. The Ethiopians living across the border spoke the same language as the Highland farmers in Eritrea, lived more or less similar ways of lives, and indeed intermarriage was quite common. The border seemed to have little to do with ordinary people, and was more a question of government. This would change dramatically in May 1998, when war broke out over the dispute of where the border should actually be defined. To most people, including those living in the border areas, the war came as a shock.

In the villages in the area I worked in, people got their information about the war through government-controlled radio and rumours. The shelling and fighting from the frontlines could also be heard. The villagers encountered the effects of the war when they could no longer travel to friends and family in Ethiopia, or near the frontlines. They felt its economic impact, when certain crops and goods went up dramatically in price, due to a total embargo on imports from Ethiopia, previously Eritrea's main trade partner. After a while, everyone was required to carry ID-cards. The highlands of Eritrea had a large proportion of migrant workers from impoverished areas of Tigray, Ethiopia's northernmost province, which borders the Highland region. These people were treated as potential spies, and ID-cards were deemed necessary to distinguish between them and Eritreans, since they spoke the same language, and wore the same types of dress, and in general had the appearance of the Eritrean Highlanders. Furthermore, many young men were dodging conscription, and would be sent away to do their service if caught without proper ID.

Radio broadcasts gave daily briefings about what horrible things the evil Weyane were up to, even in lulls between the major offensives. Ethiopian radio, which Eritreans could listen to, was speaking likewise about the Shaebia. What occupied people the most, in particular during and after the third offensive in May–June 2000, were stories about the aims of the Weyane. In the third offensive, the Weyane managed to occupy large parts of Eritrea and were reported to be carrying out horrible atrocities against the people in the occupied areas. Reports told of cattle stolen and their shepherds kidnapped and recruited to fight in the Ethiopian army; women were said to have been raped and killed, houses burned, children massacred. The general idea conveyed by these stories was that the Weyane wanted to conquer the whole of Eritrea and get rid of its people.

This was expressed on numerous occasions. When I asked people to compare the liberation war with the border war, the answer was unanimously that the border war was far worse, because there was no escape if the Weyane came – they would target people themselves. Previously people had been able to escape the fighting of the liberation war by running to the Berekha. This was possible precisely because land was heterogeneous, and because the war was over a function in the land, as seen from the villager's perspective. In the border war, by contrast, the idea of land as an entity, an object, became violently and abruptly clear to people. I argue that in this process space became homogenised.

CONCLUSION: POLITICAL SPACE AND THE LEGITIMACY OF VIOLENCE

Though the liberation war was a prolonged period of much violence, the area saw very little of the dramatic upheavals and social chaos that happened in other areas plagued by civil war. Social institutions did not break down, and most ordinary villagers carried on life as normally as they could. I argue that this is due to the fact that the violence that occurred was understandable within the framework of the particular social organisation in a heterogeneous space, where violence takes place within specific relations defined by that organisation. In a sense, the danger of violence that villagers perceived during the liberation war was not very different from other dangers inherent in the land – drought, wild animals, spirits, etc. All of these were part of an inherently heterogeneous space, where villagers themselves were merely one form of agency organised in a particular way.

With the border war, things changed. Though the area I worked in saw little direct violence, compared with the liberation war, the prevailing fear and uncertainty was far greater. Few understood what the war was actually about, but to the rural population it became clear that they themselves would be targets if the Ethiopians invaded. Previously people had used spatial strategies to survive, such as running away to uninhabited areas, when battles took place in or near their villages. But this time there was a clear impression that the Ethiopians would burn down villages, steal cattle, and kill anyone in their way. Escaping to other areas, in order to come back when things had cooled down, was therefore not an option. It became clear to the rural population that the Ethiopians were not after a certain political function in the land, but that they wanted the land itself, without the people living there. There was no place to escape to, because the Ethiopians wanted space, total space, which left nothing for the people themselves. The idea of the State with its premise of a homogenous space became suddenly and very violently clear to people. They themselves were the target of violence, based on their identity. This had been the case previously – but before, identity meant what function they were performing in space (ie, they were killed if they were seen as supporters of the other side). However, this time round, they were identified by spatial criteria: where they were born, and where they were living. They were seen, and forced violently to see themselves, as children of the space rather than children in the space. Though the atrocities during the liberation war were no less than those during the border war, the violence of that war was only judged morally when it was directed against villagers, as in the case mentioned above. The moral judgment of violence and its legitimacy depends on these particular spatial frameworks and should be understood within them. Violence caused by particular relations in the land, ie, relations between the Shifta/liberation movements and the government forces, were not judged morally. It is only when violence was directed against people because of their relation to the land that it was deemed illegitimate and immoral.

BIBLIOGRAPHY

Bauer, DF (1985) *Household and Society in Ethiopia: An Economic and Social Analysis of Tigray Social Principles and Household Organization*, Lansing, MI: Michigan State University, Northeast Africa Studies Committee, Monograph No 6, Occasional Paper Series

Connel, D (1997) *Against All Odds*, New Jersey: Red Sea Press

Crummey, D (1985) *Land and Society in the Christian Kingdom of Ethiopia*, Oxford: James Curry

Crummey, D (1997) 'Banditry and resistance: noble and peasant in nineteenth century Ethiopia', in Crummey, D (ed), *Banditry, Rebellion, and Social Protest in Africa*, Oxford: James Curry, pp 133–50

Fernyhough, D (1997) 'Social mobility and dissident elites in northern Ethiopia: the role of Banditry 1900–69', in Crummey, D (ed), *Banditry, Rebellion, and Social Protest in Africa*, Oxford: James Curry, pp 151–72

Hobsbawm, E (1969/2000) *Bandits*, London: Abacus

Pool, D (1997) *From Guerrillas to Government*, Oxford: James Curry

Tronvoll, K (1997) *Mai Weini: A Highland Village in Eritrea*, New Jersey: Red Sea Press

INDEX

NHS
See National Health Service

Norway
See Food industry in
    Norway, cultural impact of
    biotechnology in the

Philippines
See Filipina migrant domestic
    servants in Malaysia